D0871902

Word
Cultures

Word Cultures

Radical Theory and Practice in William S. Burroughs' Fiction

Robin Lydenberg

University of Illinois Press
Urbana and Chicago

Jacket photo by Gerard Malanga

© 1987 by the Board of Trustees of the
University of Illinois
Manufactured in the United States of America
C 5 4 3 2 1

This book is printed on acid-free paper.

Library of Congress Cataloging-in-Publication Data

Lydenberg, Robin, 1947–
  Word cultures.

  Bibliography: p.
  Includes index.
  1. Burroughs, William S., 1914–   —Style.
2. Experimental fiction—United States—History and
criticism. I. Title.
PS3552.U75Z73   1987   813'.54   86–30719
ISBN 0–252–01413–8 (alk. paper)

To Steven Lydenberg and Adele Dalsimer
with gratitude and affection

Contents

Preface

William Burroughs tells with pride the following story about Samuel Beckett: "He gave me one of the greatest compliments that I ever heard. Someone asked him, 'What do you think of Burroughs?' and he said—grudgingly—'Well, he's a writer.'" Considering the critical judgments of the past twenty-five years, the pleasure Burroughs takes in this minimalist commentary is understandable. Having been called everything from a degenerate and incoherent fraud to the Tiresias of the space age, Burroughs has only rarely been acknowledged as, above all, a writer. Given the flamboyant style of his private life and the shocking aspects of the worlds he describes in his fiction, it is difficult to focus on Burroughs' stylistic genius. His most experimental novels have been a major obstacle to critical recognition of his literary importance, yet it is in those works that he is most explicitly a writer, most obviously addicted to language.

Much critical work on Burroughs treats both his personal life and the idiosyncratic mythology which pervades his fiction as cultural, sociological, or psychoanalytical artifacts. His depiction of the underworld of drugs, sex, and petty crime and his exposure of the insidious power of bureaucracy, technology, and the politics of war elicit what is essentially a moral response from most critics. Burroughs is either condemned for the "unspeakable" content of his fiction or championed for his courageous and clearsighted quest for individual freedom. While these issues are surely important, they have overshadowed the significance of Burroughs' stylistic accomplishments.

My main concern throughout this book, therefore, is with Burroughs as "one who writes." I am interested primarily in his conception of language; in his emphasis on the materiality of the word and the relationship of language and the body; and more specifically in his disruption of linguistic and literary conventions, of rhetorical tropes, of the roles of author and reader. I argue that Burroughs' radical notions about language and literary production have constituted a much more substantial attack on the humanistic literary establishment than the unconventional life or the allegedly pornographic fiction for which he is often vilified.

Burroughs' literary development moves from a first stage during which his writing becomes increasingly experimental, to a second stage in which he returns gradually to more conventional narrative techniques. From his first conventional novel, *Junkie* (1953), Burroughs evolves toward the more daring mosaic style of *Naked Lunch* (1959) and then to the overtly radical "cut-up" techniques of *The Soft Machine* (1961), *Nova Express* (1964), and *The Ticket That Exploded* (1967). After the cut-up trilogy, Burroughs returns in *The Last Words of Dutch Schultz* (1970), *The Wild Boys* (1971), *Exterminator!* (1973), *Cities of the Red Night* (1981), and *The Place of Dead Roads* (1983) to what he has described (with some license) as nineteenth-century narrative.

Although the style of these more recent works is still characterized by various radical methods of narrative dislocation and estrangement, there is a tendency for critics to perceive in this phase of Burroughs' career an abnegation of his earlier experimental work. As his renewed popularity indicates, many of Burroughs' readers are relieved to see him "compromise" sensibly with narrative convention after the chaos of the cut-up novels. Burroughs himself, however, has qualified his return to "purely conventional straightforward narrative" with the insistence that he is "applying what [he has] learned from the cut-up and the other techniques to the problem of conventional writing" (*Job* 55).

It is the premise of this book that there is still much to be learned from the theories and techniques Burroughs developed and from the four major novels he produced during his ten years of experimental writing. My discussion of Burroughs' fiction and theory, therefore, is based on the period during which he evolved and revised the material for *Naked Lunch* and the cut-up trilogy, roughly between 1954 and 1964. I draw on theoretical statements by Burroughs from *The Job* (1969) and *The Third Mind* (1978) because although these books were published after his experimental phase, they represent views he held during that period. Since many of Burroughs' views and writing techniques have, in fact, changed since that time, the reader should keep in mind the historical context of my analysis.

In part 1 I discuss the four novels of the first stage of Burroughs' career, novels which constitute his apprenticeship and full development as an experimental writer. While many perceive the cut-up novels as an ill-conceived deviation from the more accessible style of *Naked Lunch*, I examine Burroughs' experimental writing as an extension of the earlier novel. In *Naked Lunch*, Burroughs has already begun his attack on the conventional structures of metaphor and morality which he sees dominating Western thought. Traditional humanistic criticism, which is based on those moral and metaphorical patterns of thought, tends to translate *Naked Lunch* into the very terms the novel sets out to undermine. I argue that the mosaic style of the novel anticipates Burroughs' determination to displace metaphorical habits of assimilation and vertical transcendence with metonymic patterns of collage and horizontal juxtaposition. In this novel, the treatment of the body, of poetic image, and of narrative structure are all predominantly metonymic—characterized by reduction, fragmentation, and a relentless literalness.

This metonymic dismemberment, which is evident in both the style and the thematic content of *Naked Lunch*, develops into the rigorous writing methods used to generate the three cut-up novels which follow. In this trilogy, Burroughs mingles straight narrative with sections of experimental prose in which he has cut and spliced his own writing into the words of other writers (Eliot, Rimbaud, Kafka), into quotations from the popular press, scientific treatises, song lyrics, and advertising. While he uses the violent figure of metonymy in *Naked Lunch* to reveal the hidden manipulations of metaphor, the cut-up technique makes explicit the coercive nature of *all* writing, of *all* symbol systems. My aim is to demonstrate that these narratives, which many critics have dismissed as unreadable, offer new ways of reading and thinking and a new kind of linguistic pleasure for which we must be trained.

The didactic quality of much of Burroughs' writing during his experimental phase stems from his intense desire to make contact with his readers, to make accessible to them the liberating effects of his techniques for manipulating language. He is acutely aware of the danger that experimental writing may *isolate* him from his audience. While he sees Beckett as an experimental writer who went too far within himself, "First he was in a bottle and now he is in the mud," he sees in Joyce's later work the risks of "purely experimental" writing which ventures too far outward: "I think *Finnegans Wake* rather represents a trap into which experimental writing can fall. [. . .] It's simply if you go too far in one direction you can never get back, you're out there in complete isolation" (*Job* 55). Refusing to be trapped within the binary oppositions of inside/outside, self/other, subjective/objective, Burroughs negotiates with care this Scylla and Charybdis of experimental writing. He develops detached, precise, scientific methods of observing and recording the world around him; he introduces chance as a factor in composition; and he embraces an ideal of contact and collaboration not only with his readers but with "many writers living and dead."

In part 2 I undertake, as an analytical experiment, a cut-up collaboration of William Burroughs with contemporary radical theorists such as Jacques Derrida, Roland Barthes, Julia Kristeva, and others. These critics challenge, as does Burroughs, our conventional notions about the status of the author in the text, about the referentiality of language, and about the dualism of Western thought. Their work has been attacked at times with a moral outrage as virulent as that of the novelist's most fierce detractors. I hope to demonstrate, through the remarkable similarities between Burroughs' experimental writing and contemporary theory, that the ideas we now recognize as characteristic of post-structuralism and deconstruction were being developed independently by Burroughs almost thirty years ago.

Burroughs and contemporary theorists share an arsenal of strategies which they use against what is now called the logocentric tradition. I examine specifically their common efforts to disrupt structures of binary opposition and hierarchy by techniques of reversal and dissemination; their exposure of the parasitic economy at work in all discourse; their refashioning of the conventional image of the body in order to extend and dissolve its borders; and their undermining of all abstractions by a provocative insistence on the bodily functions of digestion and procreation. In this intersecting network of texts, deconstruction finds a literary field in which its operations can illuminate rather than obfuscate a text, and Burroughs' experimental writing finds a critical framework in which its seriousness and complexity can be fully evaluated.

Acknowledgments

I would like to thank Boston College for several fellowship grants which facilitated my research on this project, and my department for sustaining intellectual support and encouragement. Professor Adele Dalsimer and Steven Lydenberg were dedicated readers throughout the many stages of this book. Their patience with early drafts, their editorial advice, and particularly their insistence that I proceed with the theoretical section of the study contributed significantly to the final shape of the work. My appreciation goes to Annica Lydenberg for being such a patient listener and for inventing wonderful titles for the book. At later stages of the project Jennie Skerl generously provided the invaluable suggestions and comments of a specialist and the reassurance that the manuscript was ready for publication. My thanks to the University of Illinois Press for making that process a painless one, and particularly to Professor Cary Nelson and Ann Weir for their appreciation of the submitted manuscript. A shorter version of part 1, chapter 1, first appeared under the same title in *Review of Contemporary Fiction* 4.1 (Spring 1984): 75–85. Part 1, chapter 2, is a substantially expanded and revised version of an essay with the same title published in *Contemporary Literature* 26.1 (Spring 1985): 55–73. Several sections of part 2, chapter 8, first appeared in an essay entitled "Cut-Up: Negative Poetics in William Burroughs and Roland Barthes" in *Comparative Literature Studies* 15.4 (December 1978): 414–30. Thanks to the word-processing skills of Patricia Thomas, Susan Rotondi, Jeannie Smith, and Bill Driscoll I was able to revise the book efficiently without giving up my own antiquated writing methods.

Abbreviations

The following abbreviations have been used throughout this volume to indicate the titles of Burroughs' works. Full bibliographical data can be found in the list of works cited.

Job   *The Job*
Letters   *Letters to Allen Ginsberg*
NL   *Naked Lunch*
NX   *Nova Express*
SM   *The Soft Machine*
TM   *The Third Mind*
TTTE   *The Ticket That Exploded*
Yage   *The Yage Letters*

Part One

1 | Beyond Good and Evil: "How-To" Read *Naked Lunch*

> "*Naked Lunch* is a blueprint, a How-To Book [. . .] How-To extend levels of experience by opening the door at the end of a long hall. . . . Doors that only open in *Silence*. . . ."
>
> *Naked Lunch*

The unbridgeable gap between traditional literary criticism and William Burroughs' fiction is clearly evident in the reception of *Naked Lunch*. Burroughs' project in this novel is to cure the "image addiction" and "morality addiction" of Western thought by producing a text which will defy and destroy these systems. The inability of humanistic literary criticism to account for a novel like *Naked Lunch* stems from the fact that such an approach is based on the very structures of metaphor and morality which Burroughs attacks. By laying bare the abstract mechanisms by which metaphor and morality insinuate themselves into our thinking, Burroughs throws the reader into a horizontal world of literal meaning and materiality. The grotesque physicality of *Naked Lunch*, however, is not the materiality of things as we find them in the world; it is a materiality of absence, a literal mysticism which opens up the possibility of "non-body experience" and the freedom and purity of silence.

The Moral View

Although *Naked Lunch* was brought before the Massachusetts Supreme Court on obscenity charges in the mid-sixties and still arouses dismay and disgust in many highly sophisticated readers, the critical language in which its literary importance was first proclaimed is strikingly moral. John Ciardi describes Burroughs' early novel as a "monumentally moral descent into the hell of narcotics addiction" created by an author "engaged in a profoundly meaningful search for true values" (22). Allen Ginsberg similarly judges Burroughs' intentions as "moral, like defending the good," and he lauds the author himself for the courage and idealism of his "total confession [of] exactly really what was going on inside his head" (*NL* xxxii–xxxiii). Among the most hyperbolic claims is Norman Mailer's pronouncement: "William Burroughs is in my opinion—whatever his conscious intention may be—a religious writer. There is a sense in *Naked Lunch* of the destruction of the soul [. . .]. It is a vision of how mankind would act if man was totally divorced from eternity" (*NL* xvi–xvii).

Of course, Ginsberg and Mailer were defending *Naked Lunch* not just in a literary forum but in a legal one. They felt obliged to adopt the perspective, the values, and the vocabulary of the American system of law and morality in order to win acquittal for Burroughs' work. However, since the obscenity law requires only that the work in question be proven "utterly without redeeming social value," the degree of intensity of the moral language of these critics must arise from some source other than the legal circumstances surrounding the publication of *Naked Lunch*.[1] I propose that the rhetoric of court and church and the rhetoric of mainstream humanistic literary criticism often overlap, and that the grounds for an aesthetic defense of *Naked Lunch* before the "academy" are as strictly predetermined as the grounds for its legal defense in the courtroom. The tradition of literary humanism is based on a moral vision of the universe, and on the place of art in that universe. Whether *Naked Lunch* is condemned as morally bankrupt or championed as a novel of moral quest, it is being judged within the framework of ethical dualism which dominates Western thought.

Burroughs' detractors have rejected his work primarily on the grounds that they find it demoralizing; *Naked Lunch* is denounced as negative and destructive, "on the side of death" rather than in celebration of life (Wain 21–23; Hoffman 486–89). Leslie Fiedler critizes Burroughs for evading his more personal responsibility for social reform by developing theories which locate the source of the world's problems in a conveniently distant *cosmic* disorder (*Waiting* 163–71).[2] Repeatedly Burroughs is denounced as self-indulgent because of the failure of his written work to arouse his readers to moral action in the world.

Many critics who admire Burroughs' work, have tried in turn to justify it as part of the great moral tradition of Western literature. *Naked Lunch* has been described as pursuing the sustaining "monomyth" of the quest through good and evil, through Heaven and Hell (Stull 14–29; Skerl 20–22); or compared to the medieval moral tradition which condemns the sensual realm (Peterson 30–39); or ranked among classic works of satire and didactic reform (McCarthy, "Déjeuner" 4–5; Burgess, *The Novel Now* 189). Anthony Burgess's response to Burroughs' work seems to shift depending on the context of the critical debate: he insists on one occasion that Burroughs' aims are moral and didactic rather than artistic, but then he defends the author against moralistic denunciations with the plea, "For heavens sake, let us leave morals to the moralists and carry on the job of learning to evaluate art as art" (*TLS* 9).[3] Even those critics who reject moral criteria as inappropriate for an understanding of Burroughs' work tend to set up alternative hierarchies, placing the ultimate value on such goals as scientific speculation (Moorcock 947), the exploration of the senses and "raw experience" (Creely 327; Levine 505–23), the pure exercise of will (McConnell 665–80) or—as in Burgess's case—art for art's sake. These alternative goals are inevitably set in rigid binary opposition to moral aims. As we shall see, it is not morality in general which Burroughs attacks, but the structure of hierarchy and opposition which supports moral dualism.

The deep irony of Burroughs' legal and literary status, then, is that *Naked Lunch* is most often translated into the very language and thought systems it challenges. In the "Atrophied Preface," which appears provocatively displaced at the conclusion of *Naked Lunch*, Burroughs himself gives a blunt summary of his novel which calls into question the rhetoric of his defenders and attackers alike: "Abstract concepts, bare as algebra, narrow down to a black turd or a pair of aging cajones" (*NL* 224). What becomes increasingly explicit in Burroughs' later work in the cut-up novels is that he is more interested in science and technology than in "abstract concepts," that he is more committed to the obliteration of the author and the "authority" of language than to making a "total confession" of "what was going on inside his head" (Ginsberg, *NL* xxxii).

When Burroughs concedes in an interview with Daniel Odier that he is a "great moralist," one feels he is executing a kind of semantic slide, simultaneously approaching and retreating from that ethical stance: "Q: It has been said that you are a great moralist; what do you think? A: Yes, I would say perhaps too much so" (*Job* 50). From this initial equivocation Burroughs proceeds to clarify his moral position as the demand for the destruction of three basic formulas: nation, family, and our present methods of birth and reproduction. These social and biological institutions, Burroughs argues, establish "word locks" or "mind locks" which dictate our ways of thinking and feeling, stifling spontaneous life and change. Burroughs perceives the mainstay of the nation/family/birth establishment in the dualism of Judeo-Christian morality. In referring to himself as a moralist, therefore, Burroughs is redefining the term itself in the most provocative way. Burroughs' moral position is essentially an opposition to moral dualism.

There are very few instances in which Burroughs reverts to moral categories, but they are telling exceptions. In the discussion of heroin addiction which precedes the text of *Naked Lunch*, Burroughs defines evil as the "Algebra of Need": "Junk yields a basic formula of 'evil' virus: [. . .] The face of 'evil' is always the face of total need. A dope fiend is a man in total need of dope. Beyond a certain frequency need knows absolutely no limit or control. In the words of total need: '*Wouldn't you?*' Yes you would. [. . .] Because you would be in a state of total sickness, total possession, and not in a position to act in any other way" (*NL* xxxix). Again redefining our moral categories, Burroughs condemns as evil the collapse of individual will and identity rather than the possibly illegal or immoral acts the addict in need might perpetrate. But even thus redefined, the moral terminology is kept isolated by quotation marks, quarantined like some kind of "evil" virus in its own right, never quite to be trusted. Burroughs achieves here an effect similar to Derrida's placing of key philosophical terms "*sous rature*," acknowledging the necessity of using those terms even as he calls them into question.

The "evil" virus of addiction takes many forms—addiction to drugs, sex, religion—but all are variations on a pattern of control and domination of the individual's will. As Tony Tanner points out, in Burroughs' mythology "evil" applies to anything which represses spontaneity. The most pervasive agent of repression exposed by Burroughs is the "addiction to rightness, to being in the right," the addiction to moral dualism (*Job* 144). This rhetoric of indignation manipulates the individual through disgust, shame, and guilt: "Senators leap up and bray for the Death Penalty with inflexible authority of virus yen. . . . Death for dope fiends, death for sex queens (I mean fiends) death for the psychopath" (*NL* 223). The infectious "yen" of his addiction makes the morality junky physically dependent for survival on his righteous destruction of other life. Burroughs sees moral censure itself as both evil and obscene: "[An] uglier reflection than society's disapproval would be hard to find the mean cold eyes of decent american women tight lips and no thank you from the shop keeper snarling cops pale nigger killing eyes reflecting society's disapproval fucking queers i say shoot them" (*TTTE* 216). The collection of responses to Burroughs' work which appeared in the *Times Literary Supplement* for several consecutive weeks in 1964 under the heading "Ugh" provides a panorama of such righteous indignation operating in the literary sphere. The most vitriolic of these condemnations was written by a reader who admitted (and not without some pride) that she had never read a word of Burroughs' prose (Day 27).

In Burroughs' view, such moral indignation functions as a kind of internal parasite feeding on man's "hate metabolism." In *Naked Lunch*, two Nationalists speak with distrust of an "Arty type . . . No principles" whom they suspect of experimenting with a cure for the "hate metabolism" of conflict. The Nationalists anticipate an attack on the entire "fear hate death syndrome" which maintains their power: " 'Might do almost anything. . . . Turn a massacre into a sex orgy . . . .' 'Or a joke' " (*NL* 123). Burroughs suggests that the deadly seriousness of this moral disapproval and guilt imprisons offenders and judges alike, and one primitive method of liberation offered by *Naked Lunch* is the proliferation of farcical pranks and sexual frenzies it describes. It would seem that the expulsion of this life-draining virus can only be achieved through a violent undermining of the entire dual system of morality, a system built on repression, antithesis, and conflict. Such structures of conflict represent the channeling and reduction of the infinite potential of difference into the limited realm of moral dualism. As Roland Barthes puts it, "conflict is nothing but the *moral* state of difference" (*Pleasure* 15).

Burroughs' cut-up novels are often more sober and didactic than *Naked Lunch* in their attack on the moral code, and also more explicit in identifying the danger of this code as the binary opposition of its structure rather than its "alleged content." In *Nova Express*, Inspector Lee of the Nova Police explains with scientific detachment that nothing is "right" or "wrong" in an ethical sense, but that these terms merely arise in a biological situation where one life form conflicts with the survival of another. Moral rhetoric is merely a disguise for this biological confrontation. As Lee explains further, attacking the abuses of the manipulative control systems of the oppressors with a vigilante's righteousness would merely "keep this tired old injustice show on the road" (*NX* 80), merely reinforce the dualism and hierarchy of the moral code. Thus Lee and the Nova Police offer no morally superior system to replace the Nova Mob's tyrannical control, but rather propose only a "program of total austerity and total resistance" (*NX* 13). The battle between the Nova Police and Nova Mob is not a moral battle of right against wrong, but a biological, a technological conflict. The ultimate solution is the dismantling of the machines of control—the machines of fear, shame, and guilt. At the end of *Nova Express* the narrator advises: "Shut the whole thing right off—*Silence*—When you answer the machine you provide it with more recordings to be played back to your 'enemies' keep the whole nova machine running—The Chinese character for 'enemy' means to be similar to or to answer—Don't answer the machine—Shut it off—"(*NX* 153).

While Burroughs attempts to dissolve the Chinese character for enemy, to shut down the enemy machine of moral dualism and conflict, literary critics stubbornly reconstruct that figure in their interpretations of his fiction. Whether they are defending or attacking *Naked Lunch*, critics force the novel to "be similar to or to answer" some abstract concept firmly established in our moral rhetoric. A typical example is Alvin Seltzer's analysis of *Naked Lunch* in *Chaos in the Novel: The Novel in Chaos*. Seltzer attempts to make the novel palatable by a typical humanistic sleight of hand: "the validity of the satire finally does justify Burroughs' savage treatment of the human species. Like Swift's, his contempt results from idealism, and finds expression in the most debased aspects of life" (352). In conventional humanistic criticism interpretation often takes this form of a "justification" of the text by positing a moral intention behind it. Such efforts to disguise the foul taste of *Naked Lunch* with a kind of idealistic, moral, and inevitably symbolic dressing are the norm rather than the exception.

Burroughs himself claims in the "Deposition" to *Naked Lunch* that the infamous Blue Movie sequence is a "tract against Capital Punishment in the manner of Jonathan Swift's *Modest Proposal*" (xliv). When he draws this comparison, however, he is "talking to the machine" in its own language, responding to accusations that parts of *Naked Lunch* are merely pornographic—lacking in artistic merit because they are lacking in moral purpose. We have already seen how much more far-reaching than an opposition to capital punishment are the "moral" reforms Burroughs has in mind: a revolution in our ideas of nation, family, and reproduction. He has argued that any such "halfway" measure as the reform or even the destruction of the legal system would be "like trying to abolish the symptoms of a disease while leaving the disease itself untouched" (*Job* 73).

While quite a few critics declare Burroughs a successful satirist in the Swiftian mode, David Lodge describes what he considers Burroughs' failure as a satirist. Lodge's objection is that Burroughs' narrative "suspends rather than activates the reader's moral sense" (*Crossroads* 165). In a later reexamination of *Naked Lunch* he argues that the elimination of a realistic frame for the satire robs us of our "bearings and empirical reality": the absence of "norms [. . .] by which its nauseating grotesquerie can be measured and interpreted" makes it impossible for us to "apply the episode [. . .] to the real world and draw an instructive moral" (*Modes* 38).[4]

From within the context of conventional literary humanism, Lodge assumes that "empirical reality" and moral "norms" form the unquestionable basis of all perception and interpretation of the world. Such notions are, in fact, expressions of a particular pattern of dualistic thought which measures good against evil, reality against fantasy, word against world. Lodge reasons, like Seltzer, that a satiric moral intent would "justify" or "account for" Burroughs' text. Such explanations enable the traditional critic to resolve any transgressions against moral, empirical, or even aesthetic norms. (Lodge argues, for example, that "the justification for [Burroughs'] surrealistic method is that the book expresses the consciousness of a drug addict" [*Modes* 38].)

I think Lodge is correct in his conclusion that *Naked Lunch* fails as Swiftian moral satire, but he fails to recognize the way in which Burroughs' text does succeed. Arguing that *Naked Lunch* is confused, uncontrolled, and at best an interesting failure, Lodge obscures the possibility that the ambiguity of *Naked Lunch* results from Burroughs' deliberate intention to confuse and undermine those moral norms and aesthetic conventions which claim the status of "empirical reality" and "norms." In *S/Z*, Roland Barthes describes the classical or "readerly" text as one which is limited in its plurality by certain "blocks": "These blocks have names: on the one hand truth; on the other, empiricism" (30). The traditional text owes its status to the fact that it shares with conventional literary criticism a belief in these concepts. Burroughs, on the other hand, is trying to approach the limitless plural of an ideal radical text: "As soon as we say that something is true, real, then immediately things are not permitted" (*Job* 97). His declared aim is to reverse and explode the kind of assumptions about truth, empiricism, and moral norms which form the basis of literary humanism.

The Allegorical/Metaphorical View

At least one critic points out that there can be no justifying "explanation of [the] significance" of the Blue Movie sequence, but only an appreciation of its "ecstatically kinetic . . . depiction of violence . . . only the speed of flashing sensation" (Tytell 122). Most critics of Burroughs' work, however, retreat from the immediacy and concreteness of his style to pursue, instead, elaborate figurative interpretations. For example, Lodge argues that the metaphorical connection between the Blue Movie scenes and capital punishment fails because rather than linking the themes, Burroughs' figurative language accentuates the tactile immediacy of the action. This is precisely Burroughs' intention—to offer us a naked lunch, a revelation of what is really going on and not an allegorical evasion. "If civilized countries want to return to Druid Hanging Rites," he argues, "let them see what they actually eat and drink. Let them see what is on the end of that long newspaper spoon" (*NL* xliv).

Burroughs' purpose is not to incite reform, to measure inappropriate action against a set of empirical norms, but simply to reveal a more naked truth. As Allen Ginsberg has described Burroughs' method:

> The method must be purest meat
> and no symbolic dressing,
> actual visions & actual prisons
> as seen then and now.
> .   .   .   .
> A naked lunch is natural to us,
> we eat reality sandwiches.
> But allegories are so much lettuce.
> Don't hide the madness. (*Reality Sandwiches* 40)

Nevertheless, the instinct of the humanistic critic confronted with Burroughs' writing is to dress it up as allegory and moral satire, to distance and defuse the novel by making it a mediating or disposable code serving a more abstract and therefore less threatening message.

In *The Job*, Daniel Odier asks the author to explain the "symbolism" of two passages in his cut-up fiction: one in which "two characters are split in half and rejoined to make two new persons" (114), and another in which "lesbian agents with penises grafted onto their faces" drink spinal fluid (119). Odier seems to be looking for some deeper or hidden meaning which would justify and detoxify these threatening and indigestible images. Burroughs responds patiently to the first query with a lengthy scientific explanation of bicameral brain theory which concludes, "There's no particular symbolism. It's just a possibility which I imagine in the course of time might be in the reach of medical science." Burroughs seems almost embarrassed by his interviewer's persistence in this line of questioning, and he dismisses the second image quickly as "Oh, just a bit of science fiction, really." Typically, Burroughs parries the critic's demand for symbolic explanation or moral justification with his commitment to scientific speculation and naked fact. He refuses to feed our need for allegorical explanation, our need to reaffirm the transcendent nature of language, literature, and the human condition. One detects at times in Burroughs' responses to Odier the same attitude as that expressed by the reluctant Chinese pushers in *Naked Lunch* who evade the insistent Western junky's demands with "No glot . . . C'lom Fliday" (*NL* 235).

This attitude immediately puts Burroughs at odds with conventional literary criticism which equates interpretation with metaphorical decoding and with the ethical pursuit of truth. In traditional criticism the moral and the metaphorical coincide; the same binary opposition which forms the basis of allegory, metaphor, and symbol also supports the comforting dualism of our moral code. Good/evil, mind/body, figurative/literal, meaning/text are all building blocks of the same edifice.

In Burroughs' texts, however, the moral and the metaphorical are called into question as repressive dualistic structures. We have already seen how Burroughs translates the vertical hierarchy of right over wrong into a horizontal and biological confrontation between different life forms. Similarly, the hierarchical structure of interpretation, assuming ascension to a symbolic meaning or moral intention which "justifies" a literary text, is undermined by Burroughs' insistent literalness. Rather than the transcendent "code" language of image or symbol, Burroughs offers experiments scientifically detached and uncommitted, a horizontal arrangement of shifting and random juxtapositions. Burroughs advises us to learn how to write and read horizontally: "A technician learns to think and write in association blocks which can then be manipulated according to the laws of association and juxtaposition" (*NX* 78).

Burroughs' lateralizing of discourse frustrates conventional critical analysis. Lodge, for example, rejects the very idea of a text which resists metaphorical interpretation, denouncing it as a self-destructive and self-defeating enterprise. Most intensely, however, he rejects the effect such a text would have on critical discourse, which would be reduced to merely repeating (instead of metaphorizing and displacing) the primary text (*Modes* 111). To see beyond the notion of interpretation as allegorical or metaphorical decoding, one must consider precisely this possibility. Borges considers it, certainly, in the mad project of Pierre Menard, who sets out to rewrite *Don Quixote* word for word, a critical project at once mystical and absurdly literal. Critics like Walter Benjamin, Jacques Derrida, and Roland Barthes have, I think, brought us closer to the possibility of lateral reading, a critical procedure which would consist primarily of citation and juxtaposition.

The structure imposed by the "pyramid of junk, one level eating the level below" (*NL* xxxviii) is precisely the vertical hierarchy of symbolic meaning which displaces and devours the literal text and the actual world. Metaphor and metaphorical interpretation, then, constitute an addiction: "Junk *is* image" (*NX* 15). Burroughs' distrust of allegory and image stems from his commitment to individual will. These rhetorical forms seem to screen out the literal, the fact, the signifier, to illuminate the signified idea; nothing happens, life fades and is replaced by abstraction. Frank McConnell has described Burroughs' prose as a "stern criticism of allegory," a condemnation of metaphor as "a final temptation to not-will." Burroughs' strong-willed imposition of an impenetrable literalness signifies his refusal to allow "allegorical or metaphorical translation (and avoidance)" (McConnell 669–70).

Burroughs is well aware, with Nietzsche, de Man, and many others, that there is no such thing as purely literal, scientific, or factual language. He writes to Allen Ginsberg as early as 1948: "Ultimately there is only fact on all levels, and the more one argues, verbalizes, moralizes, the less he will see and feel of fact. Needless to say I will not write any formal statement on the subject. *Talk is incompatible with factualism*" (quoted in Tytell 112). Despite this recognition, Burroughs is determined to create a language in *Naked Lunch* which will approach the literal, the concrete, the "real," which will dethrone allegory, metaphor, and symbol. Mary McCarthy heralds the success of Burroughs' attempt when she praises the power of *Naked Lunch*: "finally, for the first time in recent years, a talented writer means what he says to be taken and used literally like an Rx prescription. The literalness of Burroughs is the opposite of 'literature'" ("Déjeuner" 5).[5] McCarthy suspends in quotation marks the notion of a "literature" which is defined in opposition to literal or scientific discourse, and she perceives in Burroughs' work the author's desire to remove such restrictions from the literary work by means of a most provocative cure.

The Real Scene

A specific example of Burroughs' opposition to the moral/metaphorical order may be seen in his pointed juxtaposition of two different descriptions of the same scene in *Naked Lunch*. The narrator is explaining a particular procedure for shooting up heroin:

Provident junkies, known as squirrels, keep stashes against a bust. Every time I take a shot I let a few drops fall into my vest pocket, the lining is stiff with stuff. I had a plastic dropper in my shoe and a safety-pin stuck in my belt. You know how this pin and dropper routine is put down: "She seized a safety-pin caked with blood and rust, gouged a great hole in her leg which seemed to hang open like an obscene, festering mouth waiting for unspeakable congress with the dropper which she now plunged out of sight into the gaping wound. But her hideous galvanized need (hunger of insects in dry places) has broken the dropper off deep in the flesh of her ravaged thigh (looking rather like a poster on soil erosion). But what does she care? She does not even bother to remove the splintered glass [. . .]. What does she care for the atom bomb, the bed bugs, the cancer rent, Friendly Finance waiting to repossess her delinquent flesh. . . . Sweet dreams, Pantopon Rose." (*NL* 9–10)

The description is "put down" in quotation marks, as a voice to be distinguished from the flat factual delivery which introduces it. This description is full of just the sort of moral rhetoric that demands the reader's disgust and righteous condemnation. The rhetorical lament "What does she care for" calls up the popular domestic genres of soap opera and tawdry modern romance adventure—other familiar cultural "addictions." Burroughs counters the exaggerated and parenthetically equivocated metaphors of this manipulative rhetoric, "(looking rather like a poster on soil erosion)," with a direct, almost scientific prose:

The real scene you pinch up some leg flesh and make a quick stab hole with a pin. Then fit the dropper *over, not in* the hole and feed the solution slow and careful so it doesn't squirt out the sides. . . . When I grabbed the Rube's thigh the flesh came up like wax and stayed there, and a slow drop of pus oozed out the hole. And I never touched a living body cold as the Rube there in Philly. (*NL* 10)

Burroughs does not pursue the attack on junk and drug addiction through the whining manipulation of his first version of the scene, but straight ahead, in tactile connection with "the real scene." The hyped-up description that is "put down" in the rhetoric of moral outrage and disgust in the first part of the routine is part of the addiction itself, part of the attraction of the addiction. In his flattened, monosyllabic revision of the scene, Burroughs is trying to take the thrill out of junk, just as he tries to take the thrill out of sexual violence in the Blue Movie scene. For it is this thrill which creates a need strong enough to drive one to barter "raw material of the will." [6]

I do not mean to argue here that this detached "recording instrument" represents Burroughs' poetic voice (or lack of one). In fact, by the end of the second version of the shoot-up scene the style slides from detached objectivity to the rather stagey voice of the hard-boiled detective. We cannot locate the author or the "truth" in either of these voices "put down" in the text. We must look to the negative space between them, to the space cleared by the antithetical clash of these two ways of seeing. It is here, in the "hiatus between thoughts," that Burroughs' new poetry will show itself. This flat prose, then, is not Burroughs' answer to the first version of the scene, but merely one of many guises, one of many technical devices—along with tape recorders, scissors, pirated texts of all varieties—used by the author to undermine the hegemony of moral and metaphorical rhetoric.

One of the most common critical responses to *Naked Lunch* is the translation of the world of drug addiction into an allegory or symbol for other more abstract forms of addiction, oppression, and control. One critic argues: "The transformation of junk from fact to symbol is by far the most important result of this movement toward higher levels of abstraction in *Naked Lunch*" (Stull 16). Again we see the direction of conventional criticism toward vertical hierarchy and abstraction. Frank McConnell has astutely countered this critical tendency with the assertion that any "symbolization" of drug addiction in Burroughs' work constitutes in itself a "retreat into image-junk" (671).[7] Of course Burroughs himself makes a connection between drugs and other forms of addiction, but he is careful to explain that the relationship between the various types of "evil virus" in the "Algebra of Need" is not allegorical but logical, literal, and mathematical: "If you wish to alter or annihilate a pyramid of numbers in a serial relation, you alter or remove the bottom number. If we wish to annihilate the junk pyramid, we must start with the bottom [. . .] *the Addict* [. . .] *the one irreplaceable factor in the junk equation*" (*NL* xl). Burroughs insists further, "I have almost completed a sequel to *Naked Lunch*. A mathematical extension of the Algebra of Need beyond the junk virus" (*NL* xliv). The "evil virus," then, travels from one host to another along mathematical lines of extension or along biological circuits of need—it proceeds by literal metonymic juxtaposition and contagion rather than by metaphorical resemblance.

The literalness—mathematical, scientific, naturalistic, supernaturalistic—which pervades Burroughs' prose style is part of his campaign to free literature from morality and symbolic rhetoric, to seize for it the independence of the sciences: "A doctor is not criticized for describing the manifestations and symptoms of an illness, even though the symptoms may be disgusting. I feel that a writer has the right to the same freedom. In fact, I think that the time has come for the line between literature and science, a purely arbitrary line, to be erased" (*NL* xxxv).

This scientific or technical voice often intrudes abruptly in *Naked Lunch*, breaking in on the tone of a passage or the development of some farcical and fantastic situation. Very often these intrusions are made concrete in their own right by Burroughs' use of parentheses which represent visually the splicing in of a different voice in the text. Once again it must be stressed that these intrusions do not represent the hierarchical domination of one voice over another, but a surgical attack on all structures of hierarchy, continuity, and control. In one typical example, Clem and Jody give a banquet at which they serve couscous made from diseased wheat:

> "But you wouldn't believe it, certain disgruntled elements chased us right down to our launch."
> "Handicapped somewhat by lack of legs."
> "And a condition in the head."
> (Ergot is a fungus disease grows on bad wheat. During the Middle Ages, Europe was periodically decimated by outbreaks of Ergotism, which was called St. Anthony's fire. Gangrene frequently supervenes, the legs turn black and drop off.) (*NL* 160)

Another scene describes the narrator's plans to get rid of the Rube, a traveling companion whose uncontrollable drug habit is making him a social liability:

> I decided to lop him off if it meant a smother party. (This is a rural English custom designed to eliminate aged and bedfast dependents. A family so afflicted throws a "smother party" where the guests pile mattresses on the old liability, climb up on top of the mattresses and lush themselves out.) The Rube is a drag on the industry and should be led out into the skid rows of the world. (This is an African practice. Official known as the "Leader Out" has the function of taking old characters out into the jungle and leaving them there.) (*NL* 10)

As these examples demonstrate, Burroughs does not justify the unpleasant content of his text, as some critics would do, by pointing to a personal idealism underlying a fierce social satire, but rather by insisting, however spuriously, on the scientific and historical objectivity, on the literalness of his images.

Although the images in *Naked Lunch* are often surprisingly lyrical, nostalgic, and evocative, they are always weighted down and literalized by death, decay, stagnation:

> Carl talked to the doctor outside under the narrow arcade with rain bounding up from the street against his pant legs, thinking how many people he tell it to, and the stairs, porches, lawns, driveways, corridors and streets of the world there in the doctor's eyes . . . stuffy German alcoves, butterfly trays to the ceiling, silent portentous smell of uremia seeping under the door, suburban lawns to sound of the water sprinkler, in calm jungle night under silent wings of the Anopheles mosquito. (Note: This is not a figure. Anopheles mosquitoes *are* silent.) (*NL* 45–46)

The stern "Note" which asserts the literalness of the mosquito image is far more than an anti-metaphorical affectation. It equates the rhetorical evasion, which would domesticate the mosquito's silent threat of death into a mere "figure," with the evasion of death and disease in the conversation between Carl and the German doctor. The contempt, disinterest, and hypocrisy which characterize the doctor's treatment of Carl's "native" friend are based on the avoidance of truth: "saying without words: 'Alzo for the so stupid peasant we must avoid use of the word is it not? Otherwise he shit himself with fear. Koch and spit they are *both* nasty words I think?' He said aloud: 'It is a catarro de los pulmones'" (*NL* 45). Such rhetorical evasion is designed to distract us from the obscenity, the unthinkableness of human mortality.

In response to this evasion Burroughs returns us always to the hard facts of time, of life in the body: the sequence of the junky's days strung together on the thread of blood which flowers in the needle, the orgiast's days strung together on the thread of semen discharged by a hanged man into a black void, and the lives of all "human animals" tied to the "long lunch thread from mouth to ass all the days of our years" (*NL* 230).

Throughout *Naked Lunch* nostalgic images, memories of places, objects and actions associated with innocence and youth are punctuated by parenthetical details evoking death, silence, and decay. Evocative "train whistles" and adolescent dreams are reduced to images with no personal vibrations, no moral or sentimental impact; nostalgia and sentimentality approach silence, emptiness, a cold transparency. In that transparent landscape suddenly the evasive veil of sentiment is torn aside and we see clearly the inexorable progress of human mortality: "Time jump like a broken typewriter, the boys are old men, young hips quivering and twitching in boy-spasms go slack and flabby, draped over an outhouse seat, a park bench, a stone wall [. . .] twitching and shivering in dirty underwear, probing for a vein in the junk-sick morning, in an Arab café muttering and slobbering—" (*NL* 94). Reality is not the lubricious flow of days or words but the startling and unpredictable jump of the broken typewriter. (In the cut-up novels, as we shall see, Burroughs learns how to transform that skidding machinery into a weapon of liberation.)

In the midst of the characters' dazed wanderings in *Naked Lunch*, the narration comes into focus unexpectedly in moments of intense clarity: "Something falls off you when you cross the border into Mexico, and suddenly the landscape hits you straight with nothing between you and it, desert and mountains and vultures; little wheeling specks and others so close you can hear wings cut the air (a dry husking sound), and when they spot something they pour out of the blue sky [. . .] down in a black funnel" (*NL* 14). Here is the direct naked seeing Burroughs' prose aspires to—and what it sees is no comforting vision of transcendence but a harsh and ugly mosaic of aggression, violence, life feeding off of life, life falling to icy death "through air clear as glycerine."

Negatives and Absence

Lyricism and symbolic abstraction, then, are seen as the evasive methods of a moral/metaphorical order; Burroughs destroys them with a relentless and often disgusting concreteness. There is an accumulation of material objects in *Naked Lunch*, a cluttered mosaic, a chaotic encyclopedia of things, but they whirl by us so quickly that they never acquire the weightiness of materiality as we find it in Balzac, Dickens, or Flaubert. The concreteness which anchors Burroughs' text is instead the literalness of absence, a materiality of loss: the disappearance of the sick or aged disposed of in jungles or death-dealing sanitariums; the absence of legs lost to gangrene infection; the absence of sound ("silent wings of the Anopheles mosquito"); the absence of transcendent meaning ("TV antennas to the meaningless sky"). This absence of any central or transcendental significance, an absence which marks for many contemporary theorists the nature of all discourse, finds in the language of *Naked Lunch* a peculiarly concrete representation.

This paradoxical convergence of concreteness and absence reflects the technological mysticism of Burroughs' fiction, his scientific belief in what he calls "non-body experience." Burroughs suggests, again parenthetically, that some drug intoxications are actually "space time travel": "(It occurs to me that preliminary Yage nausea is motion sickness of transport to Yage state. . . .)" (*NL* 110). Thus, the material reality of the body's response (nausea) corroborates the experience of travel outside the body. Later in *The Job*, Burroughs argues that drugs are unnecessary, that the mind can open up space travel simply by leaving "verbal garbage behind." He clearly sees the three modes of travel— by NASA, by drugs, and by the controlled manipulation of silence—as equivalent. For Burroughs, literalness asserts not only the material facts of life in the body, but the literal possibility of escape from that body.[8]

Burroughs' philosophy and aesthetics of absence leads to a new way of thinking, a way which protects the integrity and will of the individual from the dualistic and hierarchical "mind locks" of Western thought: "It is no oceanic organismal subconscious body thinking. It is precisely delineated by what it is not.[. . .] There are no considerations here that would force thinking into certain lines of structural or environmental necessities" (*Job* 91). The strategy is clearly a negative one: "The first step is to stop doing everything you 'have to do.' Mock up a way of thinking you have to do. [. . .] Now mock up some thinking you don't have to do. [. . .] Wind up is you don't have to think anything" (*Job* 89–90). One recognizes here the deconstructive tendency to perceive sign, story, identity, or meaning as a deferred presence in which everything is, as Burroughs puts it, "delineated by what it is not." While conventional narrative, as Barthes argues, tries to "impregnate the void of what it silences by the plenitude of what it says" (*S/Z* 162), Burroughs' narratives repeatedly expose that void, accentuate that silence. His texts reveal that the true substance of writing is the hiatus it frames, the absence or gap it creates by displacing presence, reality, truth. This negative aesthetic will be carried farthest in the cut-up novels.

In Burroughs' work, then, the absence or emptiness that is language is made literal and concrete. We must learn, he warns, to "stop words to see and touch words to move and use words like objects" (*Job* 91). Not only must words become tangible (and thus controllable) objects, the entire manipulative system of Western language and thought must be made visible. This is, in a general sense, the goal of much contemporary theory which, as Said describes it, "makes visible what is usually invisible in a text" ("Problem" 674). For Burroughs, the problem is presented more dramatically as the necessity of escape from a blinding addiction. To kick the habits of Western discourse, to achieve the "total exposure" of all cultural addictions, one must follow the command to "see smell and listen" (*NL* xlv). If the word is made an object, a fact, a body, if it becomes external and visible, we can "see the enemy direct." The alternative is to be trapped in body and word forever: "LISTEN LOOK OR SHIT FOREVER [. . .] IN THEE BEGINNING WAS THE WORD [. . .] COME OUT OF THE TIME WORD THE FOREVER. [. . .] ALL OUT OF TIME AND INTO SPACE. [. . .] THE WRITING OF SPACE. THE WRITING OF SILENCE. LOOK LOOK LOOK" (*Yage* 61–62)

The View from Silence

In Burroughs' fiction clarity of vision is linked to concreteness and to silence: "I Hassan i Sabbah *rub out the word forever*. [. . .] Cross all your skies see the silent writing of Brion Gysin Hassan i Sabbah" (*NX* 12).[9] This intersection of clarity and silence is characteristic of much of the literature of the 1960s, as critics of that period have shown us. In her essay "The Aesthetics of Silence," Susan Sontag describes the "stare" induced by contemporary radical fiction. Such narratives demand of the reader a vigilant attentiveness, and offer in return a "cleansed, non-interfering vision" (16). Under this silent glazed stare of the reader words suddenly seem "palpable" and "'meaning' [is] partially or totally converted into use" (29). Sontag calls this movement away from metaphorical interpretation a "strategy of *literalness*" in which writers like Kafka and Beckett "appear to invite the reader to ascribe high-powered symbolic and allegorical meanings to them and, at the same time, repel such ascriptions" (29).[10] In his own provocative strategies, Burroughs is clearly aligned with these writers of the "literal."

The ambivalence of the text which invites allegory only to deny it is similar to the paradoxical example Sontag develops of the text which babbles its way into silence, which exhausts language by the accumulation of inventories, catalogues, and surfaces. She finds in the work of Stein, Beckett, and Burroughs the "subliminal idea that it might be possible to out-talk language" (27). The negative mosaics of *Naked Lunch* in which Burroughs juxtaposes scattered fragments, remnants, the detritus of the world, are motivated by this desire to defy and exhaust meaning, to starve out the language parasite and leave no symbolic residue. In *The Job*, Burroughs argues that he no longer believes in the possibility that certain uses of language could lead to silence (51). The only hope he retains after the 1960s for achieving the "option of silence" is grounded in the potential of hieroglyphic languages (*TM* 156), a direction he pursues to its extreme in his pictorial composite *The Book of Breeething*. Serge Grunberg points out that silence and hieroglyphics represent, for Burroughs, the possibility of the destruction of the symbolic order (132–33).

Like Sontag, Ihab Hassan sees silence and literalness as central elements in our contemporary aesthetic. He associates Burroughs with a "literature of silence [which] manages to deny the time-honored functions of literature [. . .]: it aspires to an impossible concreteness" ("Silence" 76). As we have seen, among those "time-honored functions of literature" denied by Burroughs are its functions as a medium for transcendent metaphorical meaning and as a vehicle for moral dualism. But the literature of silence, as practiced by William Burroughs, is not only a literature of denial and destruction but of liberation. "Behind the appeals for silence," Sontag argues, "lies the wish for a perceptual and cultural clean slate [. . .] the liberation of the artist from himself, of art from the particular artwork, of art from history, of spirit from matter, of the mind from its perceptual and intellectual limitations" (17–18). Like radical theory, Burroughs' fiction offers a glimpse into this space beyond limits, into the open realm which lies "beyond man and humanism."

2 | Notes from the Orifice: Language and the Body in *Naked Lunch*

To move beyond man and humanism it will be necessary, Burroughs argues, to leave behind the outdated artifacts of word and body. He insists didactically in *The Job* that the time has come to leave "verbal garbage" behind, to leave the body behind, to travel into bodiless space and silence. There will remain in his vision of the future the possibility of rediscovering word and body in some new form: word and body as they might exist outside of time, outside of binary opposition, outside of the isolated subjectivity in which we live. Burroughs approaches that rediscovery in the cut-up novels; in *Naked Lunch*, however, he is still engaged in laying bare the present conditions of word and body, in serving up the naked facts.

The narrative entrée in this naked lunch which condenses most powerfully and economically the thematic and stylistic strategies of Burroughs' fiction is the story of the carnival man who teaches his anus to talk. In this bizarre tale, Burroughs dramatizes the problematic relationship of body and mind, and the role of language in that relationship; the arbitrary violence of language as a system of naming and representation; and the possibility of an ontology and an aesthetics based on negativity and absence.

Here is the story as Dr. Benway tells it:

> Did I ever tell you about the man who taught his asshole to talk? [. . .]
>
> "This ass talk had a sort of gut frequency. It hit you right down there like you gotta go. You know when the old colon gives you the elbow and it feels sorta cold inside, and you know all you have to do is turn loose? Well this talking hit you right down there, a bubbly, thick stagnant sound, a sound you could *smell*.
>
> "This man worked for a carnival you dig, and to start with it was like a novelty ventriloquist act. Real funny, too, at first. He had a number he called 'The Better 'Ole' that was a scream, I tell you. I forget most of it but it was clever. Like, 'Oh I say, are you still down there, old thing?'
>
> " 'Nah! I had to go relieve myself.'
>
> "After a while the ass started talking on its own. He would go in without anything prepared and his ass would ad-lib and toss the gags back at him every time.

"Then it developed sort of teeth-like little raspy incurving hooks and started eating. He thought this was cute at first and built an act around it, but the asshole would eat its way through his pants and start talking on the street, shouting out it wanted equal rights. It would get drunk, too, and have crying jags nobody loved it and it wanted to be kissed same as any other mouth. Finally it talked all the time day and night, you could hear him for blocks screaming at it to shut up, and beating it with his fist, and sticking candles up it, but nothing did any good and the asshole said to him: 'It's you who will shut up in the end. Not me. Because we don't need you around here any more. I can talk and eat *and* shit.'

"After that he began waking up in the morning with a transparent jelly like a tadpole's tail all over his mouth. This jelly was what the scientists call un-D.T., Undifferentiated Tissue, which can grow into any kind of flesh on the human body. He would tear it off his mouth and the pieces would stick to his hands like burning gasoline jelly and grow there, grow anywhere on him a glob of it fell. So finally his mouth sealed over, and the whole head would have amputated spontaneous—(did you know there is a condition occurs in parts of Africa and only among Negroes where the little toe amputates spontaneously?)—except for the *eyes* you dig. That's one thing the asshole *couldn't* do was see. It needed the eyes. But nerve connections were blocked and infiltrated and atrophied so the brain couldn't give orders any more. It was trapped in the skull, sealed off. For a while you could see the silent, helpless suffering of the brain behind the eyes, then finally the brain must have died, because the eyes *went out*, and there was no more feeling in them than a crab's eye on the end of a stalk." (*NL* 131–33)

The Carny Man and His Audience

Aside from the Blue Movie scene, the carny man's tale is probably the most frequently quoted episode in critical analyses of *Naked Lunch*. We have already seen the tendency among literary critics to evade the unpleasant literalness of Burroughs' style by transposing his visions into metaphor or allegory. The carny man's story passes through several incarnations of this kind. The immediate and direct impact of the story, often described as "horrible" or "revolting," is displaced by analytical indirection and abstraction which lead us as quickly as possible away from the story's disturbing deadpan narrative to the moral and allegorical intention it allegedly serves.

Alvin Seltzer's extended analysis of the carny man routine reveals most clearly where conventional criticism is driven by Burroughs' text. Seltzer gives a chronological reading of the talking anus story and the material which directly follows it. This material, unlike the carny man tale, is blatantly didactic and provides Seltzer with a "key" to the narrative: "*Now* the story of

the talking asshole becomes a pointed one, directed toward a political statement of the evils of a democratic system. The talking asshole becomes an allegorical equivalent of bureaucracies that feed off their host. . . . The analogy
works remarkably well, not simply because it is shocking and unexpected but
because it all *works out* as a result of Burroughs' careful, conscious handling
[of what] turns out to be a highly unified sequence (346–47). I do not argue
here with Seltzer's association of the talking anus with parasitic bureaucracy,
but with his reductive mode of allegorical explanation and with his conventional notion that unity and structure "justify" a text. These stylistic conventions were, in fact, the legal criteria used in court to establish the artistic merit
of *Naked Lunch* (Goodman 212).

Tony Tanner's excellent and comprehensive analysis of Burroughs' work includes a reading of the carny man passage which retrieves precisely those
qualities of the text which Seltzer explains away, Tanner reads the story as
parable rather than allegory, a distinction that prevents him from replacing the
actual content of the tale with a coded meaning. For Tanner, the carny man's
history is a "parable of matter in a state of hideous revolt," a "paradigm" of
the ubiquitous entropic pattern in *Naked Lunch* in which lower forms of life
devour higher forms. Unlike Seltzer's conclusion that the carny man story is
not about the body but actually about the body politic (bureaucracy), Tanner
insists on the literalness of the story's content. The carny man's situation
dramatizes not just the body, but the body *as matter* (117–18).

Psychoanalytic readings of this tale also bring us closer to a direct confrontation with the story's visceral content. However, such analyses inevitably
imply, despite the critics' disclaimers, that the text provides the basis for a
clinical diagnosis of the author. These psychoanalytic interpretations also tend
to structure the texts under examination within the binary oppositions which
form the basis of psychoanalysis itself. Burroughs' work is thus drawn back
into the very structures of duality it seeks to destroy.

In Neil Oxenhandler's "Listening to Burroughs' Voice," for example, the
critic describes a recurring motif in *Naked Lunch* in which one organ or in-
stinctual drive "emerge[s] victorious from an internal conflict with the ego"
(195). Oxenhandler redefines the struggle in the carny man's story as a conflict
between two opposing drives—the oral and the anal:

> This brilliant anecdote, which shows Burroughs' tremendous power of
> improvisation, actually illustrates the genetic development of the nega-
> tive oedipus as defense against psychic masochism. There is, first, the
> struggle between the oral impulse and the anal impulse. The anal is seen
> as sadistic and searching for dominance which it eventually achieves.
> The face (the seat of orality) is sealed off by a wall of tissue, and finally
> "goes out," i.e., masochistic attachment to the giantess of the nursery

becomes completely unconscious. The domination of anal eroticism then seems complete. However, this domination is only apparent. The buried oral material retains its power and reappears [. . .]. (197)

While Tanner generalizes the conflict in this episode as an opposition of higher and lower human functions, Oxenhandler insists on the more specific struggle between the two orifices, mouth and anus. Despite a highly specialized vocabulary which can be obstructive, his reading clarifies the intense battle for domination acted out within the body sphere, and the false illusion of the victory of the anal impulse in this case.[1] He draws our attention, instead, to the inevitable and involuntary return of the oral. What is disturbing in this reading is that Burroughs' conscious control and manipulation of his material seems to have been lost in the scuffle between the oral and anal drives. Yet the story is clearly *about* control, and specifically about control *of* language and *through* language.

There are several critics whose readings of Burroughs' fiction focus profitably on language as power.[2] The most thorough analysis of Burroughs' relationship to language is Serge Grunberg's "*A la recherche d'un corps*": *Langage et silence dans l'oeuvre de William Burroughs*. In his Lacanian analysis of Burroughs' work, Grunberg combines an intense focus on the body with a heightened awareness of the relationship between the body and language; he sees the carny man tale as a "parable of writing." He argues astutely that the carny man's situation, in which the function of speech is displaced and the subject threatened by another who would talk like or for him, is the situation of *all* textual discourse, where "the other" silences the reading subject (103). Grunberg ultimately elevates the body and the body's speech to the status of an adamic language, celebrating in Burroughs' fiction what he describes as the return of the whiteness of death to its original cloacal color (104). Thus for Grunberg, the body is finally idealized as a privileged sphere of truth, and he finds "true speech" in that place where sexuality inscribes itself.[3] The limit of Grunberg's provocative and productive reading is his reluctance to imagine, or to recognize as anything but failure and self-delusion, the possibility of life without a body or without a unified subject. The prisonhouse here is not just language, but Grunberg's psychoanalytic grid which always returns us to castration, the oedipal conflict, and narcissism.

I would like to pick up where these critics leave off, to offer a reading of the carnival man story not as a political allegory or a portrait of the author's intimate psyche, but as a history of voice and body, of the relationship between language and materiality. This relationship is most strikingly dramatized in *Naked Lunch* in recurring images and transmutations of the human orifices of mouth and anus, those places where inside and outside, body and cosmos intersect. As one critic puts it—perhaps coming closest to an understanding of the carny man episode—Burroughs "focuses on where the action is, on orifices and genitals, our avenues of appetite" (Weinstein 35). In the carny man's history, anus and mouth, the sites of the digestive and the linguistic functions, become a single hole, at once an entrance and an exit. In this convergence, the binary oppositions of inside/outside, of mind/body are shown to be locked in a relationship of intense conflict, in an interminable struggle for domination.

A Tale of (against) Domination

Dr. Benway's description of the carnival man's act and its repercussions is simultaneously funny and frightening; beneath the Rabelaisian joke of a talking anus lies an ominous tale of control. The carny man story dramatizes in particular the conflict and repression at work within the body as constructed by Western philosophy and psychoanalysis. This well-ordered body is characterized by the opposition of upper and lower regions and the functions they represent: the rational sphere of the mind/the sensual sphere of the body. Critics have used these divisions and boundaries of the body as a blueprint to the carny man story, but they fail to see Burroughs' parodic attitude toward this corporeal geography.

Let us examine more closely the conventional image of the body against which Burroughs is operating. The mouth, face, and head, in their symbolic role as emblems of the higher human sphere of reason, lose their connection with the physical body. They are presented in conventional thought as not only superior to the corporeal functions of the genitals and the digestive tract, but as the very contradition of those functions. Like its internal divisions, the external boundaries of this highly structured body are also carefully designated, separating the inner world of self and subjectivity from the external world of the other.[4] In the story of the carny man, the mouth at first seems to rule the body, transforming the anus into a second, clearly inferior organ of speech. The anus's derivative status is underlined by its complaint that it wants to be "kissed same as any other mouth." In the terrifying moment when the anus grows "teeth-like little raspy incurving hooks," however, we are reminded by the grim parody that the mouth is also an organ of tearing, chewing, devouring. Thus the anus returns the mouth to its bodily function which it seeks to evade or disguise.

The impulse of the rational sphere to organize the body is evident in the immediate narrative frame for the carny man routine. Dr. Benway and Dr. Schaefer are discussing possible improvements of the human body: "We could seal up nose and mouth, fill in the stomach, make an air hole direct into the lungs where it should have been in the first place" (131). From the perspective of science, the mouth, organ of speech and ingestion, is expendable;

the scientist would retain only the minimal functions needed to keep the organism alive.

This desire to correct or improve on physical nature is also reflected in the title of the carny man's routine—"The Better 'Ole." Rather than reducing the body to its lowest common denominator, the carny man would seem to be elevating it. In acquiring language the anus is raised to the superior rational sphere of the mind. In teaching his anus to imitate a mouth, however, the man produces a kind of humiliation of nature, like performing monkeys and dogs dressed in human clothing. The surgical operations of the doctors and the routine of the carny man are similarly based on the mind's need to dominate nature and the body.

The carnival man pursues his goal of domination in a rather oblique manner by making a joke out of the idea of a dialogue between ass and face, body and mind. He plays on their similarity, but bases the comedy of his performance on their irreconcilable difference; the joke depends on the audience's certainty that the mind is in control all along. A closer look at the comic material itself reveals the ulterior motive of this routine: "O, I say, are you still down there, old thing?" "Nah! I had to go relieve myself." The mind feigns a removed indifference or obliviousness to the body, that "old thing" which is so far away "down there." The wishful fantasy behind the question "are you still down there" is that the anus *is* gone—that it has taken its inconvenient needs and processes and relieved them somewhere else, even farther away than the other end of the digestive tract. From its superior position, the mind mocks the body's weaknesses, its needs and dependencies.[5] Behind his crude joke is the carny man's desire to set up a closed circuit around the mouth, to shut down actual digestion by substituting the oral (word) for the anal (the body, the senses). The carny man's joke is motivated by an intense need for self-delusion, a need to evade the fact of his own body and his own mortality.

In his philosophical essay *Conjunctions and Disjunctions*, Octavio Paz explores man's dual nature by studying the significance of jokes or metaphors which compare the face and the ass:

> There is not much purpose in repeating here everything that psychoanalysis has taught us about the conflict between the face and the ass, the (repressive) reality principle and the (explosive) pleasure principle. I will merely note here that the metaphor that I mentioned, both as it works upward and as it works downward—the ass as a face and the face as an ass—it serves each of these principles alternately. At first, the metaphor uncovers a similarity; then, immediately afterward, it covers it up again. [. . .] Here, too, the similarity at first seems unbearable to us—and therefore we either laugh or cry; in the second step, the opposition also becomes unbearable—and therefore we either laugh or cry. When we say that the ass is like another face, we deny the soul-body dualism; we laugh

because we have resolved the discord that we are. But the victory of the pleasure principle does not last long; at the same time that our laughter celebrates the reconciliation of the soul and the body, it dissolves it and make it laughable once again. [. . .] When we laugh at our ass—that caricature of our face—we affirm our separation and bring about the total defeat of the pleasure principle. (4–5)

Paz argues that such metaphors and jokes are primarily strategies of the face, acts of repression and aggression which would impose the hierarchical dominance of the mouth within the soul-body dualism.

A perfect example of the kind of metaphor or joke Paz has in mind—and a striking parallel to the carny man's act—can be found in the historical case of a Frenchman who performed in Parisian music halls in the 1890s. Having developed the ability to draw air or water in through his anus and to expel it at will and with some subtlety of control, Le Petomane, as he called himself, performed such feats on stage as smoking a cigarette, playing tunes on a pipe, "singing," and "vocalizing" imitations of various animals and natural sounds. This apparently modest and tasteful routine (which was performed in a tuxedo) elicited just the sort of response Paz associates with the "unbearable" comparison of ass and face which makes us "either laugh or cry." In the charming account of Le Petomane's career assembled by F. Caradec and Jean Nohain, descriptions from several sources confirm the "hysterical" nature of audience responses to this music-hall specialty: "enthusiasm became delirious . . . the apoplectic faces, the streaming tears" (13), "many fainted and fell down and had to be resuscitated" (33). The audience's delight in the routine was often associated with social satire: "When I saw this Frenchman farting away professionally and people paying to hear him, I pissed myself laughing" (33); or with artistic parody: "warbling from the depths of his pants those trills which others, their eyes towards heaven, beamed at the ceiling" (73).

The narrators of Le Petomane's story, quoting authorities ranging from eleventh century health codes to Montaigne's *On the Force of the Imagination*, stress that the social proscription against farting contradicts the medical prescriptions in its favor. Le Petomane himself, like the carny man in Burroughs' novel, attracted a certain amount of medical curiosity. Caradec and Nohain reproduce the texts of several medical examinations which explain directly the displacement of the upper by the lower functions of the body: "the intestine *plays the role of* the chest . . . and the anal sphincter that of the vocal chords, the throat and mouth" (63, my emphasis).

In the case of Le Petomane, however, the issue of freedom of farting was played out most interestingly in the legal rather than the medical arena. The subtitle of his routine at the Moulin Rouge, "Le Petomane: the only one who pays no author's royalties," suggests with almost Barthesian logic that the voice of the body exists outside all conventional jurisdictions. Despite this witty claim to anarchistic autonomy, Le Petomane was sued by the directors of the Moulin Rouge who attempted to suppress the artist's free exposure of his talents to the public at large. Ironically, the episode which precipitated the suit was a demonstration given by Le Petomane at a friend's market stall, precisely in that lawless space of the popular carnival. Thus it would seem that the social taboos against the free speech of the body may be relaxed in certain circumstances, but economic exigencies will soon reimpose their own repressive censorship.[6]

Although Le Petomane's actual routine maintained a good-humored tone, innocent and earthy, the medical description of his "phenomenon" and the legal actions surrounding it remind us indirectly of the violence and repression inherent in all textual activity (which displaces the "role of the mouth" to the text) and in all cultural institutions which would control language and thought. Like the carny man tale, the story of Le Petomane raises such issues as the indeterminacy of the origin or ownership of voice and the disruption of the body/mind hierarchy. In particular, the unprecedented popular response to Le Petomane may help to explain the rather surprising prominence of the carny man story in critical analyses of *Naked Lunch*. A large part of the story's appeal is certainly its comic effect; it is a quintessential example of Burroughs' "routine" style. Yet critical references to the story do not appear in the context of discussions of Burroughs' humor. Although it was cited by the prosecution at the Boston trial, the story is not, in fact, pornographic, and it is not even the most striking example of anal-obsessive imagery in the novel. I would argue that the intense impact of this tale is due to its exposure of the dynamics of linguistic power. In the confrontation of mouth and anus, who tells the jokes and who is the victim of those jokes? Who is in control of the linguistic arsenal? Acted out within the arena of a single body, we witness what Barthes calls the "imperialism" of one language over another (*S/Z* 206).

A closer examination of the carny man's routine reveals that his attempt to establish through dialogue the similarity of ass and face, to perform his duality as a "relationship," is clearly based on bad faith. He doesn't really want to improve the body, to raise the ass to equality with the face, but merely wants to perform a comic "show" of that equality which actually reminds us of the body's inferiority. As Paz says, "Our face laughs at our ass and thus retraces the dividing line between the body and the spirit" (5). The carny man's dialogue, as it is initially conceived, is actually a monologue, ventriloquy operating as the basic weapon of control through language.[7] The carny man's anus responds to the "smiling repression of the face" (Paz 5) with violence and aggression of its own; it dominates the language function by "talking all the time night and day." The mind is reduced to using brute physical force, "beating it with his fist and sticking candles up it." Degenerating into bestial violence in response to the body's invasion of its superior territory (its language), the mind loses its position of control.[8] The vertical hierarchy of mind over body is transposed onto the horizontal plane of a battlefield.

The fate of the carny man is like that of Bubu, whose tale follows several pages later. Bubu feeds his need to dominate by consorting with a Latah, a strange creature addicted to compulsive servility and imitation. In this case, too, carnival performance turns demonic, for the Latah "imitates all his expressions and mannerisms and simply sucks the persona right out of him like a sinister ventriloquist's dummy" (*NL* 141), leaving Bubu with no self and no language. Like Bubu, the carny man can no longer speak for himself against the anus, because he has no self left. All that remains is the anus's grotesque parody of human identity—greedy, selfish, aggressive, destructive, mawkishly sentimental ("it would get drunk, too, and have crying jags nobody loved it"), and armed with a diarrhetic flow of words.

The anecdote of the talking anus challenges the comforting myth that it is language which distinguishes man from beast, man from his own bestiality. In this confrontation of body and mind, Burroughs demonstrates that language, the "human gift of tongues," is the first and easiest mental characteristic for the body to imitate and annex for itself. This successful appropriation suggests that the word has as strong, perhaps even a stronger affinity with body than with mind. What began as a comic ventriloquy show of the mind's control of the body becomes a parodic imitation by the body of the mind's pretensions, of its whining self-absorption.

What is disturbing here is the displacement or undecidability of speech. This indeterminacy appears in the carny man episode in grotesquely concrete form as the threatening phenomenon of "un-D.T., Undifferentiated Tissue which can grow into any kind of flesh on the human body" (*NL* 133). In its "degenerate cancerous life-form," this uncertain flesh forms "a hideous random image. [. . .] 3 and 4 eyes together, criss-cross of mouth and assholes" (134). In the cut-up narratives, Burroughs will use this same cement mixer of word and flesh as a breakthrough strategy of liberation. The production of indeterminacy, then, is both the sign of the disease and the method of its cure.

Burroughs' plan in *Naked Lunch* is to expose the repressive duality of body/ mind by confusing and combining word and flesh, making the abstract word literal and concrete. In this episode, Burroughs even gives speech the physical impact of a sound emitted and received by the body's lower sphere: "this ass talk had a sort of gut frequency. It hit you right down there like you gotta go. You know when the old colon gives you the elbow and it feels sorta cold inside." But this strange narrative is not a parable of the triumph of body over mind, a mere reversal of conventional hierarchy. For once the carny man's brain dies and his "blank periscope eyes" are disconnected (as all junkies' eyes) from the "seat of libido and emotion" (230), the anus too seems to fall silent. Language as we know it only persists where there is conflict and the possibility of domination. There is no winner here; this silence is not a free-dom from language and conflict but the silence of dead empty air, of the anus feeling blindly for the next host to feed its parasitic hunger.[9] Like Burroughs' god of conflict and binary opposition, Mr. Bradly Mr. Martin, the anus can do everything but see. The price of achieving the totality of the self-enclosed and hierarchically organized body is a terminal blindness to the very imprison-ment such a body constitutes.

The carny man's experience, then, enacts three basic lessons: the violence and domination inherent in the dualism of body/mind; the use of language as a basic weapon in that struggle for supremacy; and the inevitable outcome of the struggle in blindness, silence, and death. The apparently arbitrary mad-ness of many scenes in *Naked Lunch* often obscures Burroughs' consistent repetition of this basic scenario of domination and destruction. The carny man anecdote stands apart from the extravagant parade of characters and the fragmented and farcical dramatics which surround it by virtue of its clear, precise, almost flat prose style. In its clarity and concreteness, it provides us with a blueprint for understanding the radical nature of Burroughs' fiction and theory.

Reduction vs. Evolution

The carny man's story appears in a section of *Naked Lunch* entitled "Ordinary Men and Women," a cluster of routines which focus most intensely on the body/mind relationship. Burroughs populates these stories with concrete embodiments of every possible imbalance and abuse within this dual system: from paralyzed bodies numbed by the abstractions of religion and romance, to paralyzed minds imprisoned by the body's physical cravings. In every case, domination inevitably leads to a reduction of human experience and consciousness. As the tyranny of the rhetorics of religion and romance turn "live orgones into dead bullshit," the tyranny of the body turns the life energy of sex and sensory experience into the mindless mechanical responses of pure need. The organ of need (physical or spiritual) is always the orifice— mouth or anus or some vague undifferentiated hole—sucking life out of a host. Like the "blind seeking mouth" of the junky which "sways out on a long tube of ectoplasm, feeling for the silent frequency of junk" (*NL* 7), the sex addict is alienated from his own body, his own desire. He seeks blindly the same emotionless biological thrill as the junky: "He's got a prolapsed asshole and when he wants to get screwed he'll pass you his ass on three feet of in-tes-tine. . . . If he's a mind to it he can drop out a piece of gut reaches from his office clear over to Roy's Beer Place, and it go feelin' around lookin' for a peter, just afeelin' around like a blind worm" (*NL* 126–27).

Burroughs lays bare the alienation of body and mind most concretely in the experiments of the mad scientists who dominate *Naked Lunch*. These scientists explore, with inhuman detachment, possible technical improvements of the human mind and body. "Doctor 'Fingers' Shafer, the Lobotomy Kid," creates a "Complete All American De-anxietized Man" (103) whose "compact and abbreviated" nervous system turns him into a monstrous black centipede; Dr. Berger's Mental Health Hour (136–38) televises the scientific miracles of the "cured homosexual" whose muscles now "move into place like autonomous parts of a severed insect," and the "cured writer" who has been reduced to silence so that he can be dubbed.

As the rhetorics of religion, drugs, and sex in *Naked Lunch* either amputate the body or condense it to one insatiable organ of need, one orifice through which life can be absorbed, scientific improvement of the body moves similarly toward reduction and simplification: "The human body is filled up vit unnecessitated parts. You can get by vit one kidney. Vy have two?" (*NL* 182); "The human body is scandalously inefficient. Instead of a mouth and an anus to get out of order why not have one all purpose hole to eat *and* eliminate? [. . .] Why not one all purpose blob?" (*NL* 131). Like these scientific strategies, the carny man's anus also claims totality and self-sufficiency: "I can talk and eat *and* shit." What this naked parody of the mouth's desires reveals, however, is that such autonomy is won only by the repression of the other, of *all* others. The anus sneers, "We don't need you around here any more." Contrary to what Grunberg suggests, there is no solidarity of the orifices, there is only the common hunger, the common need to dominate which makes all orifices resemble each other. Each orifice, trying to fill its emptiness by devouring other life, seeks exclusive domination of the body host. Burroughs' strategy of resistance is to open *many* orifices, many holes which would dissolve and disseminate the tyranny of the single hole. In his cut-up experiments in particular, Burroughs will attempt to generate an indeterminate flux through an infinite number of textual breaks, gaps, and holes, liberating the evolutionary potential of both word and body.

The truncated creatures who grope blindly around *Naked Lunch* are dismembered remnants of human life. Dehumanized into insects, automatons, or body parts, they have been *cut off* from evolution and change. The "human evolutionary direction of infinite potentials and differentiation" (*NL* 134) which Burroughs promotes is most obviously threatened by governments and political parties. The two extreme political factions in *Naked Lunch* are the Divisionists, "flooding the planet with 'desirable replicas' [of themselves] such creatures constituting an attempt to circumvent process and change" (*NL* 162), and the Liquefactionists, a party of lubricity whose aim is the "eventual merging of everyone into One Man by a process of protoplasmic absorption"

(*NL* 146). These very different strategies of proliferation and reduction serve ultimately the same goal of replacing individuality and difference with total uniformity.

This movement toward homogeneity takes on a demonic cast in *Naked Lunch* where amoeba-like projections repeatedly threaten to assimilate or "schlup" all other life, to devour and erase all difference. The myth of democracy, to Burroughs, is merely a coverup for this parasitic absorption. As he argues in the passage directly following the carny man story, "The end result of complete cellular representation is cancer. Democracy is cancerous" (*NL* 134). In *Nova Express* he will describe the futuristic extension of this cancer in the "biologic merging tanks": "melt whole peoples into one concentrate— It's more democratic that way you see?—Biologic Representation—Cast your votes into the tanks" (132–33).

In the guise of medical progress toward simplification, in the promises of democratic representation and unity, or even in the apparently innocent form of a carnival joke, Burroughs detects the same pattern. Science, politics, the personal relations between individuals and the individual's relation to himself, to his own body—all of these are variations on the "Algebra of Need," the mathematics of reduction by whose "simple basic laws" everything keeps "simplifying away under the junk cover" (*NL* xlv). The devouring monkey who is the form of the junky's need, the Replica imitations of the Divisionist, the One Man amoeba of the Liquefactionist, or the tyrannical aggression of the carny man's mouth *or* anus, all enact the "renunciation of life itself, a *falling* towards inorganic, inflexible machine, towards dead matter" (134).

Images of amputation and death haunt the reader throughout *Naked Lunch*: "trailing the colorless death smell/afterbirth of a withered grey monkey/ phantom twinges of amputation" (234). Such poetic echoes—and they do produce a surprisingly lyrical refrain—are given more concrete and dramatic form in the final stages of the carny man's struggle. He only escapes the amputation of his head because the anus needs the eyes; nevertheless, his brain is "sealed off," virtually *cut off* from the body. This is the same sort of incision as that made by the literal slash of the surgeon's scalpel as he gleefully performs lobotomies and amputations. All of these mutilations of body and mind reflect the structure of binary opposition: body/mind. In Burroughs' literal imagination, the slash which separates body and mind, setting them in a relation of competition and conflict, is as deadly as the surgeon's knife.

Beneath the specific abuses of politics, science, or personal relations, Burroughs traces this cutting edge of domination and control to its insidious origin in language. As he warns the reader somewhat belatedly at the end of *Naked Lunch*, "Gentle Reader, The Word will leap on you with leopard man iron claws, it will *cut off* fingers and toes like an opportunist land crab" (*NL* 230, my emphasis). In the context of language as in the context of the body, all binary structures—all *relationships*—lead to reduction, amputation, death of the organism. The insistent literalness, the condensation or displacement of the whole by the part, the tendency to reduction and amputation, are all stylistic effects which link Burroughs' style with metonymy, the surgical figure par excellence.[10]

Metonymy and/or Metaphor

Metonymy has received a good deal of attention lately in critical theory, particularly in the analysis of narrative;[11] but it is defined and analyzed almost always in its relation to metaphor, in a relation of binary opposition. In the work of Roman Jakobson and his followers, metaphor and metonymy have been inflated to represent different ways of thinking and of using language. A catalogue of the contrasting characteristics most often associated with the two tropes might yield something like the following pattern:

METAPHOR	METONYMY
association by similarity, joining a plurality of worlds	association by contiguity, movement within a single world
selection and substitution of one word for another	combination of one word with another
mythic, symbolic	literal, logical
vertical hierarchy, origin, and center	horizontal linearity, play, and reversibility
transcendence	immanence
unity, order	multiplicity, change
completeness, lyrical arrest or suspension	incompleteness, temporal urgency and drive

One can easily recognize many of the elements of Burroughs' prose style in the characteristics associated here with metonymy. It would be simplistic to say, however, that metonymy is for Burroughs a superior alternative to metaphor—metaphor is bad, therefore metonymy is good. It would appear instead that Burroughs uses metonymy as a naked version of metaphor. In its extreme form, metonymy allows him to lay bare the repressive abuses of word and image which metaphor works to disguise.

Burroughs shows how the abuses inherent in binary thinking lead inevitably to a hierarchical domination of one term (or one orifice) over another. In the context of traditional rhetorical systems, whether based on two, three, or four master tropes, there is a similarly reductive tendency to construct a comprehensive dual system and ultimately to identify a single trope which dominates

that system. The single trope, which is almost always metaphor, is then inflated to represent not only all figurative language but all thought processes,
our very perception of and response to the world.[12] While Jakobson's essay
"Two Aspects of Language and Two Types of Aphasic Disturbances" directly
addresses this problem of metaphorical bias, particularly in literary criticism,
both his own system and the variations it has inspired tend to reinforce rather
than depose the hegemony of metaphor as the essential trope of literary
discourse.

Jakobson begins his essay by identifying two basic principles whose intersecting axes determine all linguistic activities: the vertical axis of selection
and the horizontal axis of combination. These functions are most economically
represented by the operations of metaphor and metonymy, of similarity and
contiguity. As he moves from the simplest level of phonetic distinctions to the
more complex levels on which texts are constructed, this model of intersection is replaced by a binary schema in which *either* the "metaphoric way" *or*
the "metonymic way" dominates. Applying this pattern to specific literary
modes, Jakobson formulates a set of oppositions which support the basic duali-
ties of conventional literary interpretation: the contrast of metaphor/metonymy
corresponds to the opposition of romantic/realistic, poetic/referential, figura-
tive/literal, metalinguistic/extralinguistic.

When Jakobson calls for a theory of metonymy, then, he sees it as characteristic of and applicable to the " 'realistic' trend": "Following the path of
contiguous relationships, the realist author metonymically digresses from the
plot to the atmosphere and from the characters to the setting in space and
time. He is fond of synecdochic details [which will] stand for the [. . .]
characters to whom these features belong" (92). Extralinguistic in its orientation, metonymy is seen by most rhetoricians as referential, repeating the contiguity of objects as they already exist in the world, while metaphor creates
new relations. In such a critical perspective, realistic narrative will rise to
the order of literature only where metonymy transcends itself to become
metaphor (Culler, *Pursuit* 188–209). Thus the paradigm which begins as a binary opposition of metaphor and metonymy slides inevitably toward the all-
encompassing rule of metaphor, or toward an intermingling of the two tropes
so complete that it renders their individual designation meaningless.

David Lodge's *The Modes of Modern Writing* is of particular interest here
because it uses *Naked Lunch* as a demonstration text. Lodge proposes to use
Jakobson's binary paradigm as the basis for a single poetics of fiction which
would encompass modernist and realist narratives, and would reconcile critical theories based on literature as imitation with those based on literature as
autonomous discourse. This desire for a reconciliation of differences is, in
itself, a highly metaphorical motivation, like Ricoeur's intention to reconcile

semiotics and semantics in *The Rule of Metaphor*. Lodge flattens the dividing line Jakobson placed between the two modes, sketching out instead a horizontal continuum along which all works might be arranged according to varying degrees of dominance of metaphor or metonymy. At one extreme, metonymy is associated with the utilitarian discourse of an encyclopedia entry; at the other extreme, metaphor is identified with poetry in verse. In the middle range, where classification would be most subtle, the two tropes are seen in a relation of polite mutual interdependence.

Those undecidable texts which refuse to combine or to choose between metaphor and metonymy are relegated by Lodge to a no-man's-land outside his typology, to the risky uncharted geography of the postmodern. His discussion of postmodern texts is, in fact, the most interesting part of Lodge's book, and one might well have expected Burroughs to be included in the company of such experimental stylists as Stein and Beckett. Lodge, however, ranks Burroughs among the metaphorical writers, where he is given the uncomfortable status of a metaphorist *manqué*. Lodge attributes Burroughs' failure in this mode to the fact that in *Naked Lunch* metaphor and metonymy are in a relationship of "obscene" confusion rather than spiritually redeeming "cooperation" (105). Like many theorists working with metaphor and metonymy, Lodge often spawns hybrid tropes like the metaphoric metonymy or the metonymic metaphor. Even Jakobson eventually abandons his notion of the "competition" between the two tropes to assert in a later essay that in poetic discourse, "every metonymy is slightly metaphorical and every metaphor has a metonymic tinge" ("Linguistics" 370).

In a chapter in *Modes* entitled "The Metonymic Text as Metaphor," Lodge attempts to reconcile the representative or mimetic function of metonymic discourse (according to Jakobson's paradigm) with the transcendent symbolic structure of metaphor. He argues that while metaphoric texts "point to their status as total metaphors" for the human condition, metonymic texts offer themselves as a "representative bit of reality." Lodge discovers here an irony which will again insure the literary hegemony of metaphor: "[metonymic narrative] is often described as a 'slice of life.' Yet this phrase . . . is itself a metaphor; and we know that it is not possible for the literary artist to limit himself to merely making a cut through reality, as one might cut through a cheese [because] his medium is not reality itself but signs" (109–10). This is precisely what Burroughs *does* propose—that reality is signs, that signs are objects, and that they can indeed be cut through like a cheese. This operation, which Burroughs pursues systematically in the cut-up novels, is set in motion in *Naked Lunch* not in the interest of representing the world, but in the interest of exposing the illusion of the referential function of language. As La Capra points out in his essay "Who rules metaphor?" the failure of the typologies of

Jakobson and Ricoeur to account for the violent tension between "dominant structures [and] more submerged aspects of the text" (20) makes them virtually unusable as methods of literary analysis.[13]

Among the literary critics writing on metaphor and metonymy Paul de Man has perhaps most accurately perceived the potential violence and provocation in the confrontation of the two tropes, and thus brings us closest to their operation in Burroughs' fiction. In *Allegories of Reading* de Man goes beyond Genette's description of metonymy as the pervasive mode of metaphor in Proust's style to expose the textual "scandal" implicit in this discovery: "The deconstruction of metaphor and of all rhetorical patterns such as mimesis, paranomasis, or personification that use resemblance as a way to disguise differences, takes us back to the impersonal precision of grammar. . . . Such a reading puts into question a whole series of concepts that underlie the value judgements of our critical discourse: the metaphors of primacy, of genetic history, and, most notably, of the autonomous power to will of the self" (16). If we apply de Man's insight about Proust to Burroughs' style, we can see that there is no intention in *Naked Lunch* to produce a cooperative interdependence of metaphor and metonymy (as Lodge would have it). Burroughs attempts instead to develop an exaggeratedly metonymic style which will expose the violence and repression inherent in all tropes, and particularly in the system of thought which stems from metaphor. Lodge's mistaken classification of Burroughs as a metaphorical writer and the predominantly metaphorical readings of *Naked Lunch* such as those discussed in chapter 1 demonstrate the failure of literary critics to perceive how Burroughs' texts undermine the very forms they use, the very interpretations they seem to invite. When contiguity collapses in Burroughs' text, it does not mark the triumph of the axis of similarity, of metaphor, but rather it realizes the author's desire to "render strange" (as Shklovsky would put it) the syntagmatic pole, to make the habitual linearity of discourse suddenly visible. When Burroughs disrupts the continuity of his narrative, it is to suggest an extension of its boundaries beyond the rules of grammar and syntax, beyond the contiguity of objects in time and space.

Metaphor has been described as a semantic impertinence which is subsequently resolved through a new figurative reading; similarly, metonymy might be seen as a syntactical impertinence which opens up the possibility of new modes of connection, new juxtapositions. As the narrative of *Naked Lunch* takes us across the country through the monotony of "U.S.A. drag," we move in and out of these disorienting mosaic composites of metonymic details:

> A train roar through him whistle blowing . . . boat whistle, foghorn, sky rocket burst over oily lagoons . . . penny arcade open into a maze of dirty pictures . . . ceremonial canon boom in the harbor . . . a scream shoots down a white hospital corridor . . . (93–94)

He plummets from the eyeless lighthouse kissing and jacking off in face of the black mirror, glides oblique down with cryptic condoms and mosaic of a thousand newspapers [. . .] to settle in black mud with tin cans and beer bottles, gangsters in concrete, pistols pounded flat and meaningless to avoid short-arm inspection of prurient ballistic experts. (75–76)

This is the poetic power of metonymy which Burroughs begins to develop in the mosaic assemblages of *Naked Lunch* and later drives to its limits in his cut-up writing experiments.[14]

Man Is an Ass/Man Is an Asshole

The implications of the complex relationship of metaphor and metonymy in Burroughs' style can be seen most clearly if we examine some examples of the tropes themselves in action. The archetypal figure of "man-as-beast," one of the most common illustrations in rhetorical treatises on metaphor, is a central figure in Burroughs' fiction. Perhaps the most brilliant realization of the metaphorical form of this analogy in a novel is to be found in Cervantes' *Don Quixote*. A close examination of Cervantes' metaphorical development of this theme will clarify the significance of Burroughs' metonymic version of it in *Naked Lunch*. The contrast of the two tropes, and ultimately of the two authors, may be seen as the difference between the metaphorical figure "man is an ass (donkey)" and the metonymic insult "man is an asshole."

In a series of adventures including the episodes of the braying aldermen, the prophesying ape, Sancho's dispute over his wages, and the enchanted boat (part 2, chapters 25–29), Cervantes develops a circular route of metaphorical recovery grounded in a classical Christian tradition: you admit you are a beast in order to transcend your beastliness. The metaphor performs a gesture of similarity which temporarily bridges the gap between man and beast; but beyond the text's play with perspectivism and reversal, it leaves the vertical hierarchy of spirit over flesh and the structural dominance of tenor over vehicle undisturbed.

In the first episode, two aldermen try to coax a lost ass out of hiding by imitating its braying; their pride in their ability to bray "to perfection" ("there's nothing between you and an ass") points to a similarity which has value only when one considers that they are in fact *not* beasts. The pattern here is very much like that of the carny man's initial joke in which the similarity of ass and face could only be enjoyed within the certainty of their difference. Because they see their similarity to the ass only in the controlled context of a performance which *contradicts* what it enacts, because they fail to recognize the sense in which they *are* beasts, the aldermen truly make asses of themselves. Ultimately they must march under the banner of the little Sardinian ass with their fellow villagers.

In the interpolated scene which interrupts this story, the metaphor is reversed as beast imitates man. On arriving at the inn, a certain Master Peter performs his own traveling carnival routine in which his ape appears to have the power to answer questions about the present and past. The misplaced faith of the audience which accepts the ape's pronouncements, like the misplaced honor and pride of the braying aldermen, transforms the questioners into beasts: "as no one examined him or pressed him to say how his ape did his divining, he made apes of them all and filled his money bags" (647). To believe in such earthly divination as that of the ape is to cut oneself off from the true wisdom of the transcendental realm, to live horizontally "less of God than of the world."

Cervantes, of course, uses Sancho Panza as the representative of this materialist tendency, particularly in his attachment to bodily comfort and money. Disgruntled by his recent beatings and despairing of more grandiose booty, Sancho demands twenty years' wages from his master, who responds with outrage: "An ass you are and an ass you must be, and an ass you will end when the course of your life is run. For it is my opinion that it will reach its final term before you realize and acknowledge that you are a beast" (655). Man becomes a beast, Quixote suggests, when he despairs of faith and hope and falls back on the horizontal immediacy of such material rewards as money. On the other hand, to admit one's beastliness in Christian humility will reaffirm a vertical hierarchy ruled by God and raise one above that beastly level.

The final episode in this series of man-as-beast analogies, and one which seems to maximize the dual power of metaphor as both meaning and event, is the episode of the enchanted boat. Quixote hopes he and Sancho will be spirited through this adventure by some enchanter who will carry them across the " 'equinoctial line which divides and cuts the opposing poles at equal distance'" (658). He would, then, carry Sancho with him across the barrier which divides them as doubting materialist and believing poet. At one pole we find the security of solid ground where the beasts Dapple and Rocinante are tied up, and at the other the uncertainty of the knight's potential adventure, the free floating of the "enchanted" boat they borrow.

Quixote and Sancho offer two very different, even opposing, attitudes toward the geography of this adventure:

"If I had only an astrolabe here with which I could take the height of the pole, I would tell you how far we have gone; though if I know anything we have passed, or soon shall pass, the equinoctial line [. . .]."

"And when we get to this noxious line your worship speaks of," asked Sancho, "how far shall we have gone?"

"A long way," replied Don Quixote, "for we shall have covered the half of the three hundred and sixty degrees of earth and water the globe contains according to the computation of Ptolemy [. . .] when we come to the line I mentioned."

"By God," said Sancho, "but your worship has got me a pretty fellow for a witness of what you say, this same Tolmy or whatever you call him, with his amputation." (658)

In Sancho's very apt misunderstanding of Quixote's technical vocabulary, he finds the "equinoctial" line which would divide him from the beasts a "noxious" one, and the "computations" by which the globe is divided a threatening "amputation."[15] For his part, the knight is determined to immobilize the beasts and escape from them, to cross over into another realm which defies the limitations of the natural world. His error, in the terms of the novel, is in trying to locate that other world of the spirit literally, geographically, horizontally on the other side of the equinoctial line.

Just when our heroes would appear to have left the beasts behind, the body reasserts itself in abundance, though in miniature. Quixote looks for proof that they have passed the equinoctial line by using the legendary sailor's test: " 'one of the signs by which they know they have passed the equinoctial line I mentioned is that the lice die on everyone aboard ship.' [. . .] Sancho felt himself and, reaching his hand gently and cautiously behind his left knee, raised his head and looked at his master, saying: 'Either the test's false or we haven't got where you worship says, not by many a long mile' " (658–59).

Don Quixote loses in reality because he cannot escape his body and attain the realm of his magical powers, and the enchanted boat episiode ends as the two heroes are sent "back to their beasts and to their beast-like existence" (661). But Quixote wins in metaphor because his longing for that spiritual world expands the space of his experience, "broadens [his] mind," and creates a unified imaginative geography which comprehends both the certain bank and the uncertain waters of his adventure.[16] Quixote wins with the power many critics ascribe to metaphor: the power of his intention to raise man above his natural state. Quixote and Sancho must maintain their faith and struggle against despair lest they turn into beasts ("griefs were not made for beasts but for men. Yet if men feel them too deeply they turn to beasts" [532]); but they must also recognize their human limitations and their proper place in a vaster hierarchy. As Sancho confesses modestly, "though I seem a man, if it's a question of going into the church, I'm a very beast" (545).

The journey of Quixote and Sancho back and forth across the imaginary equinoctial line, a journey motivated by Quixote's desire to transcend the earthly realm, blurs that boundary line, transforming it from a prohibiting border to a bridge of connection. Despite the persistent literalness given to the man-as-beast analogy in these episodes, it is also a coin of exchange in Cervantes' novel—both a material presence and the indication of an absent symbolic or spiritual meaning. Like the money which deflates those scenes where Quixote must pay his way out of a failed adventure, these beast metaphors are coins which simultaneously represent the absence of the "other world" of poetic or imaginative truth and purchase a passage to that world. As Ricoeur says of metaphor in general (and ironically, using the specific example of "Jim is an ass"), "perception of incompatibility is essential to the interpretation of the message in the case of metaphor" (186). For Cervantes, that message is the celebration of the imaginative world of the spirit, reaffirming the divine authority which arches over his novel like a protective dome (Spitzer 73). Beyond its infinitely subtle and complex play with perspectivism and reversal, *Don Quixote* seems to corroborate the association of metaphorical narrative with vertical hierarchy and transcendence.

If we consider the metaphor from Burroughs' perspective, however, it appears considerably less innocent, its promises highly suspect. Behind the ingenuous democratic gesture of metaphor (the "show" of joining or equalizing man and beast) Burroughs would detect the irreversible hierarchy of a Christian world view, the ultimate supremacy of man over beast. For him, the relationship of tenor and vehicle, like all binary relationships, always leads to domination and control. Burroughs makes this dynamics explicit and unavoidable in the metonymic image. The metaphorical "man is an ass" becomes the metonymic "man is an asshole." Man is not tentatively "like" an ass, but unavoidably attached to his own anus.

Metonymic "association by contiguity, movement within a single world" (Warren and Wellek 195), is realized and radicalized in the nightmare world of *Naked Lunch*, where the enclosed "single world" of the body is even further restricted to an alienated or amputated body part. Instead of the playful and reassuring process of metaphor, Burroughs serves up only the cold hard facts of metonymy: the carnival man is reduced to his own anus and there is no way back from that condensation or dismemberment. Instead of the recovery of meaning we find in metaphor, there is only an irrevocable literalness. Burroughs sabotages the metaphorical bridge which unites man and beast, mind and body, by making an incision—a metonymic slash which divides and destroys. The hierarchy and domination at work in metaphor—where the equivocation of the "likeness" of man and beast will allow finally for man's transcendance of his bestiality—is laid bare in the overt act of violence and suppression committed by metonymy.

Burroughs extends the notion of the violence of word and image—metaphorical or metonymic—to the linguistic functions of naming and representation. In its most elementary form, as Aristotle has observed, metaphor is a naming. For Cervantes, the poetic power of naming is seen as an expansion of the individual's identity: " 'I know who I am,' replied Don Quixote, 'and I know, too, that I am capable of being not only the characters I have named, but all the Twelve Peers of France and all the Nine Worthies as well'" (54). Roland Barthes argues that the conventional or metaphorical text actually *retreats* from name to name, approaching a single name, metaphor, or truth which finally encompasses and closes the text. In Cervantes' novel, although Quixote accumulates many names and titles, celebrating the imaginative power by which he may become many things, ultimately he returns to his true single name, Alonso Quixano the Good, and to his mortality. For Burroughs, as for Barthes, the metaphorical process takes on the sinister aspect of a reductive parasitic absorption, of a death.

Burroughs' polemic attack on the restrictions of metaphorical naming in *The Job* focuses on the copula, the "IS of identity," and his primary example is once again the man-as-beast analogy:

> You are an animal. You are a body. Now whatever you may be you are not an "animal," you are not a "body," because these are verbal labels. The IS of identity always carries the implication of that and nothing else, and it also carries the assignment of permanent condition. [. . .] I cannot be and am not the verbal label "myself." The word BE in English contains, as a virus contains, its precoded message of damage, the categorical imperative of permanent condition. To be a body, to be nothing else, to stay a body. To be an animal, to be nothing else, to stay an animal. [. . .] Whatever you may be you are not the verbal labels in your passport any more than you are the word "self." So you must be prepared to prove at all times that you are what you are not. (200–201)

In response to language's imposition of the deadly stasis of definitions, "the assignment of permanent condition," Burroughs proposes a negative strategy of resistance in which identity continually shifts, eluding any definitive form. With his own analytical scalpel, Burroughs will dissect and dismantle the most powerful weapons used by language to channel, control, and repress this evolutionary flux.

The carny man episode reveals perhaps most thoroughly the violence and aggression in the act of naming. The narrative progresses from the implicit epithet (man is "an asshole"), to a comic performance (man in a dialogue with his anus), to a literal metamorphosis (man reduced to his own anus).[17] The apparently innocent linguistic act of naming leads with terrifying logic to an irreversible change of being. While the verb "to be" paralyzes individual life within a verbal label—"You are an animal. You are a body"—in *Naked Lunch* man is not even a body, but only a body part, amputated and dehumanized. The fate of the body as seen in *Naked Lunch,* reduced by surgical amputation or parasitic absorption, is already spawned and sealed in name and image.

The particular abuses of the "IS of identity" are laid bare in Burroughs' own invention of names for his characters. These names reflect the tendency in his fiction for individuals to be dominated not just by body or mind, but more specifically and tyrannically by a single organ or orifice: Willy the Disk, the terminal junky whose entire body has rotted away except for the "round disk mouth" through which he feeds his habit; the Old Gash, a mother whose son rapes her in his attempt to "stem her word Horde," or the elusive detective known as Clem Snide Private Asshole who appears in the later cut-up narratives and in Burroughs' most recent fiction. To name, for Burroughs, is virtually to obliterate humanity and individual will, to reduce the individual to a hungry orifice, an empty sucking hole.[18] And it is always the mouth which names, always language which imposes definitions.

Burroughs perceives in the linguistic function of representation a violence similar to that at work in the restrictive process of naming. The postulate that all literature is metaphorical—the world is the tenor, the text is the vehicle— seems at first quite reasonable.[19] David Lodge suggests, for example, that all drama is metaphorical because "it is recognized as a *performance. . . . we* are spectators not of reality but of a conventionalized model of reality" (*Modes* 83). To rephrase this in less innocent terms, one might argue that whether on stage or on the written page, mimetic representation is a performance which displaces and undercuts reality with the equivocation of metaphorical "likeness." In the carny man story in particular, Burroughs reveals the potential danger and violence of all performance or imitation. As we saw in the fates of the carny man and Bubu, performance is never innocent in *Naked Lunch*; it eventually replaces life itself, the imitation absorbing and devouring the original.

The junky is for Burroughs the archetypal "performer" trying to "maintain human form" (*NL* xxxviii) despite the monkey on his back. The human form he maintains, however, is a sham, an empty cellophane skin subject to collapse in a vacuum. The junky is "without body and without feeling" (*NL* 24); he reports "absence of cerebral event" (*NL* 231). Like Bubu and the carny man, the junky has no self left, he has only the empty and artificial imitation of a self projected by his blind need. On a rhetorical level, metonymy is a similar misrepresentation in which the part masquerades as the whole. It becomes a kind of truncated double, like Gogol's "The Nose," challenging and finally appropriating the authority and identity of the individual. In *Naked Lunch*, the part never merely "stands for" the whole, as Jakobson puts it, but displaces and devours it.

Representation is perceived by Burroughs as a lethal symbiosis which reduces the world to a "copy planet," a false and lifeless imitation. In this ersatz universe, language is never to be trusted; all "documents are forgeries by nature" (*Job* 36) and all history is fiction. A knowing voice warns the reader in *Nova Express*, "You notice something is sucking all the flavor out of food and the pleasure out of sex the color out of everything in sight?" (70). The mysterious force at work here is representation itself, the alien and empty signifier absorbing the life out of the signified. For Burroughs, the relationship of word to world is not only arbitrary but destructive, carrying within it the violence of all language functions, of all binary structures.

Burroughs traces the parasitic threat at work in naming and representation beyond these functions to the basic mechanics of the reading process: "If I hold up a sign with the word 'ROSE' written on it, and you read that sign, you will be forced to repeat the word 'ROSE' to yourself. If I show you a picture of a rose you do not have to repeat the word. [. . .] A syllabic language forces you to verbalize in auditory patterns. [. . .] It is precisely these automatic reactions to words themselves that enable those who manipulate words to control thought on a mass scale" (*Job* 59). In other words, language operates like a mass ventriloquy act in which we are all dummies.[20]

Cutting Loose: The Way Out

As we saw in the carny man episode, the individual is perhaps most taken in and taken over by language when he thinks he is manipulating it for his own purposes—he is never so much the dummy as when he plays the ventriloquist. All communication through language—Burroughs calls it "one way telepathic broadcast" or "Sending"—is revealed to be terminal for the human individual. Like any junky, the word-addict or Sender is eventually devoured by his own need, the need to dominate: "A telepathic sender has to send all the time. He can never receive, because if he receives that means someone else has feelings of his own could louse up his continuity. The sender has to send all the time, but he can't ever recharge himself by contact. Sooner or later he's got no feelings to send. [. . .] Finally the screen goes dead. . . . The Sender has turned into a huge centipede" (*NL* 163). The Sender, as Burroughs explains, is no longer a human individual but "the Human Virus." Born with blank disks for eyes, the Sender's presence is traced to a sucking emptiness, the "low pressure area" generated by his parasitic need. The blind sucking orifice to which the carny man is reduced is evidence of the dead end to which domination through language brings all individual life. For Burroughs, the site of language—sending, representing, naming—is always blind and always empty. It is language which robs us of individual life and of the world itself, creating a "grey veil between you and what you saw or more often did not see" (*TTTE* 209).

To break through blindness to clear vision one must break through the mind locks and word locks of language. In the telegraphic style of his later fiction Burroughs announces, " 'Crab word falling—Virus photo falling—Break through in Grey Room—' " (*NX* 82). Such a breakthrough involves replacing the habits of metaphor, the blind prose of euphemism, automatic verbalization, and compulsive "Sending" with the totally self-conscious and concrete manipulation of the word. Once we are able to see and touch and even smell the word, its invisible power is undermined. Once the word is thus *given* body, it can be expelled or *cut loose* from the body.

Even before the explicit cut-up experiments he will use during the 1960s, Burroughs has clearly begun his surgical attack on the word in *Naked Lunch*. He shows how the precoded messages of language operate on the individual with monotonous and tyrannical predictability, like the "Regulator Gimmick" on some cosmic adding machine: "no matter how you jerk the handle result is always the same for given coordinates" (*NL* xlviii). Burroughs replaces this mathematical determinism with the arbitrary surgeon's slash: "The razor inside, sir—Jerk the handle" (*NX* 73). *Naked Lunch* begins with the flourish of that razor, "The razor belonged to a man named Occam and he was not a scar collector" (xlvi), and with the implicit claim that the random violence of his metonymic style will liberate the reader from the mechanical fixity and stasis of conventional language. The predetermined coordinates of Western discourse are shifted and shuffled; the adding machine ruled by a "Regulator Gimmick" becomes in Burroughs' prose a vast subtraction machine ruled by chance and discontinuity.[21]

The very holes that would be filled in or smoothed over by metaphorical connections in conventional discourse are opened up again by Burroughs' metonymic style as he lays bare the illusion of continuity: "Like a moving film the flow of thought seems to be continuous while actually the thoughts flow stop change and flow again. At the point where one flow stops there is a split second hiatus. The new way of thinking grows in this hiatus between thoughts" (*Job* 91).[22] Directly following the story of the carny man is a passage in which Burroughs describes how the "basic American rottonness" will always squeeze past the censor, squeeze through between bureaus, through the "space *between*, in popular songs and Grade B movies" (133). So he always looks to the silent spaces between things, the gaps through which clear vision may be glimpsed.

Burroughs' use of the central man-as-beast analogy in *Naked Lunch* draws our attention not so much to the nature of man or beast, mind or body, as to the space created *between* them—by the "IS of identity." As we saw in his polemic on "the verb TO BE," Burroughs discovers in this verbal point of intersection the naked truth about man's relationship to language: the coercion and limitation imposed by name, image, and representation. It is no accident that the most crucial episodes in *Naked Lunch* take place in a geographical space called Interzone. No balance, no hierarchy of values operate in Interzone, for it is the psychological landscape of the addict exposed to his need, conscious of his need, but not yet free of it. Interzone, as Frank McConnell has argued, is a state of flux between will and the absence of will; it is a space of confusion and contradiction, but a space where the air is clear and you can "see what you eat."

Burroughs, then, will open as many holes as possible in his texts; like Hassan i Sabbah, his call to liberation will be "No holes barred!!!" (*NL* 79). This multiplication of orifices is pursued not in a childish regression to polymorphous perversity, as some critics have suggested, but as a strategy to undermine the tyranny of the single orifice of need—the all-purpose mouth of linguistic addiction. Burroughs' strategy of resistance is always to turn the enemy's weapons against itself, to use these same orifices as the means for escape. The only hope for the carnival man tyrannized by his anus or for the compulsive verbalizer tyrannized by the word is to abandon body and word entirely, to escape *through* them to extended "levels of experience" in space and silence: "Through these orifices transmute your body. . . . The way OUT is the way IN" (*NL* 229).

The way out is through the orifices of the body, through the holes of the text. As Jacques Ehrmann argues in "The Death of Literature," everything happens "between the lines, in the interval between the words" (241), in whiteness and silence. Ehrmann describes the "incision-decision" by which meaning is coaxed out of the intertextual mass of signs as an explosion, a breaking apart that is ultimately liberating: "From this surgery a meaning bursts forth. This meaning is none other than the very break which opens the sluice gates. A trickle or torrent which does not stop signifying" (249). In the mosaic style of *Naked Lunch* and in the later cut-up experiments, the metonymic "incision-decision" is never lethal or reductive—it always proliferates: "You can cut into *Naked Lunch* at any intersection point. . . . I have written many prefaces. They atrophy and amputate spontaneous" (*NL* 224). As the "Atrophied Preface" which appears provocatively at the conclusion of his novel demonstrates, Burroughs' radical text is impervious to amputation because it is a non-hierarchial network, its parts are interchangeable and reversible: "The Word [. . .] can be had in any order [. . .]. This book spill off the page in all directions" (*NL* 229). In short, Burroughs' text is not addicted to its own image.

In an encounter with Burroughs' writing, therefore, the reader experiences a systematic program of immunization by exposure—exposure to the repressive functions of all dualisms (especially that of body/mind), to the restrictions of naming and representation, to the coercion and violence of all word and image. Overexposure to the word and to the body has a liberating and purgative effect, "the more you run the tapes through and cut them up the less power they will have" (*TTTE* 217). From the initial experiments with metonymic exposure of word and image in *Naked Lunch*, we can follow Burroughs' treatment for the diseases of Western civilization in his use of the experimental cut-up and fold-in methods of writing in *The Soft Machine*, *The Ticket That Exploded*, and *Nova Express*.

3 | The Negative Poetics of the Cut-Up Method

In 1959 Burroughs was introduced to what would become the central device in his writing in the 1960s—the cut-up method as discovered by his friend Brion Gysin, poet and painter. Having made accidental cuts through several sheets of newspaper, Gysin rearranged the fragments at random and produced the cut-up texts which appeared "unchanged and unedited" in *Minutes to Go*, published in 1959. Burroughs immediately recognized that he had already served an unconscious cut-up apprenticeship in editing and rearranging the voluminous material that finally yielded the published version of *Naked Lunch*.

What struck both Gysin and Burroughs about the cut-up method was the possibility of using this technique to make the writer's medium tangible—to make the word an object detached from its context, its author, its signifying function. They wanted to bring, as they put it, the collage to writing. Burroughs had already come a long way in *Naked Lunch* toward making word and image literal, but here the word became a substance that could actually be handled, or more accurately, manhandled. The method itself is simple: "Cut right through the pages of any book or newsprint . . . lengthwise, for example, and shuffle the columns of text. Put them together at hazard and read the newly constituted message. Do it for yourself" (*TM* 34).

Gysin explains how Burroughs extended his cut-up discovery by substituting for the "pisspoor" material of the first newspaper cut-ups his own "highly volatile material." Burroughs "loved the idea of getting his hands on his own words" (*Research* 44). Such "highly charged" works as "The Song of Songs" and Eliot's or Rimbaud's verse were cut in with scientific tracts, with the bankrupt euphemistic prose of the popular press, with various forms of popular fiction, and of course with his own writing, published and unpublished. In this way, Burroughs generated a tremendous volume of texts from which he selected, extended, and refined—an operation far more rigorous than the initial accidental cut-ups of *Minutes to Go*. While living in London in the 1960s, Burroughs collaborated with friends Ian Sommerville and Antony Balch on experiments with tape recorders and film. Gradually expanding the cut-up tools from scissors and manuscript to words on tape and images on film, Burroughs was able to transform the disembodied voice of the written word into actual magnetic patterns and frequencies.[1] With this new technology he could produce not only more complex permutations of a single text or homogeneous set of texts, but also more heterogeneous mosaics, even simultaneous multiple texts.

Burroughs openly acknowledges not only Brion Gysin's catalytic contribution to the development of his cut-up narratives, but also earlier precursors in the method. He recalls, for example, the public iconoclastic gesture of Tristan Tzara: "At a surrealist rally in the 1920s Tristan Tzara the man from nowhere proposed to create a poem on the spot by pulling words out of a hat. A riot ensued wrecked the theatre" (*TM* 29). Recognizing, too, that cut-up texts had been produced by more established writers, Burroughs includes among the literary precedents for his cut-ups Eliot's "The Waste Land" and the "Camera Eye" sections of Dos Passos's *USA*. Appropriately, a phrase from Eliot's poem—"Who is the third who walks always beside you?" (1.360)—was adopted by Burroughs and Gysin to designate the collaborative consciousness which could be generated by the cut-up method: a third mind free of the restrictions of context, culture, and subjectivity.

In a potentially infinite regression, one might trace Eliot's phrase back, as the poet himself does in a footnote, to an uncertain account of the "continual delusion" of a group of explorers that "there was one more member [on the journey] than could be counted" (Eliot 148). Liberated by Eliot from its allegedly historical and perhaps even earlier biblical sources, the phrase is then liberated by Burroughs from Eliot's text and adopted as a haunting and anonymous refrain in his own writing. Once anchored as a refrain, the phrase begins to accumulate new associations, new points of intersection. Burroughs creates, for example, the unlikely juxtaposition of Eliot's phrase with a quotation from Napoleon Hill's popular self-help manual, *Think and Grow Rich:*

> "Why am I here? I am here because you are here . . . and let me quote to you young officers this phrase: 'No two minds ever come together without, thereby, creating a third, invisible, intangible force which may be likened to a *third mind*.' Who is the third who walks beside you?" (*TM* 25)

Every phrase, in Burroughs' view, has a similarly checkered history of incarnations and migrations. The production of the cut-up text thus raises the question of who is speaking in a given phrase or fragment. Like the deconstructionists, the writer of cut-ups implies that it is always language that speaks within a network of infinite and anonymous citations.

In his theoretical explorations of the nature of cut-up writing, Burroughs comes to assert finally that all literature is cut-up. "What is any writing but a cut-up?" he asks (*TM* 8). For him, as for critics like Bakhtin, Derrida,

Kristeva, and Barthes, any literary text is an intersecting network of many texts spliced, crossed, and merged. Every writer is perceived as drawing from the language system, selecting and rearranging that material, either intersecting with and appropriating arrangements already made, or scrupulously avoiding or distorting those preexisting patterns. In either case, the writer proceeds according to a certain relationship to the body of language and literary tradition. For Burroughs, the cut-up is merely a device for making this relationship explicit.

Intertextuality and the Cut-up

The cut-up text might stand as an emblem of what contemporary theorists call "intertextuality,"[2] a concept which defines literary works not as autonomous and complete but as elements in a system of relations to other texts. In the intertextuality of the cut-up these relations are most often shifting and temporary, bringing us into a world without boundary, self, paternity, or ownership. Burroughs dramatizes this indeterminate multiplicity on a literal and scientific level in the genetic cut-ups produced in the "Biologic Courts" of *Nova Express*. These biological cut-ups are presented as "tentative briefs" which will then be subject to infinite displacement and variation.

There is some disagreement among critics using the term as to whether "intertextuality" includes non-literary and even non-linguistic systems. For Burroughs, the patterns and methods of cut-up writing extend beyond the actual manipulation of texts to our conscious and unconscious human experience. Burroughs perceives our very life in the world as a constant cut-up in which we receive subliminally and simultaneously much more than the conscious mind registers:

> Somebody is reading a newspaper, and his eye follows the column in the proper Aristotelian manner, one idea and sentence at a time. But subliminally he is reading the columns on either side and is aware of the person sitting next to him. That's a cut-up. I was sitting in a lunch room in New York having my doughnuts and coffee. I was thinking that one *does* feel a little boxed in in New York, like living in a series of boxes. I looked out the window and there was a great big Yale truck. That's cut-up—a juxtaposition of what's happening outside and what you're thinking of. (*TM* 4–5)

The aim of the cut-up, as Burroughs sees it, is to "make explicit a psychosensory process that is going on all the time anyway" (*TM* 4).

For Roland Barthes, as for Burroughs, intertextuality extends into our life in the world. In a remarkably Burroughsian moment inspired by intoxication and the image of a teeming square in Tangier, Barthes describes life in the intertext, or life as the intertext:

One evening, half asleep on a banquette in a bar, just for fun I tried to enumerate all the languages within earshot: music, conversations, the sounds of chairs, glasses, a whole stereophony of which a square in Tangiers (as described by Severo Sarduy) is the exemplary site. That too spoke within me, and this so-called "interior" speech was very like the noise of the square, like that amassing of minor voices coming to me from the outside: I myself was a public square, a *sook*; through me passed words, tiny syntagms, bits of formulae, and *no sentence formed*, as though that were the law of such a language. [. . .] this *non-sentence* was in no way something that could not have acceded to the sentence, that might have been *before* the sentence; it was: what is eternally, splendidly, *outside the sentence*. Then, potentially, all linguistics fell, linguistics which believes only in the sentence and has always attributed an exorbitant dignity to predicative syntax. [. . .]. (*Pleasure* 49)

In the cacaphony of the intertext which is constantly swirling around us, we are liberated from the sentence, from grammar and logic, from our roles as speakers or listeners, from the opposition of inside and outside.

Burroughs was, of course, similarly inspired by Tangier as an embodiment of infinite and shifting multiplicity, "the beauty of this town that consists in changing combinations" (*Letters* 154). His own brand of Yage intoxication produced visions of composite cities in perpetual architectural flux, composite races without inhibitions and open to all human potential (*Yage* 40). The intertextuality of the cut-up is discovered in geography, in architecture, in biological evolution.

In the cut-up novels one still finds the composite cities and the mosaic clusters of *Naked Lunch*, but Burroughs also develops in these later works a more explicit model of the composite writing process. Its operations range from the crudeness of a "cement mixer" for word and image, to more refined and "technical" maneuvers. Burroughs' cut-up writing machine clearly generates the activity of intertextual production:

All music and talk and sound recorded by a battery of tape recorders recording and playing back moving on conveyor belts and tracks and cable cars spilling the talk and metal music fountains and speech [. . .]—
Plays on stage with permutating sections moved through each other Shakespeare, ancient Greek, ballet—[. . .]
A writing maching that shifts one half one text and half the other through a page frame on conveyor belts—[. . .] Shakespeare, Rimbaud, etc. permutating through page frames in constantly changing juxtaposition [. . .]— (*TTTE* 64–65)

Barthes has similarly described the "text" which, in opposition to the traditional literary "work," produces by means of a "serial movement of disconnections, overlappings, variations. [. . .] the activity of associations, con-

tiguities, carryings-over" (*Image* 157). Burroughs' cut-ups realize the ideal
of this radical "text."

Extending the Boundaries

Burroughs' cut-up method and the "texts" he produces with
it make explicit the intertextual nature of all discourse and all human experience. To make explicit and to extend—these are the two directions in which
the cut-up forces our reading and our perception.[3] The advantage of the cut-up
method as Burroughs sees it is that the "use of scissors renders the process
explicit and subject to extension and variation" (*TM* 32). Burroughs' later variation on the cut-up, the fold-in method performed without scissors, similarly
"gives the writer literally infinite extension of choice." Again, the method is
simple: "A page of text—my own or someone else's—is folded down the
middle and placed on another page—The composite text is then read across
half one text and half the other" (*TM* 96). This method, Burroughs explains,
achieves in writing the effects of cinematic flashback, "enabling the writer to
move backward and forward on his time track—For example I take page one
and fold it into page one hundred—I insert the resulting composite as page
ten." Through the fold-in method, "the *déjà vu* phenomenon can be so
produced to order" (96).

Burroughs thus extends the Proustian moment of involuntary memory—
and of course the novel's access to the flashback precedes even Proust—to the
future as well. In the cut-up or fold-in narrative, reading is non-linear, every
reading already a rereading in which the whole exists simultaneously, sensed
almost subliminally by the reader in vague feelings of familiarity, dislocation,
premonition. Burroughs' experiments with narrative deny the reader all continuity, even that of a narrative persona, and the temporal dislocations of his
style cannot be framed or explained by an omniscient narrator or by the scope
of any single character's subjective perception. "It" speaks, language speaks.
Everything is always already familiar, already written, and all sensations of
déjà vu are reminders of our predetermined conditioning by language and
culture.[4]

To escape this preconditioning Burroughs extends his discourse toward the
transgression of boundaries, pushing outward the limits of language and self.
Burroughs recognized at once in Gysin's experiments, as Terry Wilson puts it,
"ways *out*—out of identity, habit, perhaps out of the human form itself" (*Research* 40). In order to extend boundaries or horizons of consciousness the
original lines of demarcation must first be exploded. So the cut-up begins as
an exercise in negativity, as a kind of Dadaist destruction. It works against the
"superstitious reverence for the word. My God, they say, you can't cut up these
words. Why *can't* I?" (*TM* 3); it works against the notion of the authorship or

ownership of words ("Since when do words belong to anybody. 'Your very own words,' indeed!"[*TM* 34]); and it works finally against the book itself in that "it is the representation of [the] negation [of the book]" (Lemaire 18). Like the intertext, Burroughs' cut-ups defy copyright and ownership, transgressing the regulations of boundary and convention.

In a work like Roland Barthes's *S/Z*, the violent and negative critical method of *découpage*—a procedure which Barthes describes as "separating in the manner of a minor earthquake" (13)—yields new points of connection, generates new and infinite associations. Similarly, while the cut-up releases the text from its binding, from its author, even from its conventional signifying function, it also enables the text to regenerate, to stretch out into multivalence and a communal anonymity. The operations of Burroughs' writing machine and tape and film experiments, the critical methods of *découpage*, the grafting techniques of deconstruction—all of these procedures create an infinite and often arbitrary network which uncovers what Burroughs calls the "live word."

Burroughs' cut-up method demonstrates how this "live word" may survive the death of the author and the boredom of the reader. The conventional notion of the immortality of literary works is slightly revised in Burroughs' claim that a cut-up of even the most familiar text will literally reincarnate the voice and creative imagination of the writer: "Shakespeare, Rimbaud live in their words. Cut the word lines and you will hear their voices" (*TM* 32); "A page of Rimbaud cut up and rearranged will give you quite new images. Rimbaud images—real Rimbaud images—but new ones" (*TM* 3–4). Thus, the same weapon that pierces the sacred untouchability of the word also releases a rejuvenating flow: "Take any poet or writer you fancy. [. . .] or poems you have read over many times. The words have lost meaning and life through years of repetition. Now take the poem and type out selected passages. Fill a page with excerpts. Now cut the page. You have a new poem. As many poems as you like " (*TM* 31).

As Barthes sees it, the "Author" can only escape his fate as the "decrepit deity of the old criticism by becoming a text like any other," by allowing himself to be "caught up in the plural of his own text" (*S/Z* 211–12). This is indeed what Burroughs' cut-up experiments attempt to achieve. Like the infinitely plural intertext, Burroughs' experimental narratives no longer have as their source an individual, but some anonymous public scribe; we do not listen to "characters" but to a "common vocal apparatus" which is language itself. He is already moving in this direction in *Naked Lunch*: "Sooner or later [all the characters in *Naked Lunch*] are subject to say the same thing in the same words to occupy, at that intersection point, the same position in space-time. Using a common vocal apparatus [. . .] that is to be the same person—" (*NL* 222–23). Characters in the cut-up text are even more elusive and interchangeable than the narrator of *Naked Lunch* who insists, "*I am never here. . . .* Never that is *fully* in possession" (*NL* 221).

Ultimately an "apparatus" of the discourse, character and narrator are only proper names around which various associations cluster, and those associations or expressions may migrate like parasites, from one host to another. Even the "I" of the reader is thus depersonalized and multiplied, and his individuality ("already itself a plurality of other texts" [Barthes *S/Z* 10]) comes to resemble the impersonal plurality it encounters in the cut-up text. The lyricism of person-to-person communication is replaced by a vibrating network of connections, juxtapositions, and intersections.

Once the ownership of language becomes in this way communal, the writer has access to a broader linguistic range beyond the repressions and habits of his own subjectivity. This sort of territorial expansion can be more problematic, as Burroughs discovers, with living authors. In *The Third Mind* he dramatizes the problem in terms of the open lawlessness of the Western frontier:

> ...fade out to room #30, 9 rue Git le Coeur, Paris, France...
>
> Yes, boys, that's me there: Patrick Bowles sits opposite.
>
> "Something on your mind, P.B.?" "Well, yes, you might say so... thought some of my words might have strayed up here..."
>
> "Free range country, feller say."
>
> "Maybe a little too free, Martin."
>
> "Don't know as I rightly understand you, P.B."—cold, distant point—
>
> "Well, you might put it this way, Martin...words have brands just like cattle. You got no call to be changing those brands, Martin...When you use my words, they carry my brand."
>
> "Sorry P.B....I been running brands for years...never could account for it." (91)

Burroughs defends his appropriation as a necessary condition for a free and living discourse: "You see, I prefer not to use my own words. I don't like my own words because my own words are prerecorded *on my bare honestie and being dead do stick and stinke in repetition*" (*TM* 92–93). In another Borgesian infinite regression, the phrase Burroughs uses to explain his preference for the "found text" is itself borrowed from Thomas Nashe's *The Unfortunate Traveler*. The language that stinks with monotony to Nashe's narrator becomes lively and provocative when displaced to Burroughs' text.

The anxiety Paul Bowles feels about the integrity of his own words—parodied by Burroughs in this Far West face-off—is also expressed by Gregory Corso and Allen Ginsberg. Although he collaborated on the cut-ups of *Minutes to Go*, Corso adds a postscript to the book in which he tries to reestablish the "sacred" inviolability of his "very own words." Burroughs and Gysin mimic that phrase in mockery of Corso's presumption: "'Your very own words,' indeed!" (*TM* 34). Although Ginsberg seems to have come farther in understanding the theoretical aims of the cut-up technique, he too admits the difficulty he had in giving up certain habitual and complacent attitudes about the role of the poet and the nature of literature:

> it threatened everything I depend on [. . .] the loss of Hope and Love; & could maybe even stand the loss of them, whatever they are, if Poesy were left, for me to go on being something I wanted, sacred poet however desolate; but Poesy itself became a block to further awareness. For further awareness lay in dropping every fixed concept self, identity, role, ideal, habit and pleasure. It meant dropping language itself, *words*, as medium of consciousness. [. . .] It meant exercises, exercises in thinking in music, colors, no-thinks, entering and believing hallucinations, altering on neurologically fixated habit pattern Reality. [. . .] But the poetry I'd been practicing depended on living inside the structure of language, depended on words as the medium of consciousness. [. . .] Since then I've been wandering in doldrums, still keeping habit up with literature. (*Beat Book* 78)

Ginsberg's response reveals again the possibility of using the cut-up as a way out—out of the structure of language, out of the restrictions of subjective conditioning, out of any fixed self-image. Burroughs too acknowledges the habit of literature, the habit of the "routine," but he is never addicted to an image of himself as a poet prophet. Burroughs is always eager to subject his "very own words" to the same destructive techniques he uses on the texts of others, for the text is no longer for him a sacred vehicle of self-expression.

The Eternal Cut-Up: Reversible and Interminable

The defining boundaries and binderies of self and book are thus transgressed in the cut-up's anonymous appropriation and permutation of texts. By means of such transgressions both text and self may escape conditioning and closure. Burroughs' indeterminate cut-up narratives resemble Barthes's ideal dream of "infinitely spread-out languages, of parentheses never to be closed: a utopian vision in that it supposes a mobile, plural reader, who nimbly inserts and removes the quotation marks: who begins to write *with me*" (*Barthes* 161). Such a reader or reading would be able to return any work to the intertext in which all texts are held, an intertext made up of "quotations without inverted commas" (*Image* 160).

Barthes argues that the ideal text's resistance to closure is not attributable so much to its possible typographical anomalies as to its metonymic energy, an energy which "can know no halt," which endlessly defers finality or totality of meaning (*Image* 147). Burroughs' inching experiments with tape recordings have the same effect as the "metonymic skid" which Barthes isolates as the essence of the reading process: "[R]eading is absorbed in a kind of metonymic skid, each synonym adding to its neighbor some new trait, some new departure: [. . .] the meaning skids, recovers itself, and advances simultaneously" (*S/Z* 92). The inching of tape and the metonymic skid of reading interrupt the sequence of lubricity which channels conventional discourse. The innovation of the cut-up text is its refusal to stop this skid with a final signature of signification.

The reversibility and flexibility of the cut-up text suggests the possibility of flight, of continual evolution and change. Instead of condensed liquefaction into a single image, Burroughs creates in his experimental writing—particularly in the cut-up narratives—a random and infinite variety of implosions and explosions, the pulsing rhythm of life itself. Medical experimenters in *Naked Lunch* amuse themselves by arresting or cutting off the life cycle of "tension discharge rest"[5] at the moment of extreme tension: "what would be result of administering curare plus iron lung during acute mania? Possibly the subject, unable to discharge his tensions in motor activity, would succumb on the spot like a jungle rat. Interesting cause of death, what?" (*NL* 131). The cut-up texts offer an antidote to this terminal paralysis in metonymic condensations that always lead to explosion, dissemination, expansion. The cycle is always recharged: "You in the Word and the Word in You is a word-lock [. . .] the word-lock that is You. Stop. Change. Start again. Lighten your own life sentence" (*TM* 61).

On a most concrete and obvious level, Burroughs' own texts resist finality by being constantly reissued in different versions, fragments large and small surfacing in new works and new contexts. The original publication dates of the three cut-up novels—*The Soft Machine* (1961), *The Ticket That Exploded* (1962) and *Nova Express* (1964)—suggest a sequence in which the critic might discover some coherent progression or development. Burroughs' habit of substantially revising manuscripts for each new edition, however, makes any rigid adherence to such a linear model rather awkward. Thus, in addition to the common base of fictional material which feeds all the cut-up novels and thus blurs their boundaries, each individual text is subject to the indeterminacy of continual revision. Beyond his challenge to the limitations of conventional linear narrative, Burroughs also attacks the equally restrictive linearity of literary history. A bibliography of Burroughs' work reads rather like Borges' catalogue of the writings of the apocryphal Pierre Menard, whose technique of "deliberate anachronism" turns history inside out.

The trilogy of cut-up novels has been described by Philippe Mikriammos as a false trilogy, a single book completed in three versions, under three different angles (*William Burroughs* 77). As we shall see in examining the three novels, the prose itself reflects this resistance to closure. Burroughs' style tends to "anamorphosis," "It rubs itself out and rewrites itself" (Lemaire 23).

The Method: Vigilance and the Risks of Chance

Released from the burden of subjectivity, of authorship and ownership, the cut-up text opens up possibilities for what Burroughs calls "space/time travel." Such futuristic journeys call for detachment, for scientific rigor and control. While Burroughs had already brought literature and science together in *Naked Lunch*, in the cut-up narratives he makes this connection even more explicit. He insists, for example, that his cut-up techniques are not arguments or "positions" but scientific experiments. The practical work of the writer is a continuous experiment; daily life is transcribed by Burroughs into scrapbook mosaics of word and image, into notebooks and diaries where clippings and photographs are accumulated and coordinated with a variety of texts.

Burroughs describes in some detail—and again in the context of "experiment"—the notebooks he keeps while traveling:

> For exercise, when I make a trip, such as from Tangier to Gibraltar, I will record this in three columns in a notebook I always take with me. One column will contain simply an account of the trip, what happened: I arrived at the air terminal, what was said by the clerks, what I overheard on the plane, what hotel I checked into. The next column presents my memories: that is, what I was thinking of at the time, the memories that were activated by my encounters. And the third column, which I call my reading column, gives quotations from any book that I take with me. (*TM* 6)

What is achieved here is a total awareness that transgresses the boundaries separating inside and outside, fiction and alleged fact, the private self and the words of others. The screening process by which the mind limits its intake is eliminated, subjective "repression and selection" are defeated. Convergence and expansion take place in the notebook's orderly structure—that is to say, beyond subjectivity. The inner world of memory or thought joins the outer world of landscape and event, and they join explicitly *outside*, on the impersonally structured columns of the notebook.[6]

Burroughs is always headed outward: "What I want to do is to learn to see more of what's out there, to look outside" (*TM* 2). The notebooks create coordinate points of intersection which offer access to a kind of time travel, travel leading out of irreversible linear time. The notebook's encyclopedic catalogue of the complex structures of a given moment—what the subject was reading, thinking, and seeing—facilitates time travel back to that moment. The notebooks aspire to the kind of total recall epitomized in Borges' "Funes the Memorious," but without the threat of immobility and congestion of Funes's non-selective and ultimately fatal vision. For Burroughs, unlike Funes, is always free to select, to extract, to cut up this accumulated material; he is never confronted with an accumulation that is sacred in its totality, never trapped within a single remembering self. Burroughs has always already moved beyond that inner isolated vision to the collaborative vision of "the third mind" spawned by the collusion of his thoughts and experiences with those of Conrad, or Eliot, or Rimbaud.

We will see in the three cut-up novels how the techniques of these "exercises" are transformed into narrative discourse. Simultaneity, time travel, juxtaposition, transgression, the confusion or obliteration of self—all of these effects are apparent in the triology. Burroughs demands of the reader the same vigilant attentiveness he develops in these exercises, "much more of the total capacity of the observer" (*TM* 6). One is always in training for this new mode of perception, even when walking down the street: "For Godsake, keep your *eyes* open. Notice what's going on around you" (*TM* 5). Acute attentiveness to the world, acute attentiveness to the text—these attitudes are intimately related in Burroughs' cut-up theory. Roland Barthes develops a similar portrait of the reader of the text as an "empty subject" strolling in a valley: "[What] he perceives is multiple, irreducible, coming from a disconnected, heterogeneous variety of substances and perspectives: [. . .] All these *incidents* are half identifiable: they come from codes which are known but their combination is unique, founds the stroll in a difference repeatable only as difference" (*Image* 159). The uncanniness of the cut-up text, its paradoxical combination of familiarity and difference, resembles this linguistic stroll.

To insure that in his cut-ups—as in Barthes's imaginary valley—"combination is unique," Burroughs adopts the use of random indeterminancy. Many critics and fellow writers have been more offended by Burroughs' use of chance in his work than by his novels' allegedly pornographic content. Burroughs relates a typical exchange about his cut-up writing: "People say to me, 'Oh, this is all very good, but you got it by cutting up.' I say that has nothing to do with it, how I got it. [. . .] Somebody has to program the machine; somebody has to *do* the cutting up. Remember that I first made selections. Out of hundreds of possible sentences that I might have used, I chose one" (*TM* 8).[7] John Cage's experiments with chance and silence have met with similar critical crankiness, and he too defends the significance of conception and selection: "There are people who say, 'If music's that easy to write, I could do it.' Of course they could, but they don't" (*Silence* 72).[8] Burroughs perceives his use of randomness as a way to exorcize habitual conditioned responses, to project one's very nervous system onto some external plane (the writing machine) where it can be studied with scientific detachment. The incorporation of chance into the writing process is thus a deliberate and conscious abdication of control which aims at an escape *from* controls—controls imposed from within or without.

Although the disruptive operations of chance and discontinuity are central to Burroughs' experimental prose, his cut-up novels do circle around certain motifs, images, patterns, and rhythms. My analysis will at times make use of these repetitions as anchors or landmarks in the midst of the uncertainty of Burroughs' cut-ups. I will attempt to orient the reader further by proceeding chronologically through the trilogy, despite the fact that Burroughs has scrambled this chronology in his revisions of the novels. It is ironic, but perhaps unavoidable, that any *explication de texte* of these narratives threatens to erase the very quality that distinguishes them, analytical selection and emphasis rendering their composition too tidy and the novels themselves too comprehensible and readable.

The cut-up novels of William Burroughs have been dismissed without ever having been rigorously examined. Even a critic as sympathetic to experimental writing as Richard Kostelanetz says, "Perhaps someone else, I am willing to admit, can make more sense of these books than I can" ("Nightmare," 129). What little is written about them tends to focus on the content of Burroughs' mythology—greeted with awe or disgust—rather than on his innovations in style or theory. And this despite Burroughs' repeated reminders that content is irrelevant, that what must be attended to in all linguistic formulations is the structure of the discourse itself, the restrictions of binary opposition, the oppressive continuity of narrative sequence and linear time. In my examination of the stylistic experiments in *The Soft Machine*, *The Ticket That Exploded*, and *Nova Express*, I will explore both the effects of chance and the evidence of selectivity and control in these narratives. I hope that the following analysis will illuminate the complexity and significance of the "cut-up effect"[9] as it is consummately practiced by William Burroughs.

4 | *The Soft Machine*

The Soft Machine was first published in 1961 in Paris by Olympia Press, but Burroughs continued to revise the novel through its first American edition in 1966 (New York: Grove Press) and its publication in England in 1968 (London: Calder and Boyars). Although he had already produced and published some earlier cut-up experiments in collaboration with Brion Gysin, Sinclair Beiles, and Gregory Corso (*Minutes to Go* and *The Exterminator*), *The Soft Machine* was Burroughs' first attempt to incorporate the technique in a full-length narrative. Michael Goodman accurately describes the novel in his bibliography of Burroughs' writing as "more an experiment than an integration of technique and theme" (23).[1] Because of its tentative and restrained use of the cut-up, however, *The Soft Machine* provides a relatively accessible introduction to Burroughs' writing experiments during the 1960s.

Even in this first cut-up novel the fragmentation of continuity and syntax makes it difficult for a reader to enter the fictional world of Burroughs' "Nova conspiracy" without a guide. Without losing sight of the paradoxes and uncertainties with which Burroughs deliberately obstructs our progress, Jennie Skerl provides a helpful mapping of the territory. She isolates in *The Soft Machine* a series of five dystopias, each covering a different historical period. These constitute the major chapters of the novel as Skerl analyzes it: the negative "creation myth" of "Wounded Galaxies"; the "anthropological fantasy" of a "preliterate" society in "Puerto Joselito"; the "historical fantasy" of a repressive ancient civilization in the "Mayan Caper"; the "contemporary capitalistic-consumer" society of "Trak Trak Trak"; and the "futuristic fantasy" of a doomed earth in "Gongs of Violence" (Skerl, *Burroughs* 54–55). My own analysis will concentrate on a single early chapter in the novel which condenses these five dystopias into a single accelerated journey through time and space.

The chapter entitled "Who Am I to Be Critical?" comes closest to the "integration of technique and theme" which Goodman and others find lacking in the novel as a whole. Burroughs exposes the sexual, religious, and political habits of Western civilization in a prose style which also explodes our linguistic and literary habits. The chapter contains only two sections where the prose has been fragmented by the cut-up method, but even the more conventional framing narrative is written in a style which distorts and exaggerates traditional prose techniques. Whether he is using conventions in a parodic manner or transgressing against them overtly in cut-ups, Burroughs generates in the reader an acute self-consciousness and alienation from the reading process.

The Frame: Speed and Immobility

The basic structure of the chapter, and of *The Soft Machine* in general, is that of the travelogue. Burroughs had already used the travelogue format in *Naked Lunch*, where the narrator's cross-country "USA drag" trip leads similarly across the border and into Mexico. Burroughs originally developed much of the material which constitutes the three cut-up novels in letters written during his travels. While he expresses several times in these letters a desire to relate his adventures clearly and chronologically, his novelistic reworkings of the same material aim instead at confusion and dislocation.

This early chapter does seem to have at least a superficially coherent itinerary. Geographically, the trip takes us south through the United States and into the interior jungle regions of Mexico. The narrator proceeds backward in time through the "good old" 1920s when it was easier to "score," through the controlled civilization of an ancient agrarian Mayan community, and finally into the primeval life of the jungle. In this most primitive outpost the narrator seems to have come full circle, rediscovering there the modern savagery of bureaucracy (the Indian Commission) and big business (the Total Oil Company).

During this circular journey, the narrator encounters a frantic series of scenes which may be condensed into the following synopsis:

> narrator and Johnny head by train for a drug cure in Lexington
> after short sex scene they disembark looking for drugs
> head south into Mexico
> join civil war soldiers who are hanging prisoners
> continue south to Monterrey
> watch burning execution
> narrator and epileptic have sex in Mexico City
> find magic man to switch their bodies
> First cut-up
> narrator in new body heads south
> finds simple life with native boy in hut
> native boy goes mad on mescal
> narrator kills him in self-defense
> flees south to Mayan community
> breaks Mayan controls
> sets up his own control rackets

discovers the Chimu tribe
breaks their "death in orgasm" control system
deeper into jungle hunting for new body
finds "live ones" among the primitive Camuyas
flees from warlike Auca tribe
ends up working for Total Oil
                                        Second cut-up

One can locate a clear thematic unity which holds these scenes together: sex need, drug need, and the need to dominate and kill all produce the same pattern of behavior. The most primitive forms of capital punishment and the most modern methods of torture are finally indistinguishable, merely variant techniques of the ubiquitous control systems which devour life in *every* civilization.

While this thematic content remains constant, the style of the narrative telescopes and distorts both time and space. The narrator's progress through the landscape of North and South America, for example, narrows down to a more surreal traveling through the body, travel into an alien body, into the alien territory of "the Other." The narrator's intense identification with a sexual partner or with a hanging victim projects him into the pleasure and pain of that other body:

> When they lit the faggots at his feet the only sound you could hear was the fire crackling and then everyone sucked in his breath together and the screams tore through me and my lips and tongue swole up with blood and I come in my pants—And I could see the others had shot their load too [. . .]—
>
> [. . .] It turned out later this kid had the epilepsy—When he got these fits he would flop around and come maybe five times in his dry goods, made you feel good all over to watch it— (19–20)

These temporary and involuntary forays into alien territory culminate in the narrator's *literal* passage into the body of the epileptic, where he "woke up the lookout different" (21).

As the spatial context of the chapter narrows down from a vaster geography to the more claustrophobic space of the body, the temporal progress of the narrative becomes similarly restricted and obsessive. The circularity with which his retreat into primitive civilization merely brings the narrator back to present conditions is repeated on a more personal level. The narrator is continually haunted by memories, fragments of disconnected and undigested images. Under the intense pressure of this temporal concentration, the narrative of *The Soft Machine* repeatedly breaks down into cut-up mosaics of memory fragments circulating hopelessly from "sad image" to "Sad image": "sad image [. . .] worn out film dim jerky far away [. . .] Times lost or strayed long empty cemetery with a moldy pawn ticket—fading whisper [. . .] Sad image circulates through backward time—" (68–70).

What is especially striking about this chapter is the paradoxical convergence of motion and stasis: the surreal acceleration with which it moves through space and time is continually contradicted by an impression of repetition and monotony. The scene is always different and new, yet it always yields the same patterns of sex, death, and control. Although the traveler continues physically in the same direction, always south and to the interior, one gets the impression of an arbitrary indifference and aimlessness in his progress. He is always heading off, beginning again, only to end up each time in a state of exhaustion and used up life, trapped in another disaster. He moans, "and that was another mistake."

The chapter accelerates gradually, moving more quickly from one stage of the journey to the next as it approaches its end. Scenes are described in less detail, often reduced to a telegraphic shorthand: "spare you the monotonous details—Suffice it to say the Upper Amazon gained a hustler" (28) The speed with which the scenes follow one another, however, is contradicted by the underlying monotony of their content. The accelerated sequence of events is also contradicted by the actual means of locomotion which become increasingly primitive: from the rapid and lively "click clack spurt spurt" of sex on the train to Lexington, to the lost car, to the abandoned train and tracks that "gave out," to travel on horseback and finally on foot. We are witnessing no ordinary journey here, but the surreal velocity produced by what Burroughs calls the "Algebra of Need." Need generates the energy which drives the junkies off the train in search of drugs and drives the narrator deeper into the jungle in search of "live ones" to replace his dead and empty self. Need generates energy, but it is a monotonous energy that never can reach satisfaction. Later in *The Soft Machine*, the jungle travels and sexual encounters of this chapter are replaced by a more sedentary and solitary journey through books; studying Mayan texts and artifacts, the narrator feels the "motion sickness of time travel" (93) but he never leaves his seat.

The metonymic drive which compels the narrator and the narrative forward is, as we learned from *Naked Lunch*, an intermittent energy of stops and starts. The narrator is repeatedly distracted by the seductive stasis of mindless prelapsarian communities: "Well maybe I would be there still, work all day and after the work knocked out no words no thoughts just sit there looking at the blue mountains and ate and belched and fucked and slept same thing day after day the greatest" (22). The nostalgic refrain "and I might be there still" recurs as each illusion of paradise erupts into consciousness, rebellion, greed, into the desire for survival that propels the narrative forward once again: "But one day we scored for a bottle of mescal and got lushed and he looked at me and said: '*Chinga de puto* I will rid the earth of you in the name of Jesus Christu!' and charges me with a machete—Well I'd seen it coming and tossed a cup of mescal in his eyes and side-stepped and he fell on his face and I

rammed the planting stick right into the base of his brain—So that was that—
And started South again" (22).

The style of the conventional framing narrative repeats and reflects the simultaneous acceleration and monotony of the journey it describes. Run-on
sentences create a breathlessness, an imperative drive that pushes the syntax
forward, avoiding or delaying any definitive ending to a phrase, sentence, or
routine: "Periodically the Chimu organize funfests where they choose up sides
and beat each other's brains out with clubs and the winning team gang-fucks
the losers and cut their balls off right after to make pouches for coco leaves
they are chewing all the time green spit dripping off them like a cow with the
aftosa—" (25). The perverse but logical extension of violent behavior in an
escalating chain reaction of destruction is described here in a style similarly
driven beyond grammatical proprieties. But the metonymic rush from phrase
to phrase invariably exhausts itself and arrives at a flat vacuity, a blank and
bovine immobility. For every refrain signaling a new start, "and woke up the
lookout different," there is a contrary refrain lamenting the oppressive familiarity of everything: "here we go again" or "been through this before."

The rhetorical conventions which normally move a narrative forward on its
way to dénouement accumulate with such speed and density in this chapter
that the reader is left spinning like a top. The most minimal signs of narrative
continuity ("So" and "Well") are repeated with an almost farcical frequency
and speed:

> *So* they strapped us to couches in a room under the temple and there was
> a terrible smell [. . .]—*So* I turn on something I inherit from Uranus
> [. . .]—I just lay there without any thought [. . .]—*So* we got out of
> there dodging stellae and limestone skulls [. . .]—So we organize this
> "fun fest" [. . .]—*So* we organize this protection racket shaking down
> the agriculturals—[. . .] *so* we packed in and shifted to the hunting and
> fishing lark—[. . .] *Well* fever and snakes and rapids and boys drop-
> ping out here and there to settle down with the locals [. . .]—*So* we hit
> this town and right away I don't like it.
>
> [. . .] *So* I am rigged up a long distance periscope with obsidian mir-
> rors [. . .]—*Well* I saw that when his neck snapped and he shot his load
> [. . .] these hot crabs hatched out of his spine and scoffed the lot.
>
> *So* we organize the jungle tribes and take Boy's Town [. . .]—*So* we
> get all the Indians and all the Green Boys with drums and flutes [. . .]
> and shattered the cubicle *so* we move in with spears and clubs and finish
> them off [. . .]—
>
> *So* down into the jungle on the head-shrinking lark [. . .]—*Well*
> there I was on the bottom when I hear about this virgin tribe called the
> Camuyas [. . .]—*So* they chucked me out and talked usefully about
> that was that [. . .]—*So* I got a job with the Total Oil Company and
> that was another mistake— (23–28, my emphasis)

These markers of narrative progress and their implied logical and causal connections gradually lose their force. Through repetition they become exhausted as signifiers and are reduced to empty habitual gestures which belie the underlying immobility of this dead-end itinerary.

One of the effects of the two cut-up sections in this chapter will be to break through the compulsive linear progress of "So" and "Well," to lay bare the fraudulent illusion of variety and change which temporarily distract us from the deadly monotony lurking beneath the surface. In the interpolated cut-up segments of the chapter, Burroughs condenses the thematic concerns and stylistic effects already at work in the framing narrative, and extends those effects to the limits of readability. While the straight narrative makes the conventions of storytelling suddenly strange and visible, the more radical cut-up sections demand an entirely new way of reading and thinking.[2]

The First Cut-Up: Dispersing the Self

The first cut-up in the chapter is quite short and relatively accessible; it is closer to the montage and mosaic style of *Naked Lunch* than to the radical cut-ups of the trilogy. The way Burroughs works this section into the framing narrative, however, is characteristic of his early attempts to incorporate dislocated prose into a larger, more novelistic scenario. He uses here a device which I will call the "situational cut-up"—a scrambled discourse that is understood to represent a subject's disturbed state of mind. Such moments usually follow the use of drugs (*SM* 11), the confusion of drug withdrawal (*TTTE* 18), the naturally blurred and jumbled workings of memory, or a moment of blackout as the subject is choked or hung (*TTTE* 86). Burroughs has argued that any film of a street scene, any moving film of *anything* is a cut-up. On this very simple level, then, the cut-up is a modest form of mimesis, merely a more truthful representation of our fragmented perception of an unordered universe.

Burroughs, however, goes beyond this modernist version of mimesis found in experiments with point of view and stream of consciousness. He moves from the natural or realistic fragmentation of reality to the unnatural—the arbitrarily induced fragmentation of the cut-up. The "situational cut-up" evolves in the later novels into descriptions of intricate technological experiments deliberately and artificially produced by film and tape and then fed into the cacaphony of street and café noises:

> He set up screens on the walls of his bars opposite mirrors and took and projected at arbitrary intervals shifted from one bar to the other mixing Western Gangster films of all time and places with word and image of the people in his cafés and on the streets his agents with movie camera and telescope lens poured images of the city back into his projector and cam-

era array and nobody knew whether he was in a Western movie in Hongkong or The Aztec Empire in Ancient Rome or Suburban America whether he was a bandit a commuter or a chariot driver whether he was firing a "real" gun or watching a gangster movie and the city moved in swirls and eddies and tornadoes of image explosive bio-advance out of space to neon— (*NX* 129–30)

Such experiments are clearly designed to extend the relatively tame degree of cut-up that exists in street or bar scenes, a cut-up effect already practiced by Apollinaire, Joyce, and others. Burroughs is committed to disrupting that lower level of mimetic cut-up with something far more radical that will call into question the very notion of reality itself.

The actual content of the "situational cut-ups" in the trilogy ranges from a series of images with relatively intact grammatical structure, the simple juxtaposition of disconnected images, to more radical forms in which the original images have been not only displaced from the linear narrative but transformed. The first example from this chapter operates on a relatively simple level; the cut-up is a clearly comprehensible condensation of the traveler's experiences up to that point in the narrative—a kind of telegraphic diary of images which come in, as the narrator says, "sharp and clear." Here is the lead-in and the text of the first cut-up:

Well we come to this village and found the magic man in a little hut on the outskirts—[. . .] he nodded and looked at both of us and smiled and said he would have to cook up the medicine we should come back next day at sundown—So we come back and he gave us the bitter medicine in clay pots—And I hadn't put the pot down before the pictures started coming in sharp and clear: the hanged boy pulling his legs up to the chin and pumping out the spurts by the irrigation ditch, the soldiers swinging me around in the harness, the burned man screaming away like a good one and that heart just pulsing and throwing off spurts of blood in the rising sun— (20)

The rapidity of this cut-up is not assisted by the refrains of "so" or "well," nor is there any temporal orientation as provided in the framing narrative by phrases like "By this time" or "We were lucky to arrive just in time." Instead, all the past moments recuperated here are thrown together in an undifferentiated simultaneity. Time is so accelerated that it produces a stationary blur, like the spinning propeller of an airplane. We find in the style of the cut-up, then, the same uncanny combination of speed and stasis which characterized the framing narrative. The merging of sex and death, of all places and all times, has already been accomplished in the thematic structure of the framing narrative. The cut-up repeats these effects—"spurts" of semen and "spurts of blood" converge to reduce the drama of sex and murder to the same monotonous emptying out of the body—but also moves beyond them.

The difference between the already radical nature of the framing narrative and the more extreme effects of the cut-up can perhaps be most clearly illustrated by comparing their representation of identity. The uncertainty or interchangeability of identity figures repeatedly in the framing narrative: first as a psychological effect of the witnesses' intense projection into the hangings they observe: "We all stood there watching and feeling it right down to our toes and the others who were waiting to be hanged felt it too" (18); then as a grotesque "performance" imitating the victim's agony: "Johnny did this dance with his tie around his neck lolling his head on one side and letting his tongue fall out" (18–19); and finally as an actual physical possibility of body exchange offered by the "magic man." Structurally, the cut-up segment functions as a bridge between the imagined or performed identity switch and the physical actuality. It is a kind of stylistic rehearsal preparing the reader for what is about to happen. The procedure dictated by the magic man requires that the narrator be hung and at the moment of death, "when I shot my load and died I would pass into his body" (20). "So" or "Well" will simply not suffice to carry the reader across this ritual passage into the world of reincarnation. While the straight narrative softens the blow of death by presenting it as an actor's performance, the non-rational discourse of the cut-up requires no such explanation. Reduced to mere textual pronouns in the cut-up, identities are as easily interchangeable as the many costumes—from "Mayan drag" to "banker drag"— which the narrator dons in the course of his travels. In the cut-up scramble of his memory, the simple shift from third to first person pronoun substitutes the narrator for Johnny in the harness rigged up by the soldiers: "the soldiers swinging *me* around in the harness." By the time the framing narrative describes the transfer of the narrator to the body of the epileptic, such a switch has already occured in the cut-up, and we witness it with some degree of familiarity.

The logic behind Burroughs' cut-up effects in this chapter and in *The Soft Machine* in general is that if the self is sufficiently fragmented, emptied out, and dispersed, one will no longer fear its loss. Beyond this shifting of identities, then, the cut-up also offers the possibility of a more radical dissolution of identity. Personal pronouns are often replaced by definite articles, "pulling his legs up to *the* chin and pumping out *the* spurts [. . .] the burned man screaming away like a good one and *that* heart just pulsing." The uncertain reference to the disembodied chin and heart and the indefinite origin of those "spurts" give the discourse a depersonalized locus which consists of haunting metonymies—dismembered organs rather than human identities. Like the carny man story in *Naked Lunch*, this sequence in the framing narrative and the first cut-up progresses from performance to actuality and finally to what the earlier novel described as the "spurting out" of undifferentiated flesh and body parts in "a hideous random image" (*NL* 133).

While the terrain of the cut-up is often frighteningly uncertain, it can also produce images of intense clarity, a perception beyond the limits of conventional seeing. The screams of the burned man which had been felt by the observer in his ecstasy ("screams tore through *me*"), are returned more lucidly in the cut-up memory to the victim, "the burned man screaming away." The detail of the irrigation ditch, unnoticed in the excitement of the actual hanging (18), mysteriously appears in the cut-up replay, noted by some more detached and alert consciousness. So the cut-up text may distort and blur habitual notions of time and identity, but simultaneously it opens up new possibilities of thinking and seeing with greater clarity and precision.

Not all cut-up texts are as manageable as this first situational cut-up, however, and most seem to obscure rather than to promote clarity. The second cut-up in this chapter produces many of the same effects as the first, but it makes more explicit Burroughs' intention to shift our focus from content to structure and style, to the mechanics of the word.

The Second Cut-Up: Dispersing the Word

While the first cut-up is logically prepared for by the narrator's circumstances, the second cut-up is anticipated only by a gradual intensification of certain aspects of the *style* of the chapter. The increasing acceleration and condensation of episodes in the straight narrative reaches a point of such dangerous velocity that it finally explodes into the telegraphic urgency of the cut-up segment.[3]

The second cut-up which concludes "Who Am I to Be Critical?" focuses not merely on the confusion, but on the explosion of identity, of linear sequence, of conventional syntax and semantics. Here is the cut-up in its entirety:

Rats was running all over the morning—Somewhere north of Monterrey went into the cocaine business—By this time fish tail Cadillac—people—civilians—So we score for some business and get rich over the warring powers—shady or legitimate the same fuck of a different color and the general on about the treasure—We rigged their stupid tree limb and drop the alien corn—spot of business to Walgreen's—So we organize this 8267 kicked in level on average ape—Melodious gimmick to keep the boys in line—I had learned to control Law 334 procuring an orgasm by any image, Mary sucking him and running the outfield—Static was taken care of that way—what you might call a vending machine and boys dropping to Walgreen's—We are not locals. We sniff the losers and cut their balls off chewing all kinds masturbation and self-abuse like a cow with the aftosa—Young junkies return it to the white reader and one day I would wake up as Bill covered with ice and burning crotch—drop my shorts and comes gibbering up me with a corkscrew motion—We both come right away standing and trying to say something—I see other marks are coming on with the mother tincture—The dogs of Harry J. Anslinger sprouted all over me—By now we had word dust stirring the 1920's, maze of dirty pictures and the house hooked for generations— We all fucked the boy burglar feeling it right down to our toes—Spanish cock flipped out spurting old Montgomery Ward catalogues—So we stripped a young Dane and rigged the Yankee dollar—Pants down to the ankle, a barefoot Indian stood there watching and feeling his friend— Others had shot their load too over a broken chair through the tool heap—Tasty spurts of jissom across the dusty floor—Sunrise and I said here we again with the knife—My cock pulsed right with it and trousers fell in the dust and dead leaves—Return it to the white reader in stink of sewage looking at open shirt flapping and comes maybe five times his ass fluttering like—We sniff what we wanted pumping out the spurts open shirt flapping—What used to be me in my eyes like a flash bulb, spilled adolescent jissom in the bath cubicle—Next thing I was Danny Deever in Maya drag—That night we requisitioned a Peruvian boy—I would pass into his body—What an awful place it is—most advanced stage—foreigner too—They rotate the symbols around IBM machine with cocaine—fun and games what? (28–29)

Thematically, the cut-up recapitulates the concerns of the framing narrative. The illusions of the "Garden of Delights" of sexual pleasure are transformed into the repeated refrains of "pants down," "trousers fell," "drop my shorts." These refrains appear here and throughout the trilogy with such frequency that they finally dissolve into a droning mechanical hum. The sex refrain even appears later as a telegram message: "Orgasm siphoned back telegram: 'Johnny pants down'" (*SM* 127). In the impersonal and condensed economy of the telegram, this urgent message contains in shorthand the entire mechanism of sex and sex control, and locates the weapon of control specifically in the sex words themselves.

In the cut-ups, the thematic connection between sex and death is not established through a fictional situation—as when spectators of an execution dissolve in orgasms—but in the simple migration of a phrase. A sex phrase from the final cut-up, "We all fucked the boy burglar feeling it right down to our toes," echoes a similar description of the hanging from early in the chapter: "We all stood there watching and feeling it right down to our toes." Sex and death are linked here simply by their intersection at the phrase "right down to our toes." The reference to the boy burglar, who does not even appear in *The Soft Machine*, extends the new cut-up lines of association beyond this chapter and this text to other texts, indeed to any text where this particular set of words assembles. The association of life and energy with death and stasis exists not in the mind or the body, but in the word; in the cut-up text Burroughs attempts to demonstrate this phenomenon and release us from these compulsive lines of association.

Unlike the first cut-up, this final cut-up segment does maintain some of the same devices as the conventional narrative: sequential refrains such as "So we score," "So we organize," "So we stripped," and temporal indicators such as "By this time," "By now," "Next thing was." While the straight narrative foregrounds these narrative markers, reducing them to compulsively repeated "tics," the cut-up completely destroys their function and significance. The reader may experience a temporary illusion of clarity, order, and familiarity when he encounters these rhetorical props, but all of his efforts to orient himself thematically, temporally, in relation to a narrative persona or to recognizable characters will repeatedly meet with frustration and resistance from the cut-up text.

There is no consistent narrative position here, no predictable narrative voice, and as pronouns shift or disappear in the cut-up text, the fundamental notion of identity becomes increasingly ephemeral. The final cut-up of this chapter, for example, adopts one form of restrictive naming—by national identity—and reduces it to absurdity. Different nationalities are accumulated with such density and are subject to such arbitrary substitutions that they begin to merge in a blur: "Spanish cock flipped out spurting old Montgomery Ward catalogues—So we stripped a young Dane and rigged the Yankee dollar—Pants down to the ankle, a barefoot Indian stood there watching and feeling his friend." In this confusion of races and nationalities, identity approaches a more total dissemination for the narrator as well: "What used to be me in my eyes like a flash bulb [. . .]—Next thing I was Danny Deever in Maya drag—That night we requisitioned a Peruvian boy—I would pass into his body—What an awful place it is—." The body and identity switch that was so carefully prepared for in the straight narrative no longer has any dramatic impact; body exchanges accelerate effortlessly in a string of meaningless impersonations. The reader can no longer locate characters by name, by body, or even by pronouns, since these too have curiously disappeared. Actions are performed without human agency as pants drop, trousers fall, jissom spurts from nowhere across a dusty floor.

The undermining of conventional notions of identity is compounded here by a deliberate confusion of verb tenses. The first cut-up is stylistically homogeneous, each verb adopting the same form: "pulling," "pumping," "swinging," "screaming," "pulsing," "throwing," "rising." There is a sense in which this early cut-up segment stands as a momentary but harmonious synthesis of the frantic activities which precede it. In the final cut-up, however, the verb forms are constantly shifting, leaving both temporal setting and identity in grammatical uncertainty: "'Rats *was running* [. . .] *went* into the cocaine business— [. . .] So we *score* for some business [. . .] We *rigged* their stupid tree limb and *drop* the alien corn [. . .] Young junkies *return* it to the white reader [. . .] *looking* at open shirt *flapping* and *comes* maybe five times' " (my emphasis). Believing that word controls time, Burroughs is able to dislocate linear sequence by dislocating grammar. Thus the cut-up offers a reading experience without limits, without orientation. Burroughs deliberately redirects the very process of reading away from any expectation of continued action.

The reader's expectation of continuity is most obviously focused on plot, but it operates in more subtle and subconscious ways in the very progress he makes or expects to make through each sentence. The itinerary of any given cut-up sentence resembles a wild amusement park ride. Consider this example from the final cut-up: "We sniff the losers and cut their balls off chewing all kinds masturbation and self-abuse like a cow with the aftosa." The first part of the sentence incorporates several details from the earlier description of the Chimu tribe in the straight narrative which describes how they "gang fuck *the losers and cut their balls off* right after to make pouches for coco leaves they are *chewing all* the time green spit dripping off them *like a cow with the aftosa*" (25). (I have emphasized the particular phrases which reappear in the cut-up sentence.) In the process of fracturing and condensing the earlier text, the cut-up version shifts the emphasis of the sentence, making more explicit the bestial nature of man's addiction to domination and control. Instead of making pouches for cocoa leaves from the victims' testicles, they now appear to chew the *testicles*, revealing the basic cannibalism of all war, all games, all human relationships. Far from obscuring the meaning of the original framing narrative, the cut-up of the original text communicates a clearer, more naked vision.

There is even more going on in this single sentence. The phrase "all kinds masturbation and self-abuse," which is spliced in with the details we have just located above, is itself a fragment of a longer refrain which recurs throughout Burroughs' fiction: "the Garden of Delights shows all kinds masturbation and self-abuse young boys need it special" (*TTTE* 3). The phrase is associated, then, with the seductive rhetoric of sexual pleasure and pain used as a mechanism for control. In the cut-up composite where it reappears, the bestiality of the war game of winners and losers is thus linked to the parasitism which arises from sexual need.

This sort of thematic pattern of association has already been accomplished by the straight narrative; what is qualitatively different in the cut-up is the actual itinerary the reader follows as he makes his way through the cut-up sentence. The reader reaches a point of intersection at the single word "all" where the phrase about the cocoa leaves ("which they are chewing all the time") intersects with the description of the Garden of Delights ("Garden of Delights shows all kinds masturbation"):

> chewing all
> All kinds masturbation

The sentence changes direction at that pivotal point, forcing the reader to proceed by a kind of looping process in which he skids, recovers, and reorients his reading to the context of the new fragment. This is again the same rhythm of "stop.change.start again" that characterized the stages of the journey in the straight narrative, or the hesitations and "dim jerky far away" of memory's movements. This stumbling or stuttering in the reading itself resembles the more technical experiments Burroughs devises in which recorded words are inched and smudged until new words emerge from beneath the damaged surface of language.

The context in which this single sentence is situated in the final cut-up produces another dislocation for the reader. The original description of the Chimu culture is now presented by the narrator in first person plural instead of third person: "*We* are not locals. *We* sniff the losers and cut their balls off chewing all kinds masturbation and self-abuse like a cow with the aftosa." The superior position from which the narrator originally viewed with contempt the Chimu's "loutish way of life" is displaced in the cut-up by a cynical acceptance of human nature. This attitude is captured in the chapter's title, "Who Am I to Be Critical?," and in the final bitter phrase of the cut-up, "fun and games what?"

In the later novels of the trilogy, and even later in *The Soft Machine*, a new narrative attitude emerges, more technical, detached, and controlled. Instead of simply substituting himself as the new agent of repression, the narrator breaks the Mayan codices and then "leaves the area." Unlike the vicious cycle created in "Who Am I to Be Critical?" these later episodes suggest the possibility of real liberation and escape which Burroughs will pursue further in *The Ticket That Exploded* and *Nova Express*.

The cut-up experiments in *The Soft Machine* are designed specifically to educate the reader out of this hopeless cycle of control and domination to a position of technical detachment and awareness. As part of his training the reader must learn to give up his desire for certainty and clarity. In a conventional text the reader is impelled forward by his desire for meaning and coherence; he grasps at familiar anchors of continuity, character, recognizable refrains, clichés, idioms. As the process of reading becomes more demanding, potentially alien and hostile, this need for clarity increases. While the individual images of the first cut-up had only to be returned to their proper place in the narrative sequence to be comprehensible to the reader, in the final cut-up the images themselves have been transformed, and some of them drawn from other texts entirely. In a characteristic section of the final cut-up—"I had learned to control Law 334 procuring an orgasm by any image, Mary sucking him and running the outfield—Static taken care of that way—what you might call a vending machine and boys dropping to Walgreen's"—a phrase like "what you might call" suggests definition or clarification. But in the cut-up text, rhetorical gestures of clarity, like narrative gestures of progress, lead nowhere and their promise is empty.

Burroughs frequently seduces and then undermines the reader's desire for clarity in *The Soft Machine* by his aggressive use of direct address: "Know the answer?—Two assholes and a mandrake—They'll do it every time" (54); or "Dead post card you got it? [. . .] Look, simple: Place exploded man goal in other flesh—" (40). Virtually anything can be plugged into the appropriate answer slot, for language's didactic gestures of knowledge, truth, and clarity are purely arbitrary.

In the paradoxical nature of the cut-up method, however, the text simultaneously reduces gestures of meaning to nonsense and elevates randomly generated nonsense phrases to highly suggestive and significant refrains. Framed as a clear and repeated imperative, a random phrase like "return it to the white reader" takes on an aura of meaning and importance. As Marcel Duchamp discovered in his own experiments with fragmenting and dislocating language, it is almost impossible to produce a text which cannot be drawn back into the mesh of meaning. Burroughs' phrase "return it to the white reader" does not simply masquerade in the rhetorical garb of meaningfulness, but actually stumbles on significance. It captures the ultimate direction in which Burroughs is always moving: the return back to the reader, to the reading of the word, to language as both the origin and the dead end of our experience.

By breaking down the limits of linear narrative, the isolation of individual texts, and the limits of identity, the cut-up text creates the possibility of a broader cosmic journey that extends across all texts, all cultural codes, all identities, across the very distinction between word and action, sign and signified. Burroughs' cut-up intervals in this chapter reorient our reading to the self-reflexive facts of life: to reality as fiction, fiction as language, and language as a system of control which can be appropriated, extended, and perhaps exploded.

5 | *The Ticket That Exploded*

The Ticket That Exploded, the second novel in the cut-up trilogy, was originally published one year after *The Soft Machine*, but its final version did not appear until 1967. During this five-year interval Burroughs extended the cut-up method to experiments with tapes and film. Perhaps as a result of these advances the cut-up effects in *Ticket* seem more controlled, more like the product of a complex machine than of dream or drug hallucinations.[1] Burroughs wields the cut-up method in *Ticket* as a war machine, a linguistic weapon against the binary thinking which generates conflict on a philosophical level (in all either/or antitheses), on a political level (in all civil or interstellar war games), and on a personal level (in all relations, sexual and non-sexual). As Inspector Lee of the Nova Police explains, this "Nova Conspiracy" to divide and devour human life is headed toward the total annihilation of the planet:

> "The basic nova technique is very simple: Always create as many insoluble conflicts as possible and always aggravate existing conflicts—This is done by dumping on the same planet life forms with incompatible conditions of existence—Their conditions of life are basically incompatible in present time form and it is precisely the work of the mob to see that they remain in present time form, to create and aggravate the conflicts that lead to the explosion of a planet, that is to nova—" (54–55)

Burroughs imagines this military emergency staged on the battlefield of language; and as a writer he declares, "I am tired of sitting behind the lines with an imperfect recording device receiving inaccurate bulletins....I must reach the Front" (*White Subway* 71).

In *Ticket* Burroughs stages actual battles in which the forces of resistance (the Nova Police) attempt to save humanity from the Nova Criminals. The enemy's strategic "Operation Other Half"—the imprisonment of human life in conflict and dualism—is countered by the revolutionaries' "Operation Rewrite," a set of techniques which would dismantle binary opposition, linear time, and eventually all word and flesh. Although Burroughs suggests various practical means of achieving this breakthrough by experimenting with tape recorders and films, with light and sound frequencies, all of the high technol-

ogy of *Ticket* is part of a single vast mechanism which dominates the novel—
the cut-up writing machine. As Jennie Skerl points out, the new hero of the
cut-up trilogy is the figure of the renegade writer (59). Even more explicitly in
Ticket than in *The Soft Machine*, the action is textual. The "soft machine" of
the body, crippled by the determinism of the codes *already written* on its
"transparent sheets" of flesh, will be dismembered and exploded by the random vibrations of the *newly written* and continually *rewritten* cut-up produced
in Burroughs' experimental fiction. This scenario for liberation is the "exploded ticket" referred to in the novel's title.

From *The Soft Machine* to *Ticket*

In *The Soft Machine*, Burroughs depicts an exotic but still recognizable world of drugs, sex, and violence in the relatively familiar genres of
the detective story and the travelogue. *Ticket* combines these genres with the
broader possibilities offered by the science-fiction narrative, extending the
novel's scope from the exotic to the cosmic. *The Soft Machine*'s presentation
of the monotonous alternation of repression and resistance is replaced in
Ticket by a final galactic confrontation in which the very survival of the human race is at stake. The same control system which dominates the world of
The Soft Machine is brought here to a state of emergency. The style of *Ticket*
is consequently more urgent, more telegraphic and intense than that of the
earlier novel.

The direct experience of the "Algebra of Need," of life trapped in the body,
manipulated by its needs and fears, is portrayed from the *inside* in *The Soft
Machine*. Both the characters and the narrator of this novel accept their situation with a listless cynicism. *Ticket*, on the other hand, examines the human
situation from *outside*: "*Your* earth case must be processed by the Biologic
Courts" (56, my emphasis). From this perspective of heightened consciousness and detachment, *Ticket* evolves a program of resistance, a possible way
out of the vicious cycle of domination which paralyzes the world of *The Soft
Machine*.

The monotony of the earlier novel in which even the most exotic or exaggerated images are reduced to the already familiar is replaced in *Ticket* by a
disorientation which renders everything defamiliarized, shifting and uncertain. The body, time, reality, and the word are all shaken loose from the blind
obliviousness of habit. The literary technique of defamiliarization, as Viktor
Shklovsky describes it, increases "the difficulty and length of perception" in
order to enhance it, to restore the "sensation of things" which automatic responses have dulled (12). Thus the difficulty and strangeness of *Ticket* demands the kind of "applied reading" Barthes describes in *The Pleasure of the*

Text, a reading which would "browse scrupulously" and slowly (12–13). Burroughs describes in *Ticket* a similar procedure for slowing down what he calls the "reality film" so that the viewer might observe, frame by frame, what is actually going on around him.

The total resistance called for in *Ticket*, however, demands more violent methods than defamiliarization. The body, time, and ultimately the word must be not only released from the predetermined patterns set by habit and routine, but more thoroughly obliterated. In *The Soft Machine* we find body transfers like the one involving the narrator and the epileptic, but the body persists, and with its weaknesses and needs the entire system of repression is insured. *Ticket* presents us with the possibility of exploding the body "into air into thin air." The earlier novel distorts time, shuffling memories and speeding up time's progress, but time still exists there and chronologies can be reconstructed. The waves of involuntary memory that confuse the characters in *The Soft Machine* are replaced in *Ticket* by a purposeful manipulation of memory lines for what Burroughs calls "time travel." The later novel carries us, in fact, to the verge of timelessness where even memory will be erased. The adventures of *The Soft Machine* may push reality to the borders of the surreal, but *Ticket* exposes all "alleged" reality, whether surreal or banal, as mere performance, no more than a badly staged carnival trick.

Like the body, time, and reality, language too is more violently distorted in *Ticket*. The cut-up intervals in *The Soft Machine* are still aberrant digressions, and as one reviewer remarks, you can still find "straightforward development of image and episode" and an "indistinct progression from one end of *The Soft Machine* to the other" (Adams 429). The cut-up disruption of narrative and grammatical continuity is the norm in *Ticket* rather than the exception, and the continuous shifting of the text makes it pulse with a mechanical flicker or vibration. This heightened frequency of the cut-up text is not an arbitrary embellishment but, as we shall see, an integral part of the war plot. Beyond the context of this science fiction battle, in the more immediate impact of the text itself, the cut-up functions as a device which might release both writer and reader from the restrictions of Western thought and language.

Reading *Ticket*

It is difficult to describe or to reproduce in analysis the experience of reading a text like *Ticket*, particularly because that experience is so radically transformed with each repetition.[2] An initial reading of this fragmented narrative is disorienting, frustrating, almost physically unpleasant. Each chapter title promises a particular focus, but it is rarely maintained; instead one stumbles repeatedly over fragments of other routines and other texts. The style, like the confused content, demands a degree of visual and mental concentration that can hardly be sustained for more than a few pages at a time. Even in those rare sections of the text where the content is continuous and homogeneous, the syntax is regularly riddled with dashes, ellipses, or parentheses. Not infrequently the reader encounters paragraphs extended through several breathless pages of fractured continuity and syntax.

At first the reader takes in little more than the visual impact of such a printed page: a cluttered mosaic which represents graphically, before the reading even begins, what Burroughs has in store for literary conventions and reader expectations. It is only after the saturation and familiarity that comes from repeated and unhurried readings that the motives and pleasures of this text begin to emerge.

This pleasure does not arise in any way from the content of the narrative. One reviewer of *Ticket* speculates incorrectly that "We cannot know what the vision means unless we experience it totally, giving ourselves up to it [to] temporarily *be* Burroughs. . . . If we read the book properly we can feel the pleasure also . . . Since we are also human, with the same polymorphous perverse background" (Davis 282). The world of violence and sex described in *The Soft Machine* and *Ticket* is never offered to the reader as a source of pleasure, but as a panorama of the *delusions* of the "Garden of Delights" where pleasure is poisoned by pain and manipulated by external forces. Burroughs attempts to destroy the power of that world and its arsenal of images by a method of cure in which the reader is immunized by exposure. As in his encounter with *Naked Lunch*, the reader is to take in the images of the trilogy as an emetic treatment, eventually purging any power they might have over him.

The real pleasure offered by a text like *Ticket*, then, is the pleasure of a new kind of mastery of the word in which Burroughs attempts to train his audience. To "temporarily *be* Burroughs" is not to be immersed in images of sex and violence, but to be in total control of the language which nurtures those images, both from within and without. The reader is thus detached from the text's images and drawn instead to its style. Because he cannot reassemble the material of *Ticket* into a coherent linear narrative, the reader must hold the entire chaotic text in his mind at once; because his perspective must be inclusive and simultaneous, the reader achieves a secular equivalent of divine vision. Free to chart his own course through an inexhaustible network of textual associations and digressions, the reader is everywhere present in the limitless and reversible space of the cut-up text.

This effect of simultaneity is particularly heightened by Burroughs' use of the fold-in method in this novel. "The *déjà vu* phenomenon," as he explains, can be "produced to order" by folding page one into page one hundred and then inserting the composite in the text as page ten. Thus even a first reading of *Ticket* will have the haunting quality of a rereading, of a return to mysteriously familiar terrain. Actual rereadings will obviously intensify this effect to a startling degree. The reader experiences the flash of recognition as a single word spliced into one episode condenses and recalls an entire routine from some distant chapter. He also feels the pleasure of release as a cryptic image held suspended in mystery from an earlier cut-up collage reappears, finds its context at last, and expands.

Frequencies and Alternations

A reading of *Ticket* continually pulsates with such expansions and contractions. Brion Gysin describes a very similar pattern of images moving in and out of focus through the effects of his stroboscopic "Dream Machine": "regulated to produce interruptions of light at between eight and 13 flashes a second, complementing the alpha rhythms in the brain, or eventually bringing the two into phase, and at that moment, immediately, one begins with sensations of extraordinary, bright colour and infinite pattern, . . . changes of pattern which follow each other in apparent random order, and then give way, at a certain point, to things recognized as dream images, imaginary events occurring at a certain speed, much like a speeded-up movie" (Palmer 51). In Burroughs' cut-up text, as in Gysin's stroboscopic flickering images or in the intoxication of certain drum music, what is powerful and significant is not any specific content but pattern and rhythm.

In Burroughs' description of the cut-up writing machine in operation, our attention is drawn away from any shifts in content to the stylistic patterns of alternation itself:

Sheets of magnetized calligraphs drew colored iron filings that fell in clouds of color from patterns pulsing to metal music, off on, on off—[. . .] Photomontage fragments backed with iron stuck to patterns and fell in swirls mixing with color dust to form new patterns, shimmering, falling, magnetized, demagnetized to the flicker of blue cylinders, pulsing neon tubes and globes [. . .] characters walk in and out of the screen flickering different films on and off— (*TTTE* 62–64)

Burroughs explains that in cut-up experiments with tape recordings "the content of the tape doesn't seem to effect the result"; the power is in the rhythm, in patterns "alternating [. . .] 24 times per second" (18–19). Content is reduced to the irrelevancy of the "so-called context" (163), shifting the reader's attention to the structures and rhythms of the text's surface.[3]

One might argue, of course, that all good prose has a distinct rhythmical patterning. But there is more at work here than the natural pacing of the good storyteller or comedian; this pattern of expansion and contraction, of speeded up accumulation and subsequent slowing down or breaking down of the narrative is the compulsive pattern of Burroughs' creative imagination. In an early letter to Allen Ginsberg, Burroughs describes this creative pattern as "the routine [which] pounces on [him]" (*Letters* 122); it is defined as spontaneous and beyond his control (113). The routine alone can lift him out of the hopeless monotony of his drug addiction, physical discomfort, or loneliness, out of the Beckett-like bleakness of his vision of human life. It provides a "moment's freedom from the cautious, nagging, aging, frightened flesh" (*Letters* 79).

In one letter to Ginsberg, we can actually see the routine work its magic (*Letters* 40–42). The letter begins with a series of complaints about his painful physical condition, his feeling of being isolated and rejected by everyone. He mentions another bad luck character similarly "washed up" in Tangier. His initial short summary of "The Saga of Eric the Unlucky" seems to dissolve his discontent and send him off on a lively routine in which he enumerates Eric's many disasters. Desperation itself, in its fertile richness and variety, becomes a source of energetic hyperbole and pleasure, the catalyst for the sort of "good canter" that Beckett's Didi and Gogo periodically enjoy. Despite Burroughs' claim that there is "no such thing as an exhaustive routine" (*Letters* 78), these moments of energy and comic relief always do run down. Relief from the "nagging, aging, frightened flesh" is only temporary. The routine can lift him out of himself, out of his "blank and narcoticized" state (*Letters* 153) or out of his physical suffering, but it will always return him to that same condition. The saga of the medical disasters suffered by Eric the Unlucky tolls Burroughs back to his own problems: "This [condition of paralysis] has got worse while I wrote the letter. Now I can hardly move" (*Letters* 42).

There is a crucial distinction to be made here between the spontaneity and immediacy of Burroughs' letters and the deliberate composition and editing of his fictional texts. In the cut-up narratives, the alternation of high and low energy, of the expanded routine and the breakdown to despair, is deliberately and even mechanically produced. Despair is stylized in long cut-up mosaics of death, absence, and endless sad farewells. When these accumulated images threaten to paralyze the text, Burroughs jolts the narrative back to life with the rush of a new routine and the performance of a new voice. These alternations between stark glimpses of the banality of despair and surreal flights of the imagination have no subjective emotional content. The involuntary and spontaneous seizures of the routine have been controlled and replaced by the workings of the "writing machine."

The movement from the involuntary to the controlled, from memory to text, is not only a strategy for writing but a strategy for living. Burroughs has a tendency to textualize himself even beyond the distancing effect achieved by any writer who transcribes lived experience. Commenting on the collection of his correspondence with Allen Ginsberg, Burroughs automatically turns the

letters into a cacaphony of "vaudeville voices," a grotesque series of impersonations. Referring to himself in the third person or merely as a disembodied
"querulous voice," Burroughs mocks the banality of his own complaints, the
"ancient saga of a moaning man of letters" (*Letters* 1). He cuts up and re-
assembles fragments of his own correspondence to expose the consistent
drone of his self-centered preoccupations and demands. Burroughs acknowledges that the letters, like all writing, give the reader a vision of experience
"transmuted into what we call art." His rereading of his correspondence pro-
vokes further transmutation of that experience, further distancing and manipulation. The letters to Ginsberg are finally condensed by Burroughs into
his three-page cryptic preface to the edition entitled (with relentless self-
mockery) "UN HOMME DE LETTRES. UN POEME MODERNE."

It is clear from what we have already seen in *Naked Lunch* and in *The Soft
Machine* that Burroughs' artistic metamorphosis moves in the direction of depersonalization. The reader of *Ticket* is being trained in a similarly depersonalized and detached method of reading. While the images in this novel, as
in Burroughs' earlier works, may often be arbitrary and repulsive, the rhythmic patterns of images, sentences, and narrative sequences are rigorously
controlled and highly purposeful. The reader's mastery of this new way of
reading and thinking promises to release him from the power of involuntary
word and image, from the insistent demands of memory and desire.

"Combat Troops in the Area"

In order to explore more fully the radical impact of Bur-
roughs' experimental writing in *Ticket*, I will focus on a single chapter, "combat troops in the area." Located at the very center of the novel, this chapter
depicts one battle in the ongoing war in which invaders from Venus and the
fictional planet Minraud attempt to control humans through addiction to sex
and power. The ultimate strategy of the guerilla resistance fighters is "time
travel" along memory lines, escape out of the present moment in which their
survival is threatened.

On the broadest level, the content of the chapter breaks down into two sections: one concerning direct and immediate combat with interplanetary invaders (102–11), the other focusing on personal memory (111–18). Typical
of the elusive and paradoxical nature of *Ticket*, the chapter moves in two contradictory directions: outward to the cosmic battleground of Venus, Mercury,
Uranus, and Minraud; and inward to the mind's most private recesses of nostalgia and desire in two memories involving "John and Bill" as adolescents
and then as young men. Moving outward into the cosmos, the narrative opens
up access to Burroughs' most surreal inventions of omniscient machines, of
crab and insect life with superhuman intelligence; telescoping inward, it re-

veals the monotonous banality of human life weighted down by physical desire, memory, and language.

These thematic alternations are further complicated by stylistic alternations between relatively conventional and radically experimental prose. As
they intersect, these binary oppositions in content and style dissolve into fluid
patterns of shifting juxtapositions—the vibrating frequency of the cut-up machine. Our disoriented reading of the chapter functions as a decisive element
in the battle being fought in *Ticket* for the liberation of human consciousness.

Once one is familiar with the general outlines of the Nova mythology, the
opening section of the chapter is relatively straightforward.[4] It narrates one
confrontation among many between the Nova Police (the resistance or revolutionary forces) and the Nova Mob, alien invaders from Venus, Minraud, and
beyond who have gained parasitic control of human life on earth by trapping it
in word and flesh:

> As the shot of apomorphine cut through poisons of Minraud he felt a
> tingling burning numbness—his body coming out of deep freeze in the
> Ovens—Then viscera exploded in vomit—The mold of his body cracked
> and he stepped free—a slender green creature, his hands ended in black
> claws, covered with fine magnetic wires that extended up the inner arm
> to the elbow—He was wearing a gas mask to breathe carbon dioxide of
> enemy planet—antennae ears tuned to all voices of the city, each voice
> classified on a silent switchboard   green disk eyes with pupils of a
> pale electric blue—body of a hard green substance like flexible jade—
> back brain and spine burned with blue sparks as messages crackled in
> and out—
> "Shift body halves—Vibrate flesh—Cut tourists"—
> The instructions were filed on transparent sheets waiting sound forma-
> tion as he slid them into mind screens of the planet—He put on his
> broken body like an overcoat—Silent and purposeful under regulating
> center of the back brain, he went into a bar and stood at the pinball ma-
> chine, his hard green core sinking into the other players writing the resis-
> tance message with magnetic wires—The machine clicked and tilted in
> his hands, electric purpose cutting association lines—Enemy plans ex-
> ploded in a burst of rapid calculations—Vast insect calculating machine
> of the enemy flashed the warning—
> "Combat troops in the area"—
> [. . .] Too late the crab guard saw the jade body and the disk eyes
> pounding deep into his nerve centers—The eyes converged in a single
> beam forcing the guard back like a fire hose—The pressure suddenly
> shut off as the eyes vibrated in air hammer synchronization—pounded
> the guard to writhing fragments— (102–3)

Despite the surreal quality of this sequence, the main figures are identifiable
(the revolutionary agent with the jade body and his opponents, the crab guards

of Minraud) and the action is continuous. The style is appropriately abrupt and telegraphic, reflecting the immediacy and urgency of the attacks and counterattacks.

As we look more closely, however, even this straight segment of the narrative produces the disorienting effect of a cut-up text. The identity of the jade man is mysterious and anonymous (he may or may not be the agent K9 referred to later in the chapter) and his portrait is a metonymic catalogue of dismembered parts: "antennae ears," "green disk eyes," "body of a hard green substance," "back brain and spine." Free not only of name but also of the limits imposed by the conventional notion of a total organic body, the agent manipulates his separate body parts like an arsenal of high-tech weapons. While the action as a whole is continuous, particular actions tend toward fragmentation: the jade man's body "cracked and he stepped free," messages "crackled in and out," he infiltrated the barroom by "cutting association lines," and finally he reduced the crab guard to "writhing fragments" with his vibrating stare. Language too is dismembered, tied as always in Burroughs' work to the fate of the body. The dash predominates throughout, replacing the terminal period with a frantic metonymic drive. Pronouns and articles are omitted, as the text proceeds by disjointed contiguous phrases. Dismemberment and fragmentation, whether of the body or the word, seem to have the positive effect here of a *liberation* from control, a freedom from predetermined patterns.

As the battle intensifies and its scope widens, the narrative erupts periodically into battle cries of the revolutionary troops: "messages crackled in and out—'Shift body halves—Vibrate flesh—Cut tourists,'" or "dictating message of total resistance—'Shift linguals—Cut word lines—Vibrate tourists—Free doorways'" (104). These refrains take the form of imperative commands telegraphing the dangers of dualism and the necessity of escape from the limits of word, image, and flesh. They dictate procedures for cutting, shifting, and vibrating all established codes. While they appear at first as "situational" refrains announced by the narrative, these emergency directives eventually slip in and out of the text unannounced along with many other disembodied voices. As the refrains accumulate in permutating fragments they begin to lose their specific meaning, operating instead with the impact of verbal punctuation marks. Like the ubiquitous dash of this first section of the chapter, they generate a tone of urgency and an insistent rhythmic pattern.

In many ways, the battle described in this chapter is a confrontation of frequencies, of different rhythmic patterns. The "vast insect calculating machine" of the alien invaders manipulates human will by alternating pain and pleasure at "supersonic speed like a speed up tough and con cop routine—" (111). Burroughs demonstrates this technique at some length in *The Job*, where the "tough and con cop routine" is compared to contradictory commands imposed by advertising and the daily press:

So the modern ceremonial calendar is almost as predictable as the Mayan. What about the secret calendar? Any number of reactive commands can be inserted in advertisements, editorials, newspaper stories. Such commands are implicit in the layout and juxtaposition of items. Contradictory commands are an integral part of the modern industrial environment: Stop. Go. Wait here. Go there. Come in. Stay out. Be a man. Be a woman. Be white. Be black. Live. Die. Be your real self. Be somebody else. Be a human animal. Be a superman. Yes. No. Rebel. Submit. RIGHT. WRONG. [. . .] Present. Absent. Open. Closed. Entrance. Exit. IN. OUT, etc., round the clock. [. . .] The controllers know what reactive commands they are going to restimulate and in consequence they know what will happen. (45)

The frequency produced by the rapid alternation of contradictory commands functions as "an artifact designed to limit and stultify on a mass scale" (*Job* 193). In the disorientation induced by this technique, the subject is left defenseless, and the controller may impose any subliminal suggestion. The resistance troops in *Ticket* counter this conflict-oriented programming of human life with a deprogramming machine, similarly impersonal, superhuman, and technical. The guerilla forces do not, as in *The Soft Machine*, simply replace the enemy's control machine with their own, for they are "galactic shock troops who never colonize." Using random techniques of cut-up, fold-in, and permutation, the resistance machine explodes all structures of conflict and continuity. As the lubricious flow of the narrative is thus broken open like the jade man's body, there is a temporal as well as a linguistic breakthrough: "It was over in a few stuttering seconds [. . .] Electric static orders poured through nerve circuits in stuttering seconds [. . .] stuttering distant events" (104–6).

The resistance message stutters in telegraphic refrains and the message *is* to stutter—to cut, shift, and vibrate the word. Thus the narrative represents simultaneously the military strategy of the nova plot and the actual composition of the novel's style—and those two operations become one. The narrative moves beyond isolated refrains which describe the cut-up methods ("shift linguals" or "Word Falling") to extended sections of more radically dislocated prose which constitute the *results* of those methods. The reader finds himself thrown into the strangely deterritorialized and timeless terrain of Burroughs' most experimental writing:

Body halves off—appropriate instrument pinball color circuits—Sex words exploded in photo flash—Nitrous fumes drift from pinball machines and penny arcades of the world—Photo falling—Break through in grey room—Click, tilt, vibrate green goo planet—Towers, open fire—Explode word lines of the earth—Combat troops show board books and dictate out symbol language of virus enemy—Fight, controlled body prisoners—Cut all tape—Vibrate board books with precise shared meals—scraps—remains of 'Love' from picture planet—Get up off your rotting combos lit up by a woman—Word falling—Free doorways—Television mind destroyed—Break through in Grey Room—'Love' is falling—Sex word is falling—Break photograph—Shift body halves—Board books flashed idiot Mambo on 'their dogs'—with pale adolescents of love from Venus—Static orders pour in now—Venus camera writing all the things you are—Planet in 'Love' is a wind U turn back—Isn't time left—Partisans showing board books in Times Square in Piccadilly—Tune and sound effects vibrating sex whine along the middle line of body—Explode substitute planet—Static learned every board book symbol with inflexible violence—color writing you out of star dust—took board books written in prisoner bodies—cutting all tape—Love Mary?—picture planet—Its combos lit up a woman—'Love' falling permutated through body halves—Static orders clicking—Word falling—Time falling—'Love' falling—Flesh falling—Photo falling—Image falling—

[. . .] Galactic shock troops break through moving in fast on music poured through nerve circuits—stuttering distant events—In a few seconds body halves off from St. Louis—Ghost writing shows board books—Vibrate dead nitrous film streets—Fight, controlled body prisoners—Cut flute through board books—Scraps to go, doctor—cleaving new planet—Get up, please—Television mind destroyed—Love is falling from this paper punching holes in photograph—Shift body halves in the womb—a long way from St. Louis—total resistance—cobblestone language with inflexible violence—Combat troops clicked the fair—a Barnum Bailey world— (104–6)

Some fragments within this cacophony will already be familiar to the reader: actions repeated from the combat scenes such as exploding, flashing, falling, shifting, breakthrough; fragments of the battle refrains of the resistance troops ("Photo falling—Image falling"); and the thematic focus on the dangers of dualism ("Body halves off"). These familiar allusions, however, function in the cut-up without any order or continuity, as floating textual references. The fragmented voices seem to come from all directions at once in a simultaneous multilevel discourse, a transcription of an anonymous and infinite intertext.

This cut-up not only scrambles elements from the scenes which immediately precede it and from Burroughs' other works, but introduces voices from the culture at large, particularly the popular culture of song lyrics and television. As the cement mixer of Burroughs' writing machine processes its material, new combinations displace the "rotting combos" imposed by the rhetoric of sentimentality and the "sex whine" of desire. Isolating "Love" in quotation marks, splicing love and sex into the language of war and violence, Burroughs suggests their hidden affinity and exposes the role of romance in the enemy's Nova plan. Once the dead end of "Planet in 'Love' is a wind U turn back" is publicly exposed in Times Square and Piccadilly, its subliminal power will be dispersed.[5]

As Burroughs argues in *Naked Lunch*, the ugly truth always spurts out from the spaces between the lines. The cut-up text multiplies those cracks or gaps by vibrating, "stuttering," and "clearing" its way through the enemy's war plans. It exposes the Venusian "Love" gimmick which transforms love into vampirism, and explodes the more comprehensive "word and image banks" of the "board books" of control. All predetermined limits of identity and time ("Venus camera writing all the things you are") are shaken loose and rewritten. The cut-up reaches back into the past, to Burroughs' childhood memories of St. Louis, in order to disperse and escape its manipulative sentimentality: "Stuttering distant events—In a few seconds body halves off from St. Louis," or "Shift body halves in the womb—long way from St. Louis."

Cutting into/Cutting up the Past

The cut-up text may liberate the subject from haunting and obsessive memories by shifting and permutating their fixed forms (the "womb" memories of St. Louis), or it may give access to more liberating memories of innocence and freedom. These chosen remnants of the past can then be manipulated by the subject at will, allowing extensions of consciousness in "time travel."

The heterogeneous clutter of one cut-up passage from the chapter's combat section, for example, seems to catch on a single snapshot image from the past—"Kiki stepped forward." Burroughs expands this particular memory from his Tangier days, allowing it to displace the science-fiction war scenario. This brief memory detour rehearses the longer digression into memory which will constitute the second half of the chapter:

> —His street boy senses clicked an oven in transient flesh—Call in the Old Doctor—heavy twilight—A cigarette deal?—Kiki stepped forward—
> "True? I can't feel it"—
> "Yes, smiling"—
> The man was only a face—Sex tingled in the shadow of street cafés—On the bed felt his cock stiffen—open fly—stroked it with gentle hands—Healed scars still pulsing in empty flesh of KY and rectal mucus—flicker ghost only a few years older than Kiki—Outskirts of the city, masturbated under thin pants—orgasms of memory fingers—Blue twilight fell on his Scandinavian skin—shadow beside him, KY on his slow fingers—As you listen fill in with a pull—teeth ground together the track—Muscles relax and contract—Kicked his feet in the air—steady stream of drum music in his head—forgotten scent of pubic hairs in other flesh with loud snores—

"Without you i on pavement—Saw a giant crab snapping—Help
me—Sinking ship—You trying Ali God of Street Boys on screen?—
So we turn over knife wind voices covered—From the radio interstellar
sirocco"—
   The room was full of white pillow flakes blowing out from a conical
insect nest of plaster—Scorpions crawled from the nest snapping their
claws—He felt the conical nests attached to his side—white scorpions
crawling over his face—He woke up screaming: "Take them off me—
Take them off me"—
   The dream still shuddered in milky dawn light—Kiki lay naked in a
strange bed. (106–7)

In the confusion of memory, the scene's characters, action, and setting are
multiple and indistinct. The vision is haunted by shadowy ghosts, dismembered and anonymous body parts—face, hands, fingers. Kiki's "loud snores
of sleep" lead into a nightmare dream mosaic of threatening giant crabs and
white scorpions, flashes of surreal creatures from the science-fiction combat
sequence. In this intersection of memory, sex, and dream we find the same
uncanny merging of the surreal and the ordinary which characterizes the alternations of the cut-up narrative of *Ticket* as a whole.
   When Kiki awakens from his dream, "his street boy senses clicked back."
The narrative style also "clicks back" from dislocated memory and dream
cut-up to a relatively conventional style. The entire sexual encounter between
Kiki and the shadowy man begins again, to be replayed in three pages of detailed and realistic linear narrative:

—His street boy senses clicked back: standing in a doorway his collar
turned up against the cold Spring wind that whistled down from the
mountains—The man stopped under a blue arc light in the heavy twilight—He put a cigarette to his mouth, tapped his pockets, and turned
his hands out—Kiki stepped forward with his lighter extended smiling—
The man was only a few years older than Kiki—thin face hidden by the
shadow of his hat—They had sandwiches and beer at a booth where a
kerosene lamp flickered in the mountain wind—The man called a cab
that seemed to leave the ground on a long ride through rubbly outskirts of
the city—It was a neighborhood of large houses with gardens—In the
apartment Kiki sat down on the bed and felt his cock stiffen under thin
pants as the man stroked it with gentle abstract fingers— (107–8)

All of the disconnected details of the cut-up version are meticulously ac-
counted for here. Instead of the confusing multiple setting of the cut-up, the
straight narrative traces a linear itinerary of the two men's motions from street
café, to suburbs, and to bed; the mysterious effects of flickering light and
shadow are explained by kerosene lamps and a hat which obscures the man's
features. Objects which appear randomly in the cut-up are now logically inte-

grated in the realistic setting. Instead of the cut-up confusion of "shadow beside him, KY on his slow fingers [. . .] steady stream of drum music in his head," the narrative describes Kiki taking the tube of KY from the nighttable, and the man putting a recording of Arab drum music on the tape recorder. The only surreal effect which remains in this second version is cautiously equivocated: "the man called a cab that *seemed to* leave the ground on a long ride through the rubbly outskirts of the city" (my emphasis).

We know from the "Atrophied Preface" to *Naked Lunch* what Burroughs thinks of this sort of realistic linear narrative:

> Why all this waste paper getting The People from one place to another? Perhaps to spare The Reader stress of sudden space shifts and keep him Gentle? And so a ticket is bought, a taxi called, a plane boarded. We are allowed a glimpse into the warm peach-lined cave as She (the airline hostess, of course) leans over us to murmur of chewing gum, dramamine, even nembutal.
> "Talk paregoric, Sweet Thing, and I will hear."
> I am not American Express....If one of my people is seen in New York walking around in citizen clothes and next sentence Timbuktu putting down lad talk on a gazelle-eyed youth, we may assume that he (the party non-resident of Timbuktu) transported himself there by the usual methods of communication.... (*NL* 218)

Why then is the reader given this sedative in *Ticket*? On one level, we might see this as part of Burroughs' "shock troop" strategy. The reader is lulled into a sense of security by the familiarity of both content and style here, only to be abruptly returned to the surreal science-fiction scenario. (Kiki is eventually attacked in the streets by the "giant crab claws" of his prophetic dream, and rescued by "Ali God of the Street Boys"). Our acceptance of the detailed realism of the second version of the Kiki memory is thus transferred metonymically to the surreal nova mythology, giving it a more concrete impact.

On another level, this extended conventional narrative offers a temporary relief from the telegraphic pounding of battle scenes and the embattled cut-up prose. The relief is not only logical and grammatical, but emotional; the machine-like vigilance of the troops is replaced in the memory of Kiki by a gentleness and pleasure which appear here for the first time in *Ticket*. Without the overt violence of military conflict, or the covert violence of sentimentality, a human contact is made in this encounter. Desire is straightforward and rhetoric minimal: "Kiki took the man's hand and closed the fist and shoved a finger in and out— / 'I fuck you?'— / 'Si'—" (108). Instead of the "sex" words and "Love" words which were satirized in the earlier cut-up permutation, this scene takes place almost in silence, accompanied only by the pulsing rhythms of the Arab drum music and the pulsations of life energy in which "muscles relax and contract." Free of the cultural repressions of guilt or sentimentality, the two men are in total control of their bodies. They synchronize their orgasms by counting together; and their desire, though detached and impersonal, is also playful and innocent: "Kiki blew the smoke down through his pubic hairs and said Abracadabra as his cock rose out of the smoke—[. . .] He was in fact very tired after the street, yawned as he crawled under the covers and snuggled against the man's back—" (109). There is no victory in orgasm, but it does offer a temporary retreat from the relentless battle of the streets.

Burroughs associates the pleasure and release of orgasm with dream and with memory—all experiences in which the limits of the present moment and of the body are transcended. In its shifting permutation of different bodies, voices, times, and levels of consciousness, the cut-up method achieves a similar transgression of boundaries. While Kiki slips off into post-sexual prophetic dreams, the shadow man is described as "seated at a table" perhaps composing the very cut-up permutations of the sex scene. When Kiki wakes up he finds only traces of this ghostly scribe in a heap of crumpled clothes (109). There is a clear sequence in this first half of the chapter from the extended resistance message cut-up, to the isolated cut-up memory of Kiki's orgasm and dream, and finally to the straight narrative of the sexual encounter. It is almost as though the readers, and perhaps the narrator, must pass through the liberating linguistic and temporal scramble of the cut-up passages before they can experience the innocence and directness of the Kiki memory.

Memory Retreat

A similar pattern of alternations between cut-up and conventional prose characterizes the second half of this chapter—the memory sequence involving John and Bill. The narrative proceeds from an initial cut-up which intertwines the two memories, to a straight narration of the earlier scene of John and Bill in the basement, to another composite cut-up of both memories, and finally to the straight version of the second meeting, ten years later, in John's loft apartment.

These two memories are more developed than the Kiki scene and their content extends beyond sexual play to more abstract discussions about language and time, and to actual experiments with radio frequencies, written texts, and scrambled tape recordings. While the earlier cut-up in the combat section seemed to stumble on the Kiki memory accidentally, through involuntary "orgasms of memory fingers," the John and Bill memories are introduced as a conscious and purposeful military maneuver. From resistance headquarters a directive is broadcast to the guerilla troops: "operation of retreat on this level involves shifting three-dimensional coordinate points that is time travel on association lines. Like this:" (111). The memory permutations then follow as an actual example of the possibilities offered by such "time travel."

Unlike the combat section, the basic content of this second part of the chapter is relatively homogeneous and realistic throughout. Burroughs shows here an uncharacteristic respect for continuity of plot and character, and the nostalgia and longing which the memories evoke are communicated without irony. The two boys have a clear relationship as teacher and initiate and as sexual partners:

> "I'm trying to fix it so we can both listen at once."
>
> He was opening a headphone on the bench with a screwdriver the two heads so close John's fluffy blond hair brushed Bill's forehead.
>
> "Here hold this phone to your ear. Do you hear anything?"
>
> "Yes static."
>
> "Good."
>
> John cupped the other phone to his ear. The two boys sat poised listening out through the dusty window across back yards and ash pits the tinkling metal music of space. Bill felt a prickle in his lips that spread to the groin. He shifted on the wooden stool.
>
> "John what is static exactly?"
>
> "I've told you ten times. What's the use in my talking when you don't listen?"
>
> "I hear music" . . faint intermittent 'Smiles.' Bill moving in time to the music brushed John's knee . . "Let's do it shall we?"
>
> "All right." (113)

This sort of conversation is very unusual in Burroughs' fiction—an exchange between friends uncomplicated by ulterior motives of control and domination. There is a desire for understanding which is genuine and communal. Even the difficulties of communication ("What's the use in my talking when you don't listen?") are familiar and oddly affectionate.[6]

The second memory takes place ten years later, when John and Bill meet in a poolhall and return to John's loft apartment. In this encounter the earlier radio experiments are replaced by drug experiments (marijuana), but lead to the same sexual play:

> St. Louis summer night outside the pool hall smell of coal gas the moon red they walked through an empty park frogs croaking John lived over a speak-easy by the river . . a loft reached by outside wooden stairs.
>
> "Come up for a while," he said
>
> "All right." Bill felt a tightening in his stomach. A room with rose wallpaper had been partitioned off from the loft like a stage set. As John turned on the light Bill saw a work bench tools and radio sets in the loft. On the door to the bedroom John had painted a number like a hotel door No. 18 . .
>
> "Sit down" . . John took a cigarette from a box on the night table. It was rolled in brown paper.
>
> "What is it?"
>
> "Marijuana. Ever try it?"

"No" . . John lit the cigarette and passed it to Bill. "Take it all the way down and hold it . . That's right . ."

Bill felt a prickling in his lips. The wallpaper seemed to glow. Then he was laughing doubled over on the bed laughing until it hurt his ribs laughing. "My God I've pissed in my pants."

(Recollect in the officers' club Calcutta Mike and me was high on Ganja laughed till we pissed all over ourselves and the steward said "You bloody hash heads get out of here.")

He stood up his grey flannel pants stained down the left leg sharp odor of urine in the hot St. Louis night.

"Take them off I can lend you a pair."

Bill kicked off his moccasins. Hands on his belt he hesitated.

"John I uh . ."

"Well so what?"

"All right." Bill dropped his pants and shorts.

"Your dick is getting hard . . . Sit here." John patted the bed beside him. (117)

The basic content of the two memories is so similar that they are almost interchangeable. The identical mechanics of seduction and response recurs; the decision to masturbate together in the basement ("lets do it shall we?" / "All right") is repeated ten years later ("Come up for a while," he said. / "All right."). As in the Kiki encounter, the rhetoric of seduction is minimized here, condensed to a direct, non-manipulative exchange. The locked basement storage room where the boys retreat to "do it" in the first memory is literally reproduced in John's loft as "a room with rose wallpaper [. . .] partitioned off [. . .] like a stage set." The storage room and its mock-up stage reproduction both contain technical work tools and radio sets, but also nostalgic details like the lamp shade "with parchment roses" in the basement and the "rose wallpaper" in the loft.

The actions described in these two memories—experiments with the crystal radio set, with marijuana, with sex—are essentially realistic and familiar. As experiments, however, they all involve a testing of limits, a gesture toward communality, silence and space. The boys attempt to synchronize their listening (to radio static, to frogs croaking, to "metal music of space") and their sexual excitement—as though to listen together and to reach orgasm together would take them outside of themselves, their action, the present moment they occupy. Even the adolescent sexual competition at masturbating ("Lets see who can shoot the farthest") becomes in this context a provocative gesture outward, beyond the limits of present time and body, "Over the hills and far away."

While the dialogue in the first memory is uncharacteristically conventional for Burroughs, the content of the boys' discussion brings the narrative to the borders of the surreal. They are debating the possibility of time travel through silence:

"John is it true if we were ten light-years away we could see ourselves here ten years from now?"

"Yes it's true."

"Well couldn't we travel in time?"

"It's more complicated than you think."

"Well time is getting dressed and undressed eating sleeping not the actions but the *words* . . What we *say* about what we do. Would there be any time if we didn't say anything?"

"Maybe not. Maybe that would be the first step . . yes if we could learn to listen and not talk." (114)

These particular memory segments facilitate time travel, escape from the present moment of military emergency, because they dramatize the same desire to travel outside the limits of time and body. Already in the didactic interval of the boys' conversation, the homey basement memory verges on a more cosmic or mystical experience.

In the straight versions of the two memories quoted above the recurrence of the same details and phrases suggests the circularity of time, the obsessiveness of memory. In the cut-up versions of the same scenes, on the other hand, the two memories intersect not in metaphorical similarity but concretely, in the actual text. We are no longer trapped in repetition but vibrated free of its constraints; the movement of the memory cut-ups is more explicitly a movement in and out of time:

John is it true on Market St. Bill leaned touching dials and "if we were ten light-years away we across the table and wires with gentle precise fingers could see ourselves here John goosed him with "I'm trying to fix it so we can both ten years from now? a cue and he collapsed listen at once." "Yes it's true." "Well couldn't we across the table laughing . . he was opening a headphone on the bench travel in time?" they had not seen much with a screwdriver . . "It's more complicated than you think" of each other in the two heads so close John's "well time is past ten years . . (112)

This first cut-up of the two memories foregrounds, almost as a refrain, gestures of physical extension as in the repeated phrase "we across the table." These physical gestures reinforce the extension of consciousness achieved as the cut-up leaps across the gaps which separate events in time and bodies in space.

Conventional notions of setting, action, and identity are thus distorted and expanded to the breaking point:

"I'm trying to fix it so we can both . . Bill saw a work 'I hear music' ten years from now listen at once" he was bench tools and radio faint intermittent 'Smiles' . . opening travel in time sets from the light John Bill moving in time to the with a screwdriver" hold this turned on . . the music brushed John's knee. [. . .] "Let's do it shall we?" anything maybe not maybe the two hotel door No. "All right" boys poised listening out through 18 . . "Sit down" John took out a John put down the headphones on the dusty window would cigarette from a box on the bench. [. . .] Bill Bill turned on a lamp parchment shoulders looking down at feet a prickling in his shade with painted roses the stiffening flesh flower smell lips . . the wallpaper chairs upside down on a desk of young hard-ons [. . .] "I'm trying to fix it so we can both ten years from now listen at once." opening travel in time with a screwdriver (114–15)

Human presence disappears into the inanimate furniture; the recognizable identities of John and Bill are doubled or stuttered ("Bill Bill turned on a lamp" or "John took out a John put down the"). At a later point the random intersection of the two memories produces a single composite creature, "John Bill moving in time." Actualizing the desire for communality and for surreal mobility, this image defies all laws of linearity and identity. It is the perfect emblem of the cut-up text.

In the memory cut-ups the most ordinary and practical aspects of the two scenes achieve surreal transformation. The mundane screwdriver used on the earphones in the basement scene is suddenly a magical space age instrument "opening travel in time with a screwdriver." The radio static the two boys listen to and listen through opens up access to another level of experience, another language: "two boys poised listening out through the dusty window would be the first step across back yards and ash pits yes if you could learn the tinkling metal music of space" (115–16).

One of the most frequently repeated images in this chapter is of windows or doors opening out onto vaster territories of space and time. Like the telegraphic refrains which announce the guerillas' imminent victory—("Word falling—Photo falling—Breakthrough in Grey Room")—these refrains of escape and expansion repeatedly announce a liberation that is never quite achieved. Escape in *Ticket* is always uncertain, slightly out of reach; access through the window is always difficult, "dusty" or obscured. The chapter seems to end on a note of lost opportunity, of failure to reach those wider realms of timeless space. We are reminded that this itinerary of time travel was merely a temporary retreat from the cosmic disaster, not a definitive victory:

"All right," he decided his gentle precise fingers on Bill's shoulder fold sweet etcetera to bed—EE Cummings if my memory serves and what have I my friend to give you? Monkey bones of eddie and bill? John's shirt in the dawn light? . . dawn sleep . . smell of late morning in the room? Sad old human papers I carry . . empty magic of young nights . . Now listen . . ugh . . the dust the bribe . . (precise finger touching dead old path) . . was a window . . you . . ten-year-old face of laughter . . was a window of laughter shook the valley . . sunlight in his eyes for an instant Johnny's figure shone to your sudden "do it" . . stain on the sheets . . smell of young nights . . (118)

Despite the glimmers of hope and joy in the contemplation of innocence and youth—"was a window of laughter shook the valley.. sunlight in his eyes for an instant"—these fragments are finally empty and fleeting. The "dead old paths" of nostalgia are as useless and worn out as an aging junky's tired veins. It is not only the haunting accumulation of personal memories of moments lived and lost which threatens to immobilize us, but the textual memories of everything read or written which swells the bulk of "sad old human papers [we] carry." Among the textual baggage Burroughs carries is the E. E. Cummings poem alluded to here, "My sweet old Etcetera." This poem serves very well as a coda for the chapter because its juxtaposition of war and love repeats Burroughs' intermingling of combat scenes and memories of lost lovers and friends. In Cummings' poem, as in Burroughs' novel, the personal context of remembered affection is seen as a retreat from the mindless brutalities of war. While these memories do preserve and communicate the desire for the non-destructive human contact of "gentle precise fingers," both writers finally reduce all the platitudes of nationalism and the euphemisms of love to an "etcetera" or a fading ellipsis.[7]

For Burroughs, as for many writers, memory is always textual, always trapped or preserved in language. But if it is the word that traps us in the past, in time and our bodies, the word can also be manipulated to liberate us from time's constraints. The boys in the basement perceive this when they argue that what imprisons us is not action but word, "What we *say* about what we do" (114). Words, Burroughs has insisted, must be at our disposal. Just as the resistance fighter in the opening sequence breaks free of his body which he can then put on or take off like a costume; just as the nostalgic past of the early basement scene is contained and controlled by John as a "stage set" in his loft; so language can be transformed from a seductive trap into a carefully manipulated means of escape. To this end the cut-up will shift the memories away from sentimental content, transforming them into pure conduit, a way out.

The Perforated Text

Conventional content and identity are repeatedly dismissed in *Ticket* in a medley of memory refrains exposing the sham reality which has trapped us in body, time, and word: "Remember i was a battery of tape recorders at the door" (68), "Remember i was the movies— [. . .] Remember i was the ship gives no flesh identity" (136). Repeated with multiple and apparently arbitrary predicates ("Remember i was your account" [137]), these refrains point always to the void at their center, the void at the center of any articulation of human experience or identity. Burroughs' writing techniques continually break open the body of the text, making holes in its representational function: "wind through dusty offices and archives—board books scattered to rubbish heaps of the earth—symbol books of the all powerful board that had controlled thought feeling and movement [. . .]—The whole structure of reality went up in silent explosions [. . .]—dead nitrous streets of an old film set—[. . .] and in the black silver sky great rents as the cover of the world rained down in luminous film flakes—" (30–31).

To pierce the illusion of a reality which limits human experience, which locks it into patterns of binary opposition and conflict, is to make holes which may serve as points of intersection, points of entrance and exit—the "way out" of the stalemate of nova conflict. Burroughs has described the narratives of *Naked Lunch* and *The Soft Machine* as a subway: "Glad to have you aboard reader but remember there is only one captain of this subway" (*SM* 167). The subway text is pure transit, not a geographically bounded space but a gap, a space between, a free interzone in which all is change, vibration, freedom from stasis. As Burroughs explains, in underground jargon the subway is known as "The Hole." His text, then, does not simply create holes in its continuity, it is itself a hole rattling madly through darkness.[8]

Burroughs offers a concrete emblem of this perforated universe in the visual impact of the punctuation of this chapter. Parentheses, dashes, ellipses, slashes, or simply blank spaces mark the points of intersection of multiple texts and voices in the cut-up narrative. Punctuation, like the word, is always concretely alive and literal for Burroughs. In his early letters he describes his fear of falling "into a great gray gap between parentheses" (*Letters* 117), or a fear that parentheses may "pounce on [him] and tear [him] apart" (*Letters* 113). In the cut-up narratives, however, this power is under his control; parentheses tear apart conventional narrative continuity and chapters often defy closure by drifting off in parenthetical refrains, sucked into an image of monotonous repetition: "(The shallow water came in with the tide and the Swedish River of Gothenberg)" (*NX* 115).

The punctuation of the "combat troops in the area" chapter has been manipulated by Burroughs with particular precision. The alternations of content between the surreal combat scenes and the familiar sex memories are reinforced by a stylistic alternation in tone and rhythm (fast/slow, high/low energy) and in structure (expansion/contraction). The stylistic contrast between the telegraphic urgency of the galactic war segment and the more nostalgic and dreamlike atmosphere of the memory sequence is reflected in the shift from an accumulation of breathless dashes to the drifting effect of repeated ellipses.[9] In the memory sequences, the cut-up proceeds without any respect for conventional punctuation; quotations are closed without ever having been opened, new sentences begin in the middle of an unfinished phrase. While the telegraphic discourse stutters and jumps its jerky way forward in the war narrative, the elliptical memory discourse seems continually to circle back on itself, recovering textual fragments in an endless operation of reconstruction and recuperation. These two tendencies capture the complexity of the reader's experience moving through the cut-up narrative; the compulsion to complete, to connect, to reconstruct continuity alternates with the contrary desire to give up all conventions, to defy all boundaries and enter a wider, if wilder, territory.

As in the boys' radio experiments, the reader listens through the static of the cut-up text, poised for scraps of continuity. The remembered gestures of the boys reaching across, leaning across, listening and seeing across gaps in time and space are reproduced in the reader's groping across cut-up discontinuities to reconstruct syntax and sense. The cut-up fades in and out of focus, alternately satisfying our need for completion and frustrating it. The goal is to be able to read on two levels at once: on one level following the compulsion of conventional grammar and meaning, and on another level experiencing the text as a hypnotic non-grammatical incantation.

The opening cut-up composite of the two memories of John and Bill is the site to which the reader keeps returning as those fragments find their context in the straight versions of the scenes which follow. The repetition of familiar memory fragments or refrains leads the reader on a circuitous path, a continual return to certain images or phrases by which he anchors and orients himself in an otherwise unnavigable discourse. Such refrains nurture our compulsion to obey and impose conventional order. At the other extreme, however, the reader of *Ticket* has been lifted out of conventional linear sequence and thus he may savor delay, digression, and dislocation instead of being frustrated by these devices. Only after he has assimilated the entire text can the reader wander freely through its confused geography, abandoning what Laurence Sterne calls the "rules and compasses" of literary form for what becomes, in reading Burroughs' more radical discourse, a kind of oriental passivity.

Circle or Spiral?

Burroughs' experimental methods of writing—cut-up, fold-in, permutation—transform the repetitions of obsessive memory into an escape route. Unlike Sterne, Burroughs does not feel obliged to return to his story from digressions, for there really is no story, there is only the texture of the cut-up. Burroughs' text *can* break free: "He slipped out of time in a—His camera gun blasted memory" (31). The narrative, which is in many ways the nameless protagonist described in these words, does literally "slip out of time" in a dash—in the cut between texts, in the break of syntax or continuity. Like the "rent in the sky" torn open by "supersonic film vibrations," space, time, and identity are distorted and made surreal as the cut-up method reveals the open cosmos of a new script.

Can the reader slip through these holes in the text, through the free spaces marked by parentheses, dashes, slashes, or blanks? Does this narrative subway go anywhere? Does it ever let the reader off above ground? There can be no definitive answer to these questions, just as there is no certain progression from the dangers of obsessive involuntary memory to the deliberate manipulation of memory lines for "time travel." The circling or looping back of the narrative creates an alternation between the hopefulness of imminent escape and the hopeless despair of stasis, between a cold and impersonal control and an excruciating sorrow and loneliness.

This alternating pattern continues through the final chapter of the novel, "silence to say goodbye." Burroughs returns here to the memories of John and Bill, but they have been transformed and expanded. John offers to demonstrate for Bill his recent experiments combining different texts on a tape recorder with a special splicing mechanism. John asks his friend to read "something from [his] novel," and what Bill happens to have with him is a description of the earlier scene in the basement. That memory, then, has been transformed into a text, distanced and depersonalized. John's input is similarly detached; he picks up a magazine and reads at random into the recorder. Instead of the subjective impression of memories merging in the mind's confusion, this final chapter produces an explicitly mechanical composite of two *texts*. The wistful conversations of "combat troops in the area" are replaced here by the detached behavior of two technicians: " 'All right . . go ahead . . And try not to crackle the paper.' [. . .] 'That's enough . . one minute . . Now I will read.' [. . .] 'Now I am going to cut the cylinder into sections and rejoin the sections alternating your voice with mine . . take me an hour or so' " (185–87).

Memory has passed through many metamorphoses on its way to this final chapter: from the actual experiences in basement and loft, to Bill's novelistic account, to an impersonal recording of that text, and finally to the cut-up permutations produced by John's splicing experiment. The scenes have moved farther and farther away from any human center or presence. The resulting cut-up discourse, as John and Bill discover, is "scarcely recognizable as human voices." The cadence of vibration from the spliced tape has the power to send the listeners spiraling out beyond identity, body, and language: "Bill felt a rush of vertigo as if the sofa was spinning away into space. Blue light filled the darkening room. Bill was breathing a soft electric silence that sent the blood pulsing to his crotch . . the two boys naked bodies washed in blue twilight shivered and twitched in spasms . . He was spiraling up toward the ceiling" (187). The vibration of words alternating on the tape migrates to the boys' bodies, "naked bodies [. . .] shivered and twitched in spasms," and they break free of word and body in a blast of silence. Nagging and seductive memory, the "steady stream of distant voices coming in," is finally left behind as "Image no matter how good must die in time blockade exploded" (188).

What is it that the young men hear on that scrambled tape that sends them spiraling up to the ceiling? At the beginning of *Ticket*, Burroughs describes cut-up tape experiments in which voices are smudged and inched on a tape recording. As the patina of meaning and rhetoric is scraped away by the tape's distortions, the words are laid bare in their primitive essence ("They snarled and whined and barked"); their hidden meanings, words "not in the original text," are exposed (118). What is finally shaken loose and revealed as the two voices are alternated on tape "24 times per second" is a third subliminal voice, the voice of language itself: "A familiar sound I had heard it for years barely audible . . loud and clear now a muttering hypnotic cadence" (19). What John and Bill hear is the frequency which signals the presence of parasitic life—the parasitic organism of the word which locks us in body and in time. Like a virus, the past prerecords your future: "all actions are prerecorded and doped out and there is no life left in the present sucked dry by a walking corpse muttering through empty courtyards under film skies of Marrakesh" (189). Once the subliminal mutterings of language have been made conscious, audible, and concrete (as magnetic dust on tape), the writer can escape from word, image, and time.

The narrative of *Ticket*, however, has been announcing this liberation since the first chapter, only to be repeatedly drawn back down to earth. The apparently victorious spiraling up of John and Bill through blue silence does not save this final chapter from the return of memories and regrets. Thus "silence to say goodbye" forms another circle or loop in the narrative. The chapter ends as it began with a long series of farewells from various Nova characters, including the narrator who bids a courageous goodbye to his lost innocence and youth, his dreams, his very self: " 'stale face stale late face in the late summer morning mouth and nose sealed over [. . .] sure you dream up Billy [. . .] didn't exist you understand . . ended . . stale dreams Billy . . [. . .] boy I was who never would be now . . a speck of white that seemed to catch all the light left on a dying star . . and suddenly I lost him . . my film ends . . I lost him long ago . .' " (201–2). The incantatory beauty and simplicity of "stale face stale late face in the late summer morning" gives way to a more detached and definitive avowal, "my film ends . . I lost him long ago." In the alternation between the draw of nostalgia and the determination to maintain detached control, Burroughs achieves moments of powerful lyricism, but a lyricism without sentimentality. This poetic quality is perhaps only accessible to those who have the courage to give up the self, to move beyond its boundaries. The remnants of memory which still resurface in *Nova Express* most often take the form of this impersonal lyricism. No longer carrying the weight of nostalgia, they burn with an abstract clarity of vision untroubled by personal regret: "Piece of a toy revolver there in nettles of the alley . . . over the empty broken streets a red white and blue kite" (*NX* 104).

Such moments come and go in the flicker of the cut-up text of *Ticket*. In the final paragraph of "silence to say goodbye," the narrative is still shifting and changing direction. It swings back from the silent void of abandoned memory and identity to the expansive high energy of the excited storyteller: " 'lips fading—silence to say good bye—' See the action, B.J.? This Hassan I Sabbah really works for Naval Intelligence and . . Are you listening B.J.?' " (202). These final questions return us to the novel's first chapter (entitled "see the action, B.J.?") and bring the narrative full circle once again.

Beyond the closed circle of this chapter, however, Burroughs extends two gestures. The first is a page of Brion Gysin's calligraphic permutations of the phrase "silence to say good bye," and the second is Burroughs' essay "the invisible generation" which was appended to the later editions of *Ticket*. This essay functions as a didactic coda of practical advice on applications of the cut-up techniques. Just as *The Soft Machine* seemed to begin again and again, *Ticket* seems thus to end repeatedly. Each of the three endings evades conventional finality: the "silence to say good bye" chapter is suspended on a question ("Are you listening B.J.?"); Gysin's calligraphy dissolves the chapter's title into purely abstract design; and Burroughs' didactic essay fades out into repetition and blank space ("cut the prerecordings into air into thin air   "). In the last two endings, Burroughs has explicitly distanced himself from the narrative: the calligraphy page is a grafting onto his text of the work of another artist in another medium, and the end of the essay is borrowed from Shakespeare's *The Tempest* (act 4, scene i, 1.150).

These gestures of displacement and depersonalization, of a self-reflexivity that eventually cancels its "self" out, mark the general direction in which Burroughs is headed during the sixties. Everything that is vibrated into the freedom of indeterminacy by *The Ticket That Exploded*—the body, time, identity, and word—is sent hurtling through space on the *Nova Express* in the final subway ride of Burroughs' cut-up trilogy.

6 | *Nova Express*

The strongly didactic purpose Burroughs pursues in *Nova Express* most clearly distinguishes it from the two earlier cut-up novels. In a predominantly impersonal and technical style, the third novel offers the reader a good deal of information and clarification. The blueprint of *Nova Express* is "Operation Total Exposure"—the author's most overt attack on all conventional notions of reality, the body, and identity. In this final cut-up narrative, everything is revealed to be a sham, a derivative "dummy" which language produces to replace the authentic life it has devoured.

Despite this radical distrust of language, Burroughs must still use it in *Nova Express* to clarify the theoretical intentions which have motivated his experimental works. Like all of Burroughs' writing, however, *Nova Express* is fraught with paradox: although the narrative perspective tends to externalize and dissect all human responses, it is also marked by a painfully human and urgent appeal to the reader. This narrative insistence reflects Burroughs' desperate desire to make contact with someone or something outside the text, to be understood by his audience. While the actual reading difficulty posed by the cut-up style would seem to defeat the author's desire to make contact, Burroughs' development of the cut-up in *Nova Express* is aimed, at least in theory, at precisely this goal.

In Burroughs' writing career from *Naked Lunch* to *Nova Express*, didacticism increasingly displaces entertainment. Burroughs avoids a potentially pompous authoritarianism, however, by his willingness to submit even his most official pronouncements to the same cut-up operations he has used to deflate the writing of others. For example, after delivering two speeches at the International Writers' Conference in Edinburgh in 1962, Burroughs cuts and splices his own words into an assortment of other materials from the conference brochures. He describes the resulting mosaic, published later that same year, as "a composite of many writers living and dead" ("Censorship" 5).

In the "Foreward Note" to *Nova Express* Burroughs describes that novel's composition in the same terms: "An extension of Brion Gysin's cut-up method which I call the fold-in method has been used in this book which is consequently a composite of many writers living and dead." We have in *Nova Ex-*

press, as in the Writers' Conference cut-up, a hybrid text which asserts the author's intentions and beliefs while it simultaneously denies, displaces, or multiplies the authorship and conventional authority of the text. Ironically, the dissemination of the authorial self into a communal collaboration fulfills an intense personal need for contact which is apparent in Burroughs' earliest writings and which persists even in the depersonalized technical atmosphere of *Nova Express*. The cut-up or fold-in method, which had been used in *Ticket* to disrupt and dislodge continuity, becomes in *Nova Express* primarily an exercise in collaboration and citation. The aim of this new mode of cut-up is to explode the notion of ownership of voice, name, and word.

Nova Express is not a purely theoretical work; there are still remnants here of the jungle swamps and villages of *The Soft Machine*, of the cosmic battlefields of *Ticket*, of personal memory cut-ups and sexual encounters. These fictional contexts, however, are interrupted and framed in *Nova Express* by a technical purpose which brings us back always to the present moment of the reading of the text, to the immediacy of the reader's relationship to the word. In the confrontation of the forces of resistance (Nova Police) and the forces of control (Nova Mob), Burroughs' readers are clearly cast among the former as revolutionary cadets in training. In fact, reading the two previous cut-up novels has been a training program in new ways of thinking and perceiving, of reading and writing. *Nova Express* is an advanced seminar review of what the reader *should* have learned from these earlier fractured texts.

The self-reflexive focus on language and writing which was more indirect in *The Soft Machine* and *Ticket* is insistent and unavoidable in *Nova Express*. The revolutionary Nova Police are identified explicitly as writers, manipulators of the word and thus of history. Their method of resistance involves the appropriation of the enemy's writing machines which regulate external patterns of the culture and internal patterns of thought and sensation. The revolutionary Nova Police are taught, above all, the necessity of the ultimate obliteration of all linguistic weapons and of the disbanding of the revolutionary troops themselves once the planet has been liberated. "Operation Total Exposure" leads to the obsolescence of word and self, of our conventional notions of writing and identity.

Like the Nova Police, the text of *Nova Express* is a regulative device which is not meant to outlive its initial function: "The Nova Police can be compared to apomorphine, a regulating instance that need not continue and has no intention of continuing after its work is done. Any man who is doing a job is working to make himself obsolete" (50). The narrative of *Nova Express* is perpetually signing off in official postscripts and depositions, the lyrical farewells of the earlier novels reappearing in a more technical and detached form.

There is a discernible progression in Burroughs' work toward an increasingly intense and inclusive skepticism. In *Naked Lunch* he acknowledges that all fictional characters are arbitrary artifice, interchangeable pronouns and names reducible to the same "vocal apparatus"; in *Ticket* the "monikers" of these characters accumulate and dissolve in long farewell litanies. In *Nova Express*, the dismissal of all sham realities and obsolete mechanisms extends to the outer frames of the text to include the author as well as his friends and collaborators: "Long time between suns behind—Empty hunger cross the wounded sky—Cold your brain slowly fading—I said by our ever living poet dead—Last words answer your summons—May not refuse vision in setting forth the diary—Mr Martin Mr Corso Mr Beiles Mr Burroughs now ended— These our actors, William—The razor inside, sir—Jerk the handle—That hospital melted into air—Advance and inherit the insubstantial dead—Flakes fall that were his shadow—" (73). At the end of *Nova Express* even the book itself is dismissed, relegated to the shadowy ranks of the "insubstantial dead": " 'Mr Bradly Mr Martin?'— You are his eyes—I see suddenly Mr Beiles Mr Corso Mr Burroughs presence on earth is all a joke—And I think: 'Funny— melted into air'—Lost flakes fall that were his shadow: This book—No good junky identity fading out" (152).

Having known the isolation of addiction, the paralyzed existence of the junky alone in his room staring at his shoe for months on end, Burroughs looks to his writing to rescue him from that deadly stasis. Just as Kafka saw his own work as a repeated leave-taking from his father—the source, Kafka argued, of his own paralyzed life—so Burroughs' writing might be seen as a continual leave-taking from addiction, from the addiction to any and all delusions. The central locus of all addiction, as *Nova Express* didactically demonstrates, is the addiction to language, and more particularly to writing. Burroughs' relationship to his writing is highly ambivalent: he needs it as an escape from his isolation but he fears that it will become, or already has become, a need which restricts his freedom. Of all his novels, *Nova Express* in particular traces this ambivalence.

Making Contact

In the letters he wrote primarily to Allen Ginsberg during the composition of *Naked Lunch* (1953–57), Burroughs reveals an intense need for a contact that will relieve his loneliness and isolation. The letters are filled with such laments as "I do wish I had somebody to *talk* to" (*Letters* 80), or "It is really a deprivation to be without intelligent conversation. I evolve concepts, but no one to communicate with" (98). From within the solitude of writing and drug addiction, his correspondents seem to offer an indispensable "point of reference" (130) which keeps Burroughs from slipping away. The audience redirects the energy of Burroughs' writing habit outward: "Routines like habit . . . . I have to have receiver for routine. If there is no one there to receive it, routine turns back on me and tears me apart, grows more and more insane" (27). The audience functions here as the "Regulator Gimmick" that gives direction to the writing, saving it from the final explosion into madness. Burroughs has a nightmare vision of himself lost in a routine, "so far out one day I won't come back" (154); so he seizes his audience aggressively like some Ancient Mariner: "This letter is for you and Jack and Peter" he writes to Ginsberg, "Now listen" (164). This imperative surfaces in the fiction as well, where the narrator repeatedly demands of the reader of *Nova Express*, "Pry Yourself Loose and Listen" (15).

Burroughs alleviates some of the dangers of writing in his letters by carefully selecting an audience for each routine. Despite his acute awareness of the isolating nature of writing, he tries to infuse his transatlantic communications with the immediacy of conversation. He warns Ginsberg, "it always annoys me when someone ignores a question in one of my letters" (125), or scolds, "Write me on this point" (164). For Burroughs, any response to his letters is of crucial importance, and his frustration with the distance imposed by correspondence becomes at times almost pathetic. "Which letter of mine did Neal groan when he read?" he asks Ginsberg.[1]

The most obvious connection between these early letters and the cut-up novels Burroughs published during the sixties is the overlapping of the content of the routines themselves. More instructive, however, is the anxiety about failed or obstructed communication that pervades the letters and the novels alike. Many of Burroughs' routines are about the need for human contact and the fear of isolation, and he often expresses these feelings in epistolary images. One of the more familiar motifs of *The Soft Machine*, for example, is the "dead postcard":

> We are digested and become nothing here—dust air of gymnasiums in another country and besides old the pool now, a few inches on dead post cards—here at the same time there his eyes—Silver light popped stroke of nine.
> Dead post card you got it?—Take it from noon refuse like ash—Hurry up see?—Those pictures *are* yourself—Is backward sound track— That's what walks beside you to a stalemate of physical riders— . . .
> [. . .] Ghost of Panama clung to our throats coughing and spitting in the fractured air, falling through space between worlds, we twisted slowly to black lagoons, flower floats and gondolas—[. . .]—Dead post card are you thinking of?—What thinking? (*SM* 40–41)

Burroughs is haunted by the fear of incomplete communication, of the text without an audience consigned to death and oblivion. The fate of writing too often resembles for him "sending letter to a coffin" (*SM* 122), or "dead post card falling through space between worlds" (*SM* 143).

In contrast to the iconoclastic pleasure Burroughs finds in producing cut-up collective texts, personal communication through the mails seems to elicit his conservative side. He writes bitterly, to Ginsberg, "more letters are lost than delivered. These people have no sense of responsibility" (*Yage* 19). In another letter he relates a nightmare about his correspondence being tampered with at American Express: "*Every letter has been opened*, and they are all jumbled together, typewritten pages, so *I can't tell whose letter it is*. I keep shuffling the pages looking for *the end of the letter* and a signature. I never find it." What he *might* have perceived as a felicitous emblem of the liberating cut-up text evading the stasis and finality of a single signature is seen instead as a harbinger of danger and evil, a terrifying moment of lost contact: "I walk out along a dry, white road. There is danger here" (*Letters* 69).[2]

The problem, as it persists in *Nova Express*, is how to make contact and communication work, how to "intersect across wounded galaxies" without giving up the freedom from restraint achieved by the cut-up and fold-in methods. The emblems of this anxiety have become more abstract and stylized in *Nova Express*, refined down from purely sexual images of "making contact" in *The Soft Machine* and *Ticket* to recurring glimpses of an anonymous boy gesturing in an obscure code from some window:

> Again at the window that never was mine—Reflected word scrawled by some boy—Greatest of all waiting lapses—Five years—The ticket exploded in the air—For I don't know—*I do not know* human dreams—Never was mine—Waiting lapse—Caught in the door—Explosive fragrance—Love between light and shadow—The few who lived cross the wounded galaxies—Love?—Five years I grew muttering in the ice—[. . .] Its goal? That's more difficult to tap on the pane [. . .] And I became the form of a young man standing—My pulse in unison—Never did know resting place—Wind hand caught in the door—cling– Chocada—to tap on the pane (*NX* 75)
> —The Boy, driven too far down the road by some hideous electric hand—I dont know—Perhaps the boy never existed—All thought and word from the past—It was in the war—I am not sure—You can not know the appalling Venusian Front—Obscure hand taping all messages in and out— [. . .] The Boy had never existed at all—A mouth against the pane—muttering—Dim jerky far away voice: "Know who I am? You come to 'indicated accident' long ago . . . old junky selling Christmas seals on North Clark St. . . . 'The Priest' they called him . . . used to be me, Mister" shabby quarters of a forgotten city . . . (88)

From within his isolation, abandoned in "greatest of all waiting lapses" and "caught in the door," the vague figure of "some boy" or "form of a young man" is suspended in his efforts to communicate. Ultimately the boy is reduced to an "obscure hand," a "mouth against the pane—muttering"—dismembered metonymic fragments of the author's need to make contact. The poignant failure to bridge the gap which separates him from his past and his desire leads Burroughs finally to deny that boy image, "that boy had never existed at all," and to escape the sad snares of nostalgia and need.

In *Nova Express* Burroughs attempts a final leave-taking from such sentimental gropings, displacing them with the more immediate and practical problem of critical misreadings of his novels. Instead of turning only in on itself, the self-reflexivity of *Nova Express* also aims outward to its audience and critics in a most detached and professional manner. Sad lyrical laments over the lost postcard or the abandoned boy are undermined in *Nova Express* by Burroughs' aggressive and imperative defense of his works:

> "*Listen*: Their Garden Of Delights is a terminal sewer—I have been at some pains to map this area of terminal sewage in the so called pornographic sections of *Naked Lunch* and *Soft Machine*—Their Immortality Cosmic Consciousness and Love is second-run grade-B shit—Their drugs are poison designed to beam in Orgasm Death and Nova Ovens—Stay out of the Garden Of Delights—It is a man-eating trap that ends in green goo [. . .] Flush their drug kicks down the drain—*They are poisoning and monopolizing the hallucinogen drugs—learn to make it without any chemical corn*—
> [. . .] The purpose of my writing is to expose and arrest Nova Criminals. In *Naked Lunch*, *The Soft Machine* and *Nova Express* I show who they are and what they are doing and what they will do if they are not arrested. Minutes to go. [. . .] With your help we can occupy The Reality Studio and retake their universe of Fear Death and Monopoly—" (*NX* 13–14)

Burroughs insists on the theoretical nature of his texts and on his own scientific detachment:

> And let me take this opportunity of replying to the criticisms of my creeping opponents—It is not true that I took part in or instigated experiments defining pain and pleasure thresholds—I used abstract reports of the experiments to evolve the formulae of pain and pleasure association that control this planet—I assume no more responsibility than a physicist working from material presented to an immobilized brain—I have constructed *a* physics of the human nervous system or more accurately the human nervous system defines the physics I have constructed— (*NX* 78–79)[3]

Burroughs is forced to adopt this didactic and authoritarian tone because in order to produce the new kind of writing he has in mind he must reach an understanding with his readers.[4] In place of the hierarchical structure in which an author's words and ideas are imposed on passive readers (the "one-way Sending" described in *Naked Lunch*), Burroughs tries to generate in the cut-up a collective writing. The creative power of the writer, that which gives him

life ("only live animals write anything" [*TTTE* 149]) and distinguishes him
from a mere machine ("the machine can only repeat your instructions since it
can not create anything" [*NX* 78]), is passed on to and shared with the audience. His writing aspires to the indeterminancy of "stage performances programmed at arbitrary intervals so each performance is unpredictable and
unique allowing any degree of audience participation" (*TTTE* 213). Burroughs' method of "making contact," then, involves an unusual degree of
self-effacement or anonymity for the writer, and may be ultimately directed
toward his definitive obliteration: "Departed have left spectators involved"
(*TTTE* 68).

It is clear from his early letters that Burroughs sees his correspondents or
readers not simply as auditors, but as editors and even collaborators. When he
feels overwhelmed by the energy of the routines that are spilling out in his
letters, Burroughs looks to his friends for help. "I wonder how collaboration
might work out . . . I think it might be terrific" (*Letters* 183). He is torn between his need to isolate himself with his files until he can "work out [his]
method alone" (182) and the conflicting need for human contact with other
minds collectively devoted to perfecting the routines. He appeals to Ginsberg
repeatedly for editorial assistance on the smallest stylistic details: "I have four
alternative phrasings which I submit for your judgement. I have worked over it
so much I can't judge" (61).[5]

It is hardly unusual for a writer to solicit this sort of editorial response from
other writers and friends. In Burroughs' case, however, this tendency is inten-
sified by an anxiety about communication which is basic to his temperament
and to his system of composition. The cut-up writing machine is conceived as
a mechanism which combines not only multiple written texts, but multiple
responses to those texts:

> Characters walk in and out of the screen flickering different films on
> and off—Conversations recorded in movies taken during the exhibit ap-
> pear on the screen until all the spectators are involved situations per-
> mutating and moving—[. . .]
> [. . .] The spectators are invited to feed into the machine any pages
> of their own text in fifty-fifty juxtaposition with any author of their choice
> any pages of their choice and provided with the result in a few minutes.
> (*TTTE* 64–65)

The resulting cut-up is a hybrid of chance and choice, of authors and readers.

Along with Lautréamont and Tzara, Burroughs asserts that art is for everyone. This means, for Burroughs, that not only does every person have the
potential for artistic creation, but all existing art belongs to everyone. Ultimately, the collaboration of the cut-up text does not involve just author and
reader but all of literary history. This new collaborative text evades the re-

pressive restrictions of subjectivity and ownership and the stasis of an established literary canon. Burroughs imagines a vast communal text which embraces non-hierarchically the high art of Shakespeare, the radical poetics of Rimbaud, the popular genres of science fiction and spy thrillers, and even the discourse of popular science, journalism, and advertising.[6] From this heterogeneous mass, the cut-up technician surgically detaches some fragment and then subjects that found text to further fragmentation, juxtaposition, and reintegration in a new context.

Burroughs' increasing incorporation of found texts into his narratives reflects an effort to escape from personal identity and memory and to focus on the immediate practical activity of writing. Personal memory is displaced in *Nova Express* by the memory of texts written or read, by a purely literary recall. In *The Soft Machine* the incorporated textual fragments are almost all drawn from Burroughs' own work, early routines, letters, and memory pictures. The continuity is fragmented but the text remains hermetic, sealed up as the expression of a single subjectivity. In *Ticket*, Burroughs seems to emerge from the solipsism of the earlier work to acknowledge and extend the ideas of other science fiction writers with whom he finds fortuitous points of intersection. In *Ticket*, for example, Burroughs acknowledges his debt to Henry Kuttner's *Fury* and J. Barryngton Bayley's "The Star Virus" (*TTTE* 22, 156). In *Nova Express* he reaches not only beyond his own subjectivity but beyond the literary context of science fiction to actual scientific texts, both popular and technical.

The juxtaposition of scientific fact and imaginative fantasy in literary narratives has a history much older and more established than the popular genre of science-fiction. The technique as practiced by writers like Ovid or Rabelais is meant to assert the wonders of the natural world itself, more rich in variety and mystery than any fiction. This ambiguous narrative gesture, then, enables those authors to proclaim the superiority of nature over art and at the same time to defend their wildest inventions against accusations of non-verisimilitude. However, Burroughs' allusions to the laws of nature—as presented to us by scientific investigation or speculation—have none of the joy and wonder in nature expressed by these earlier texts. Instead, one senses the author's grim satisfaction in discovering allegedly factual or scientific evidence to corroborate his most bleak intuitions about the universe.

These cut-up collaborations in general constitute a form of found art, like that practiced by visual artists like Marcel Duchamp or Robert Rauschenberg and by composers like John Cage. In Burroughs' method, a found text may be "found out," exposed as empty rhetorical gesture or as a system of manipulations; or a found text may prove to be for the author a fortuitous "find," a text which corroborates or extends his own theories. In this latter situation, Burroughs' narrative finds in this other text its own double, and the text may ultimately become a complex double-talk text.

The Found Text "Found Out"

Let us take first the simplest and most familiar use of the found text, a method which Burroughs inherited from the Dada and Surrealist artists. One common target of both Burroughs and his avant-garde predecessors is journalistic prose, and their aim is to undermine the media's claims to objectivity and truth. Removed from its protective context and status, journalistic prose can be subjected to a more lucid scrutiny; it is only by isolating and *cutting up* limited segments for analysis that we can begin to see the bare mechanisms of control at work. Beyond the experiments of the Dada and Surrealist groups, beyond theorists of popular culture like Marshall McLuhan and Roland Barthes, Burroughs further alienates the media languages by not only cutting segments out of context but by further scrambling them in new permutations and combinations.

A short chapter from *Nova Express* entitled "Extremely Small Particles" (80–82) offers an interesting example for analysis. Burroughs appropriates the title itself from one of the found texts he will cut up in this chapter—an article describing recent scientific investigations of "high density silica as extremely small particles." By detaching part of this phrase from its original context and reconstituting it as a title, Burroughs has transformed the function of the words. The material which furnishes the *content* for the cut-up becomes a self-referential description of the cut-up style, composed from "very small particles" of found texts. This appropriated phrase is now Burroughs' description of his own method; and yet he did not compose this definition, he merely found it. In the very title of the chapter we have already entered the labyrinth of theoretical problems raised by Burroughs' techniques.

The opening lines of the chapter situate us temporally in the actual time of the publication of (or Burroughs' reading of) the texts he will use in the cut-up: "December 17, 1961—Past Time—" (80). Temporal travel to "past time" is no longer an extension along personal memory lines, as in *Ticket*, but the reconstitution of a particular moment of reading or writing. The situational frame for this cut-up text is no drug-induced confusion but rather a controlled and detached reading experiment.

As Burroughs has repeatedly asserted in interviews, anyone can play this game of cut-up collaboration with found texts: take two or more articles from a newspaper, fold in half, match up the halves of different articles and read across. This game comes with no guarantee of quality; thousands of pages of notes and experiments may yield barely a hundred pages of good routines.

Many of the shorter cut-up chapters in *Nova Express* are of little or no stylistic interest, and might be, as Burroughs concludes in one section, "irrevocably committed to the toilet" (146).

The best of these found text cut-ups, however, can be remarkably funny, and the "Extremely Small Particles" chapter produces some wonderful incongruities:

> Attorney General For Fear announced yesterday the discovery that cries of nepotism might "form a new mineral damaging to the President"— Insidious form of high density silica as extremely small particles got into politics with Lyndon B. Johnson, wife of two Negro secret service men—Another Mineral American formed by meteorite impact—"And it would make a splendid good talker," he said—
>
> At these tables there is virtually jostling diplomats—Some displacements of a sedate and celebrated rose garden but ideal for the processes of a quiet riverview restaurant—Police juice and the law are no cure for widespread public petting in chow lines the Soviet Union said yesterday—Anti-American promptly denounced Kennedy's moribund position of insistence:
>
> "Washington know-how to deal with this sort demonstration in Venezuela of irresponsible propaganda—Outside Caracas I am deeply distressed at the Soviet Union's attempt to drag us back just when we was stoned in violation of the administration's twenty billion dollar solemn word" (*NX* 82)

After an initial comic impact, there follows the rather uncanny recognition that the cut-up is not so different from the original found texts. Despite all distortion of content, the basic tone and rhetorical effect of the media prose remains intact. What we really take in here is the journalistic posturing of objective and accurate reporting of the truth. We register almost subliminally such introductory clauses as "The supreme court said yesterday" or "Attorney General for Fear announced yesterday" or "The Soviet Union said." In this stylized journalistic rhetoric, statements are repeatedly attributed to abstract or institutional entities, there is never really anyone behind this prose. The catch phrases of cold war chauvinism—"Damaging to the President," "Anti-American," "irresponsible propaganda"—continue to communicate a particular emotional attitude and political position even without any coherent context. Such phrases or gestures, the cut-up shows us, have nothing to do with their content—or the content is so arbitrary and meaningless that we might plug anything into the blank in the rhetorical structure. The found text here is "found out": the governmental propaganda of the "Administration's twenty billion dollar solemn word" is revealed to be a counterfeit coin in a discourse of bankrupt signs. The found text is forced to denounce and to deconstruct itself.

These words are not simply operating in a vacuum for they have become part of Burroughs' narrative, and that new context subjects them to yet another startling transformation. Not only does this cut-up text still resemble in its essential characteristics the original found text, but it bears a remarkable resemblance to Burroughs' wildest mythologies. We can now reread this same cut-up as if it were written by Burroughs as part of his own idiosyncratic vision. For example, the cut-up tells us that the government imposes itself on the populace at an insidious microscopic level: "insidious form of high density silica as extremely small particles got into politics with Lyndon B. Johnson." Recalling Burroughs' theory of the parasitic invasion of the word virus, we read this sentence as a denunciation of political manipulation by means of language. The cut-up describes how this linguistic invasion instills fear in the victim and reduces all affective animal life to a fossilized and controllable organism, "Another Mineral American." The mechanical dummy thus produced is, as the text explains, a "splendid good talker," for the tyranny of the word always displaces human life. The cut-up also seems to predict a revolt against this inhuman metamorphosis, and the victims' riotous demands for sex and food threaten the forces of repression: "Police juice and the law are no cure for widespread public petting in chow lines." Phrases that appeared at first as ridiculous incongruity suddenly make thematic sense. The found texts are not only forced into self-contradiction, they are forced to express the very position of their revolutionary enemies.

Corroboration—The Found Text as "Find"

While the cut-up is used in *Ticket* and *Nova Express* to attack and unmask the "blind prose" of journalism and government propaganda, the later novel tends more toward selecting found texts for corroboration, assimilating rather than exploding their authority. As Burroughs says, such a technique "takes some experimentation":

(This takes some experimentation)—The old mind tapes can be wiped clean—Magnetic word dust falling from old patterns—Word falling— Photo falling—"Last week Robert Kraft of the Mount Wilson and Palomar Observatories reported some answers to the riddle of exploding stars—Invariably he found the exploding star was locked by gravity to a nearby star—The two stars are in a strange symbiotic relationship—One is a small hot blue star—(Mr. Bradly)—Its companion is a larger red star—(Mr. Martin)—Because the stellar twins are so close together the blue star continually pulls fuel in the form of hydrogen gas from the red star—The motion of the system spins the hydrogen into an incandescent figure eight—One circle of the eight encloses one star—The other circle encloses the other—supplied with new fuel the blue star ignites"— Quote, *Newsweek*, Feb. 12, 1962— (*NX* 69)

The found text is barely tampered with here; it is carefully identified by Burroughs and maintains its own continuity. His interruption of the text consists only of two parenthetical asides pointing to the parallels between his own mythology and the symbiotic structure described in the article. What Burroughs implies here is that the scientific account of the stars' relationship reproduces in a cosmic context the basic conflict of duality which dominates Western language and thought. Burroughs has embodied this destructive duality in the double character Mr. Bradly Mr. Martin.

Following the quotation from *Newsweek*, Burroughs extends the theory of "supernova or exploding star" into a more elaborate routine. The news article's objective and disinterested account of the fuel exchange between twin stars is elaborated on grotesquely by Burroughs in a heightened drama of global conspiracy and its impact on daily life:

> Before they blow up a star they have a spot picked out as many light years away as possible—Then they start draining all the fuel and charge to the new pitch and siphon themselves there right after and on their way rejoicing—You notice we dont have as much time as people had say a hundred years ago?—Take your clothes to the laundry write a letter pick up your mail at American Express and the day is gone—They are short timing us as many light years as they can take for the getaway [. . .] And the Nova Law moving in fast—So they start the same old lark sucking all the charge and air and color to a new location and then?—Sput— You notice something is sucking all the flavor out of food the pleasure out of sex the color out of everything in sight? Precisely creating the low pressure area that leads to nova—So they move cross the wounded galaxies always a few light years ahead of the Nova Heat— (69–70)

Burroughs' frequent assertions that his images are to be taken literally is supported by this intersection of science and myth; in the *Newsweek* article, his paranoid vision of a universe ruled by domination and parasitism is externalized, objectified, and corroborated.

Burroughs' corroborating texts are not always scientific; certain literary texts also carry the authority of an established external source. In a chapter entitled "This Horrible Case" Burroughs invents a futuristic genetic legal system—the Biologic Courts—where cases of biological conflict are resolved by the production of infinite evolutionary possibilities. Faced with a classic case of "Oxygen Impasse" in which the survival of "Life Form A" necessitates its parasitic invasion of "Life Form B," the Biologic Court turns not to a scientific or legal but to a literary precedent:

Brief for the First Hearing
Biologic Counselors must be writers that is only writers can qualify since the function of a counselor is to *create* facts that will tend to open biologic potentials for his client—One of the great early counselors was

Franz Kafka and his briefs are still standard—The student first writes his own brief then folds his pages down the middle and lays it on pages of Kafka relevant to the case in hand—(It is not always easy to say what is and is not relevant)—To indicate the method here is tentative brief for The First Hearing in Biologic Court:—A preparation derived from one page of Kafka passed through the student's brief and the original statement back and forth until a statement of biologic position emerges—From this original statement the student must now expand his case—(120–21)

The writing of legal briefs here follows the same process as the production of cut-up texts, and the infinite permutations produced in both cases involve both choice ("It is not always easy to say what is and is not relevant") and chance. The thematic point of intersection of Kafka (*The Trial*) and Burroughs is clear here: while the former reveals the threat to the individual posed by all social institutions, the latter exposes the origin of this problem on a technical and biological level in two conflicting life forms, in the structure of binary opposition. The resulting cut-up combines intense psychological drama and detached technical description; the common image which unites these two extremes is the basic threat to survival—the difficulty of breathing:

> Brief for First Hearing//
> Case of Life Form A
> They sometimes mutate to breathe "here"—The gentleman *is* Biologic Court Building "here"—You see it's only "here" fixes any case from The Ovens—Not in other places—after buying the relatively fresh air—Life Form A arrives on worst thing that could happen to a space craft—Life Form A breathes from the atmosphere of alien planet—Form A directs all behavior withdrawn from the advocate into channels calculated to no longer achieve health and intersect of the host—The case had simply reached to space stage—Assistance was ruled out—Even the accused was beyond years—Life Form A's room was in the very top—
> "I fancy," said the man who was on alien planet, "that crippled faintness is due to the 'oxygen'—There is no 'oxygen' this gentleman feels but by invading and occupying 'the office air' they can convert the 'oxygen' up from the stairway of Life Form B." (122)

The "tentative brief" produced by the above cut-up may not be particularly interesting in itself, but its purpose has been clearly circumscribed. The cut-up collaboration with Kafka is not meant to stand as a product, but merely to indicate and initiate a process, to help the Biologic Counselor or writer expand and liberate his ideas. The cut-up is the transitional space between an idea and its subsequent extension or its genetic permutations. It is the anonymous and unhampered third mind generated by all cut-up collaborations. What remains essential in this intersection with Kafka is the idea that the enemy machine of language can be reprogrammed for revolutionary change, for survival rather than destruction.[7] Word fictions, Burroughs seems to suggest here, can be used to transform the world. Far from perceiving all literary history, with Harold Bloom, as a series of oedipal struggles and confrontations, Burroughs surveys the expanse of all that is "already written," searching out fellow conspirators like Kafka or Rimbaud, collaborators against repression and control.

The Double Text

The collaboration of minds achieved by the cut-up finds a most graphic representation in *Nova Express* in a kind of double text in which lengthy footnotes on the lower half of the page run parallel to the main narrative. This double-talk text is in some ways an extension of the device Burroughs uses in *Naked Lunch* where brief parenthetical asides to the reader provide definitions or alleged historical sources for particular expressions or events. In the more complex structure developed in *Nova Express*, the definitional aside loses its derivative status as clarification of the primary text and takes on a life and energy of its own. This "other" voice of the footnotes has a more complex relationship to the main narrative, producing a multiple text of indeterminate origin and shifting hierarchies.

The existence of footnotes in *any* text draws our attention immediately to the geography of the page—to its borders or limits. By convention, the footnote stands outside the text, and yet it is intimately grounded within it. Textual annotation implies a hierarchy of the discourses in which the footnote is subordinated at the bottom of the page or even at the end of the text; yet the very existence of the footnote attests to an urgency strong enough to interrupt or cut into the main text. Footnotes often draw our attention to the separation of primary from secondary text, distinguishing between the author's words or ideas and those of other writers. When it is included in a work of fiction the footnote structure most often implies the subordination of fiction to the external and objective authority of fact. Any conventional use of footnotes, then, reinforces basic binary oppositions of self/other, subjective/objective, fact/fiction, inside/outside.

The problematic nature of these binary oppositions marking off the conventional borders of a text have been most thoroughly pursued by Jacques Derrida. In his essay "Living On," he argues that "all those boundaries that form the running border of what used to be called a text [. . .] the supposed end and beginning of a work, the unity of a corpus, the title, the margins, the signatures, the referential realm outside the frame and so forth" have been replaced in recent years by "a differential network" which "overruns all the limits assigned to it" (83–84). His own essay is accompanied throughout by the

overrun of a running footnote which doubles his discourse. In the "Border-
lines" of his extended footnote Derrida interrupts his interruption of the essay
to remark: "This would be a good place for a translator's note, for example,
about everything that has been said elsewhere on the subject of the 'double
bind,' the double band, the double procession, and so forth (a quotation *in
extenso*, among others, of *Glas*, which itself . . . and so forth): this, as a measure of the impossible" (79–80). The binary oppositions which would place
and define each text are dispersed as the text extends into the infinite plurality
of the intertext which accompanies, precedes, follows, and contains it.

This transgression of the limits of the text, of course, does not happen for
the first time in critical theory but has its roots in the evolution of narrative
fiction, in the works of such writers as Rabelais, Cervantes, Swift, Sterne,
and Joyce. The annotated fictional texts of these authors speak in many voices
at once. Reading such a text, therefore, resembles in many ways an encounter
with the "multilevel" discourse of Burroughs' cut-up or fold-in narratives.
The indeterminancy we have come to accept within the body of Burroughs'
fiction—the uncertainty of character, plot, syntax—extends in the double text
of *Nova Express* to the fiction's outer boundaries, to the place (in the footnotes) where we expect to get things straight. Like the footnotes in Swift's
Tale of a Tub or Eliot's "The Wasteland" (two literary precedents Burroughs
might have had in mind), those in *Nova Express* will frustrate rather than sat-
isfy that expectation, will open and extend rather than close the text.[8]

Burroughs' attraction to the extended footnote of the double text, however,
may stem primarily from its potential as a meeting ground of writer and
reader. In the footnote, the writer often identifies himself as a reader of texts,
so writer and reader become equal collaborators in their effort to control
rather than be controlled by the unwieldy mass of the "already written," the
ubiquitous intertext.

"Smorbrot"

In the chapter of *Nova Express* entitled "Smorbrot," Burroughs works out a training program which might lead to such a collective
reading, and both the form and content of the chapter reflect the success of
this project. The double text which constitutes the first half of the chapter is
resolved in the final pages where the main text and footnotes merge again into
a single narrative. This coming together is enacted in the content of the chapter as well, for in order to arrive at his final liberated state the hero of "Smorbrot"—the revolutionary cadet K9—must learn a new sense of body and
identity, a new pansexuality, and a new language. This training program will
find its analogue in the reader's experience of the double text.

The content of "Smorbrot" can best be understood as a response to the preceding chapter which describes a demonic Amusement Garden where the enemy drives people into communal immersion tanks to reduce them all to "a single concentrate." The revolutionary training described in "Smorbrot" involves the use of the same techniques to achieve the opposite results, aiming instead at the *expansion* of body outlines, at a collective multiplicity which transcends the repressions and anxieties of the individual psyche. The narrator describes the positive potential of experiments with sense deprivation tanks: "Cadets enter the tank naked and free floating a few inches apart—permutate on slow currents—soon lose the outlines of body in shifting contact with phantom limbs—Loss of outline associated with pleasant sensations—frequently orgasms occur—" (135).

The overall goal of the training program is control and detachment through the directed use of drugs, sex, and sense withdrawal. For example, instead of a sexuality which is helplessly epileptic, "struggling for control [. . .] careening through dream flesh" (141), the training aims at a sexuality which is curiously weightless and suspended: "I took off my clothes and practiced balancing naked in a chair—The balance point was an electrical field holding him out of gravity—The charge built up in his genitals and he came in a wet dream the chair fluid and part of this body—That night made sex with the boy I met in Neuerhaven for the first time with each other in space—Sure calm wire acts balanced on ozone-blue electric spasms—" (139–40). Control is achieved, it would seem, by first expelling from the body all structures of repression; body outlines separating individuals are blurred and dissolved, the force of gravity (physical and emotional) is left behind as partners enter the weightlessness of ozone or salt water.

The most crucial prerequisite for liberation, however, is the expulsion of the word from the body: "K9 took off his clothes in a metal lined cubical with a Chinese youth—[. . .] they let themselves down into the tank [. . .] There was a sudden sharp spasm in his throat and a taste of blood—The words dissolved—His body twisted in liquid fish spasms and emptied through his spurting penis—" (135–36). This exorcism of the parasitic language which traps us in the narrow confines of the body, in individual identity, in repressive anxiety and fear, makes way for a mysterious new language of "bird calls" and "color writing" in which everything comes together: "color-music-smell-feel to the million sex acts all time place." Like Rimbaud's systematic *dérèglement* of the senses, like Burroughs' cut-up technique in general, the revolutionary training described here involves a deliberate abdication of control as the paradoxical means by which a higher and more conscious control is achieved.

The above summary of the chapter's content, however, is deceptively simple. It omits the immediate problem presented to the reader by the doubling of the text on the page. Following the opening words of the chapter, "Operation Sense Withdrawal," an asterisk immediately sends the reader to a lengthy footnote. In describing this chapter, the critic can easily defer the footnotes until the main narrative has been summarized, but in the actual experience of reading the text one is confronted with the necessity and the impossibility of a simultaneous reading of the main narrative and the extended footnote. Just as the immersion tanks dissolve the outlines of the body, this footnote interruption of a narrative that has barely begun dissolves the text's borders.

In contrast to the high level of stylistic cut-up confusion in the main text of this chapter, the footnote style is logical, coherent, and grammatical. The reader's expectation that the footnote will function as a device of clarification seems at first to be satisfied. Here is the footnote in its entirety:

> The most successful method of sense withdrawal is the immersion tank where the subject floats in water at blood temperature sound and light withdrawn—loss of body outlines, awareness and location of the limbs occurs quickly, giving rise to panic in many American subjects—Subjects frequently report feeling that another body is floating half in half out of the body in the first part—Experiments in sense withdrawal using the immersion tanks have been performed by Dr. Lilly in Florida—There is another experimental station in Oklahoma—So after fifteen minutes in the tank these marines scream they are losing outlines and have to be removed—I say put two marines in the tank and see who comes out—Science—Pure science—So put a marine and his girl friend in the tank and see who or what emerges— (135)

As in most of his footnotes, Burroughs begins by offering the reader some scientific or objective support of the narrative's wild routines. He then further proposes experiments which might be staged to test the basic principles controlling his apocalyptic mythology. Under the guise of scientific or mathematical precision, Burroughs' footnotes gradually lead us back into a world as mad as that of the main fictional text. In this example from "Smorbrot," objective technical details are gradually displaced by a playful speculation, the dissemination of an endlessly permutating routine, "I say put two marines in the tank [. . .] put a marine and his girl friend in the tank."

Like the genetic potentials produced by the Biologic Court's cut-up, these scientific experiments with sense withdrawal are merely variations on the basic principles governing the cut-up writing machine. In the footnotes' proposed experiments, there is no guarantee, there is only the energy of speculation and surprise—"see what comes out." "Science—Pure science" is indistinguishable from textual play; what is happening to the *cadets'* bodies is precisely what is happening to the *text's* body. Like the cadet, the reader must learn to give himself up to free floating, to a reading without expectations or outlines which will accommodate the undifferentiated and non-hierarchical structure of the double text.

The interdependence and intersection of footnote and main narrative are perhaps most clearly seen in the chapter's second footnote. Here again the initial tone is scholarly and objective as Burroughs summarizes the theories and experiments of Wilhelm Reich.[9] He stresses in particular the scientific approach to sexuality in Reich's study of orgone energy. On the simplest level, this second footnote presents the reader with a perspective from which the orgiastic activities described in the accompanying narrative can be viewed not as scandalous fantasy but as material for scientific experimentation. The footnote, then, becomes not simply a vestigial digression from the narrative but a running commentary, an instruction manual on how to read the main text itself.

Burroughs shifts his focus in the footnote from factual reference to a concern with the immediate reading process, from science to art: "It has occurred to this investigator that orgone energy can be concentrated to disperse the miasma of idiotic prurience and anxiety that blocks any scientific investigation of sexual phenomenon—Preliminary experiments indicate that certain painting—like Brion Gysin's—when projected on a subject produced some of the effects observed in orgone accumulators—" (137). Using Reich as a collaborative and quasi-scientific point of departure, Burroughs envisions the possibility of a new kind of writing to replace the expelled parasitic word, a new writing which will operate like the orgone by intense concentration leading to powerful discharge of energy. This is, as we have seen repeatedly, the lively rhythm of the expansion and contraction of both the mosaic and the cut-up text. The "investigator" who speaks in the footnote is primarily a *writing* technician, and his experiments take the form of purely *linguistic* postulates.

An example of this new writing is found in the main narrative cut-up which runs parallel to the second footnote. Here all content dissolves in wild fragments unified only by the text's self-referential allusions to a new "writing" replacing the old:

Projectors flashed the color writing of Hassan i Sabbah on bodies and metal walls—Opened into amusement gardens—Sex Equilibrists perform on tightropes and balancing chairs—Trapeze acts ejaculate in the air—The Sodomite Tumblers doing cartwheels and whirling dances stuck together like dogs—Boys masturbate from scenic railways—Flower floats in the lagoons and canals—Sex cubicles where the acts performed to music project on the tent ceiling a sky of rhythmic copulation—Vast flicker cylinders and projectors sweep the gardens writing explosive bio-advance to neon [. . .] he came in spasms of light—Silver writing burst in his brain and went out with a smell of burning metal—(137)

Here the footnote's discussion of new directions for reading and writing has been dramatized in the fictional field of action.

Burroughs thus defeats the structural oppositions on which the conventions of the footnote are based. In the last page of the chapter where the double text is reunified into a single narrative, we find wild mosaics of sensual and sexual imagery merging with technical explanation and experiment. Suddenly we seem to be reading simultaneously what were the two separate strains of the double text:

> open shirts flapping over the midway—Silver light popped in my head and went out in blue silence— Smell of ozone You see sex is an electrical charge that can be turned on and off if you know the electromagnetic switchboard [. . .] Now take your sex words on rose wallpaper brass bed—Explode in red brown green from colors to the act on the association line—Naked charge can explode sex words to color's rectal brown green ass language [. . .] Substitute other factors for the words— Arab drum music—Musty smell of erections in outhouses—Feel of orgasm— (140)

The chapter's content reenacts this coming together; the shifting pronouns, names, and nationalities circulating in the sex scenes of "Smorbrot" culminate in the final triumphant rollercoaster ride which ends the chapter: "Hans laughed pointing to my shorts—Pants to the ankle we were the only riders— Wheee came together in the first dip open shorts flapping genitals—Wind of morning through flesh—Outskirts of the city—" (142). In this weightless sex, as in all forms of cut-up collaboration, identity becomes plural and then dissolves; "we" is transposed to "Wheee," anonymous and pure expression of pleasure and release. The body here is permeated with air and the outlook is toward a new time and a new space, a morning beyond the boundaries of the city, the body, and the page.

Against Death and Ending

Burroughs' *Nova Express* is headed for the outskirts and beyond, determined to leave no trace of its passage. Like sky writing, the cut-up text is designed to dissolve in the wake of its own production, resisting the entropic effects of permanence: "The great skies are open. I Hassan i Sabbah *rub out the word forever*. If you I cancel all your words forever. And the words of Hassan i Sabbah as also cancel" (12). In this perpetually shifting discourse every word constitutes a farewell to language, a deposition or "last word" of the word itself; resistance forces "sound the words that end word." Transformed by Burroughs' cut-up operations the word no longer carries referential content, it no longer functions as mimetic representation or subjective expression; it is only the sign of an absence and an abdication: "Nothing here now but the recordings" (154).

As early as *The Soft Machine*, Burroughs attempts to wipe the slates clean with a kind of negative writing: "Metamorphosis of the Rewrite Department [. . .] We are digested and become nothing here [. . .] Nothing here now—Metamorphosis is complete" (40–41). Everything that resists change, evolution, and mobility must be left behind—the body, individual identity, the word. In a chapter of *The Soft Machine* entitled "Dead Fingers Talk," Burroughs quotes the last words of the diary of Yves Martin, who "presumably died of thirst in the Egyptian desert with three companions." Martin's final words, "*Finnies nous attendons une bonne chance*," capture the uncertain quality of all of Burroughs' endings, at once hopeful and hopeless. The uncertainty of this diary entry, however, extends beyond its ambiguous tone: "Just who died is uncertain since one member of the party has not been found alive or dead and identity of the missing person is dubious [. . .] it seems the party was given to exchange of identifications, and even to writing in each other's diaries" (175). Confronted with death, the explorers cast off the restrictions of private identity and ownership of the word to achieve the ultimate collaboration—to write in someone else's diary. The result of this abdication of exclusive self-expression is that "Dead Fingers Talk." Having pooled their identities into an anonymous collectivity, all the members of the expedition have eluded death. Like the cut-up collaboration with "many writers living and dead" the collective diary defies the temporal finality of last words, the fixity of the finished text.

Burroughs tries to keep his endings similarly open and uncertain. The last words of his cut-up novels are displaced, repeated, drawn out or truncated, manipulated in so many ways that they begin to lose the very quality that defines them as endings: "Now here is a calculating machine—of course it can process qualitative data—Color for example—[. . .] Or feed in a thousand novels and scan out the last pages—That is quality is it not? Endingness?" (*NX* 79). In the final pages of *Nova Express*, Burroughs attempts to sabotage the certainty of this calculating machine, the finite quality of "Endingness." Like some ham tragedian drawing out his death scene until it collapses into farce, Burroughs keeps signing off, repeatedly announcing definitive escape and silence:

> Fade out muttering: "There's a lover on every corner cross the wounded galaxies"—[. . .] Slowly fading—I told him you on tracks—All over for sure—[. . .] [. . .] So leave the recorders running and get your heavy metal ass in a space ship—Did it—Nothing here now but the recordings—Shut the whole thing right off—*Silence* [. . .] Now slow—slower—*Stop*—Shut off—No More— (152–54)

Burroughs compounds the indeterminacy of these endings by doubling his final gesture in the novel:

> Well that's about the closest way I know to tell you and papers rustling across city desks . . . fresh southerly winds a long time ago.
> September 17, 1899 over New York
>
> > *July 21, 1964*
> > *Tangier, Morocco*
> >
> > *William Burroughs*

The text signs off and is dated, but the time and place of signature are doubled and uncertain. Can this printed name of the author constitute a bona fide signature and ownership of the text?[10]

As closely as he may approach silence, Burroughs is always "caught in the door" of the prison house of language; his promise of silence must still be made in words, and often rather loudly in capital letters. While his cut-up technique will allow him to collaborate in a positive way with "many writers living and dead," he must also collaborate (in the term's more negative political sense) with the enemy—with language. That collaboration taints him, it seduces and infects him with the need for language, for the word-fix. The endings of *Ticket* and *Nova Express* in particular enact Burroughs' attempts to shake the writing habit: "Yes sir, boys, it's hard to stop that old writing arm—more of a habit than using—Been writing these RXs five hundred thousand years and sure hate to pack you boys in with a burning down word habit—[. . .] My writing arm is paralyzed—ash blown from an empty sleeve—do our work and go" (*Ticket* 198); "No More—My writing arm is paralyzed—No more junk scripts, no more word scripts, no more flesh scripts" (*NX* 154).[11]

For Burroughs the verb "to write" always carries the connotation it has in junky's jargon—to write a prescription for drugs: "hit this old country croaker for tincture with the aged mother suffering from piles in the worst way there is line and he wrote like a major" (*SM* 17). When Burroughs announces that his writing arm is paralyzed this is no failure of creativity or imagination but rather a reflection of the author's courage to kick the habit, the refusal to feed the monkey that straddles his back and that of his reader.

But writer and reader always come together again in their addiction to language, for despite its inherent parasitic threat the word still provides the potential for making contact. Friendship and collaboration are necessary for survival and sanity, but such contacts also carry for Burroughs the potential for intellectual and emotional vampirism. The dilemma of the writer resembles that of the revolutionary agents of the cut-up trilogy, caught between the imminent threat of assassination and the persistent need to reach out beyond the isolated self: "None the less we are reasonably gregarious since nothing is more dangerous than withdrawing from contact into a dead whistle stop" (87). The code of these provocateurs may help us understand why, despite his deep distrust of language, Burroughs continues to write, publish, and even perform his work.

Part Two

Introduction

"But then who am I to be critical?"

The Soft Machine

I have explored in part 1 the ways in which Burroughs' experimental writing produces an indeterminacy of meaning, narrative structure, and authorial voice. In these texts Burroughs forces his readers to test the limits of the sentence, the page, the book, and ultimately of reality itself. As Inspector Lee is warned during his orientation as a revolutionary agent in *Ticket*, "There is no certainty. Those who need certainty are of no interest to this department" (10). Such uncertainty often embarrasses and offends traditional humanistic criticism which relies on a belief in truth, center, origin, presence, and boundary. Those radical contemporary critics who embrace and even multiply indeterminacy provide, therefore, a more sympathetic context for Burroughs' iconoclastic theory and practice. One explanation for the fact that Burroughs' writing has been enthusiastically received by some French critics may be that the French tradition in particular, from Rabelais to Derrida, is attuned to an amoral intellectualism which celebrates the infinite and uncertain play of possibilities.

The remarkable parallels between Burroughs' writing and the work of radical contemporary theorists (many but not all of them French) have been briefly noted by several critics. I will pursue these similarities in depth by constructing a cut-up juxtaposition of Burroughs' experimental writing with critical texts by such theorists as Jacques Derrida, Roland Barthes, Julia Kristeva, J. Hillis Miller, and others. As Burroughs makes imaginary journeys into "space/time travel," contemporary theory also traffics in cosmic pioneering, pursuing a horizon or vanishing point that is "ceaselessly pushed back, mysteriously opened" (Barthes *S/Z* 12). The "naked astronaut" of Burroughs' experimental novels travels comfortably in the company of those radical critics Geoffrey Hartman has called "Skywriters." Similarly extravagant and provocative, the skywriting of William Burroughs and of these contemporary theorists will "intersect across wounded galaxies" in the following chapters.

7 | Binary Opposition

Is it still possible today to imagine, with Ovid, the creation of the world, the first metamorphosis of the universe from chaos into a dwelling place for men and beasts?

> Before the ocean was, or earth, or heaven,
> Nature was all alike, a shapelessness,
> Chaos, so-called, all rude and lumpy matter,
> Nothing but bulk, inert, in whose confusion
> Discordant atoms warred: [. . .]
>
> . . . .
>
> Air without light, substance forever changing,
> Forever at war: within a single body
> Heat fought with cold, wet fought with dry, the hard
> Fought with the soft, things having weight contended
> With weightless things.
>   Till God, or kindlier Nature,
> Settled all argument, and separated
> Heaven from earth, water from land, our air
> From the high stratosphere, a liberation
> So things evolved, and out of blind confusion
> Found each its place, bound in eternal order.

(*Metamorphoses*, Book One, lines 5–9, 17–27)

This benign pacification of chaos seems necessary, even "natural," simply the demarcation of geographical space into air, land, and water. The ordering of the world is presented by Ovid as "a liberation," the democratic model of a "great globe / Even on every side" where no single force "holds dominion." Yet binary opposites that contend "within one body" in the reign of chaos are maintained in the new world where they are hierarchically "separated" according to some divine real estate plan of "Division, subdivision" (line 34). This mapping out of the universe, then, is not just an horizontal but a vertical plan, distinguishing "heaven from earth . . . our air from the higher stratosphere."

The evolution toward a geography in which man orients himself as in an orderly dwelling is the evolution of a system of hierarchical repression which denies him access to other realms, other identities, other orientations. Ovid's epic poem is powerful precisely because it explores that life energy which cannot be "bound in eternal order," the infinity of transgressions and metamorphoses which constitute the flow of life itself. Ovid identifies metamorphosis as the seed of chaos ("substance forever changing") which survives within and despite the separation into binary opposites imposed by creation. Without this energizing disruption of continual change and transgression, Ovid often seems to suggest, life would be stifled within its very dwelling place.

Our contemporary poet of metamorphosis, William Burroughs, also perceives the highest values in life as evolution and change, and he marshals these forces against all threats of stasis and repression. In his fiction, the enemy of "evolutionary potential" is most often represented by the structure of binary opposition, the "Aristotelian Either/Or" which he sees as the basis of Western thought. One can recognize immediately here the common project of Burroughs' fiction and much of contemporary critical theory, particularly deconstruction: critical analysis of the basic dualism underlying our civilization, and the development of a methodology which attempts to break through the strictures and structures of binary opposition into a more free and open space.

While Ovid's description of the creation sets up the binary oppositions governing matter (wet/dry, heavy/light, hard/soft), both structuralism and deconstruction are concerned with the binary oppositions which form the basis of Western philosophy and logic: mind/body, nature/culture, presence/absence, essence/appearance, truth/falsehood. As theoreticians focus more narrowly on the central role of language within this system, a new set of problematic oppositions is identified: speech/writing, thing/sign, reality/image, literal/figurative, metonomy/metaphor. These same pairs and the hierarchy of privilege implied within each pair also constitute the major targets of Burroughs' fiction and theory.

Either/Or

When asked if he thinks classical philosophical thought has had a damaging effect on human life, Burroughs singles out in his affirmative answer the dominant and destructive effects of binary thinking: "as Korzybski . . . has pointed out, the Aristotelian 'either/or' . . . is one of the greatest errors of Western thinking. . . . There are certain formulas, word-locks, which will lock up a whole civilization for a thousand years" (*Job* 48–49).

Similar versions of Western history as stasis appear in deconstructionist accounts of our culture, such as this statement by J. Hillis Miller: "the sad alternatives of nihilism and escape beyond the world could be evaded if man would only reject twenty-five hundred years of belief in the dualism of heaven and earth" (*Disappearance* 359). What seems in Ovid's account of the creation an innocent and natural method for geographical clarification appears from this modern perspective as a double-bind trap which excludes the possibility of life beyond the current "sad alternatives" offered by our binary thinking. Burroughs perceives this double cross throughout history from the Mayan calendar to the contradictory commands directed by advertising and the popular media in strategies "designed to limit and stultify on a mass scale" (*Job* 193). A contradictory command, Burroughs explains, "gains its force from the Aristotelian concept of either/or. To do everything, to do nothing, . . . to have it all *or* not any, to stay present *or* to stay absent" (*Job* 200). These commands, he reasons, may "seem harmless, and in fact unavoidable" (193), but they constitute a parasitic invasion of the individual's will and his potential to evolve.

Burroughs' mythologies dramatize the same mechanics of repression which are uncovered by critics like Michel Foucault, Roland Barthes, and Félix Guattari. Edward Said describes the general focus of Foucault's work, for example, as an investigation of "the machinery of corporeal and mental control throughout Western history . . . the process of exclusion by which cultures designate and isolate their opposites and its obverse, the process by which cultures designate and valorize their own incorporative authority" ("Problem" 705). In a hierarchical pattern of binary opposition, what is inside dominates by exclusion what is forced outside.

The dangers of oppression do not begin in politics, but are already inherent in metaphysics. As Derrida argues, "in classical philosophical oppositions we are not dealing with the peaceful coexistence of a *vis-à-vis*, but rather with a violent hierarchy" (*Positions* 41). Burroughs traces this ubiquitous formula of conflict and control from Western logic and metaphysics to its ultimate deadly repercussions: "EITHER/OR is another virus formula. It is always you OR the virus. EITHER/OR. This is in point of fact the conflict formula which is seen to be an archetypal virus mechanism. . . . Basically there is only one game and that game is war. . . . There are no games where everybody wins" (*Job* 202).

The conflict formula of binary thinking is explored with particular precision in the work of Roland Barthes. One of the premises of *S/Z* is Barthes's challenge to the hierarchy and closure produced by Western discourse. He designates the structure of binary opposition, represented by the figure of "Antithesis," as one of the most stable fortifications of traditional thought. Because antithesis erects a wall forbidding passage, a wall which "separates for eternity," it is seen as "inexpiable" and ultimately tyrannical. Barthes's highly provocative reading of Balzac's "Sarrasine" translates that story into a parable of the contamination, castration, or hemorrhage which will follow any breach in the ruling "Wall of Antithesis": "The Antithesis is a wall without a doorway. Leaping this wall is a transgression . . . there is an explosive shock, a paradigmatic conflagration. . . . Antithesis cannot be transgressed with impunity: *meaning* (and its classifying basis) is a question of life or death" (*S/Z* 65–66). Language, reproduction, and the economics of exchange are all dependent on and ruled by the structure of binary opposition: "the dividing line, the paradigmatic slash mark which permits meaning to function (the wall of the Antithesis), life to reproduce (the opposition of the sexes), property to be protected (rule of contract)" (*S/Z* 215).

There are increasing numbers of writers who, like Ovid's Pyramus and Thisbe, persistently look for the chink in the wall or, as J. Hillis Miller puts it, for the "loose stone which will pull down the whole building" ("Stevens' Rock II" 341). Contemporary radical theorists and William Burroughs approach the deconstruction of binary thinking with a similar set of strategies: tracking binary opposition to its origins in language, reversing its implied hierarchies, and finally disrupting its dual structure with an unassimilable third element.

Language as Origin

Julia Kristeva locates the beginning of all control and repression in the specific linguistic functions of naming and differentiation: "Naming . . . and hence differentiating . . . amounts to introducing language, which, just as it distinguishes pleasure from pain as it does all oppositions, founds the separation inside/outside" (*Powers* 61). Similarly, Burroughs describes an original parasitic invasion of the human individual by the alien word. Lodging itself within the body, the word dominates and possesses the individual, subjecting him to a dual life, to the restrictions of binary opposition: "The human organism is literally consisting of two halves from the beginning word . . . planet based on 'the Word'" (*TTTE* 52). From the beginning of this "planet based on 'the Word'" Burroughs charts a history of conflict and domination monotonously repeating itself like a worn out carnival routine: "the angle on planet earth was birth and death—pain and pleasure—the tough cop and the con cop—It's an old vaudeville act" (*TTTE* 142).

This old vaudeville act is no mere entertainment, for it is presided over by the divinity of binary opposition, "Mr. Bradly Mr. Martin, who invented the double cross." Burroughs elaborates on this figure in *The Third Mind*: "Mr Bradly-Mr Martin, in my mythology, is a God that failed, a God of Conflict in two parts so created to keep a tired old show on the road, The God of Arbitrary Power and Restraint, Of Prison and Pressure" (97). The immediate danger posed by this power, as Burroughs sees it, is the enemy plan to reduce all human life to "simple binary coding," to condense and assimilate the entire planet: "The cyclotron processes image—It's the microfilm principle—smaller and smaller, more and more images in less space pounded down under the cyclotron to crystal image meal. We can take the whole fucking planet out that way up our ass in a finger stall—[. . .] A *stall* you dig—Just old showmen packing our ermines you might say—" (*NX* 44). Burroughs' strategy of resistance consists of attacking the power of this "simple binary coding" and thus of all language codes with his own word power. "Rewrite Mr Bradly Mr Martin," he advises. Language, as Derrida and others have suggested, is both the poison and the cure.

Double Science and the Logic of the Third

The rewriting of binary opposition is envisioned by Burroughs and by many contemporary theorists as a "double science," an austere strategy in two stages. First the binary hierarchies of Western culture are reversed, their values turned upside down in a carnivalesque provocation. Deconstruction seems to evaluate writing as previous to and superior to speech, elevating absence over presence, nihilism over faith. Derrida and others repeatedly insist, however, that a mere reversal of hierarchies accomplishes nothing, leaves us still operating in the same terrain (*Positions* 42). Many critics of Burroughs' work have similarly followed his strategy only half way, denouncing him for revering body over soul, evil over good, anarchy over democracy. Burroughs argues in his own defense that to respond to the forces of repression with righteous indignation—to reverse the moral hierarchy by redefining and asserting *your* good over *their* evil—is merely to keep this "tired old injustice show on the road."

The gesture of reversal, then, is ineffective without the second stage, the "eruptive emergence" of a third term which cannot be absorbed into a binary structure and which, in fact, confounds and disperses it. Derrida's notions of "supplement," "difference," and "trace" are all elusive versions of that third element. Their characteristic role is to evade structural assimilation, to dwell within and explode the dual structure.

Burroughs too harnesses the power of the third to disrupt or dislodge binary structures. In his technical manifestos he advises experiments in which tape recordings of two sides of an argument are spliced in with a third tape of totally irrelevant and thus unpredictable material (*TTTE* 163). Focusing more specifically on the binary pairs of reader/writer or writer/text, Burroughs again conjures up a third term to unsettle fixed patterns of conflict and ownership. In *The Third Mind*, where he and Brion Gysin elaborate on their methods of dismantling the word by cut-up and permutation, Burroughs discusses a "third mind" which results from such experiments and collaborations. This third is neither author nor reader and is not even present except as "an absent third person, invisible and beyond grasp, decoding the silence" (Lemaire 18).

As habitual patterns of binary opposition and hierarchy are disrupted by this third, discourse erupts into an uncharted space, risky and indeterminate. Barthes explores this chancey third realm in the context of film interpretation. He defines what he calls a "third meaning" embedded in Eisenstein's film stills, a meaning which "appears to extend outside culture, knowledge, information" (*Image* 55).[1] In the context of psychoanalysis, Julia Kristeva locates something analogous to Barthes' elusive and disturbing "third meaning" in the notion of a "Third Party," a version of the self which appears as some wandering stray excluded from all systems of logic and control, a third self without identity or limit. She designates the territory inhabited by this third as the space of the abject, the habitation of everything we reject and repress as monstrous and defiled. Kristeva asserts finally that all literature inhabits this space, that every literary work is a "version of the apocalypse" (*Powers* 207). While one may resist this association of *all* literature with the uncertain, the monstrous, the abject, one certainly recognizes in Kristeva's description the world of William Burroughs' fiction.

Difference Within

What is finally monstrous to us in Burroughs' fiction and in radical literary theory is that they threaten the very structures of binary opposition on which our conceptions of the world, society, and man rest. In keeping with the perversity of their logic, deconstructionists argue that what is mistakenly perceived as the difference *between* their theory and humanism is really a difference *within* humanism itself. J. Hillis Miller, for example, insists that he does not seek to oppose metaphysics *with* nihilism, but rather to reveal the nihilism which is already embedded *within* metaphysics ("Host" 230). In a deconstructionist reading, each element in a binary opposition is shown to contain, already, its opposite; every presence is based on the necessity of absence, all speech is predicated on the concept of writing, every inside is defined by what it pushes outside. This paradoxical logic might explain why in their efforts to understand the central forces of our culture writers like Burroughs, Derrida, and Kristeva focus their analyses on what has been excluded from that culture as marginal, trivial, or monstrous.

In his exploration of the marginal underworld of drug addiction and sexual deviation, Burroughs also shifts our attention from the difference between to the difference within, to the inner complexity of the simple binary pairs which people his fictional universe. Beneath the opposition of hustler/mark or pusher/

junky each subject is already divided within himself, possessed by an alien and unnecessary need. The master is himself enslaved by his need to dominate; the pusher is addicted to contact with his clients, even the god of conflict Mr Bradly Mr Martin is possessed by and dependent on the "human dogs" who are his victims. Everyone is ruled by a "Man Within" or a "Mark Inside" which has invaded the individual along the life line of words.

The common problem for Burroughs and contemporary theory is how to bring what is hidden to light, how to expel the tyrant word and the binary structure through which it functions. One strategy, as we have seen, is to disturb the binary opposition which establishes the structural foundations of logocentrism, to make a hole in the Wall of Antithesis. In a more poetic strategy, these radical texts also spawn images—often disturbingly concrete—which compel the reader to see the repressive mechanisms of the established order spread out like a "naked lunch." The abstract threat posed by dualistic thinking is perhaps most dramatically represented in Burroughs' fiction and in radical theory in the relationship of parasite and host.

8 | The Parasite

In 1980, the French theorist Michel Serres published *Le Parasite*, an enigmatic and provocative work in which he asserts that the key to our culture, to our modernity, is the parasitic relationship. Serres uncovers the parasite at the origin of all cultural institutions, in the operations of all bureaucracies which establish their power by imposing structures of inclusion and exclusion. Ironically, the parasite one would identify as alien and excluded is shown to be "always already" inside, already usurping the place of the master or host. Serres asks problematically, "who is the host and who is the guest?" (23). The binary opposition of parasite/host thus dissolves into indeterminacy in Serres's analysis; the dual structure of parasite/host is constantly interrupted and disrupted by the intervention of a third element which shifts all the roles.

Serres explains that when we discover the invading parasite which has become the master and "runs the household," we have uncovered "our system itself," the bureaucracy which we inhabit. The parasitic power of bureaucracy is based on the control of information and the power of speech, particularly that imperialistic speech which silences all other speakers: "[the parasite] commands, he has the power, his voice has become that of the master, he speaks so he is heard everywhere, no one else can talk" (38). Parasitic communication is based on an economy of exchange, not a free exchange but a "flow [which] goes one way, never the other" (5). The parasite takes but gives nothing in return. At the same time, however, Serres demonstrates how that irreversible flow is in fact continually disrupted; there is always interference in the channel. In French, *bruit parasite* is the term for "static" or "interference"; there is always a new noise to interrupt the voice of the parasite, to make the parasite move over into the position of displaced host.

For Serres, then, the parasite is the archetype of all relations of power; but it is also the agent of change which disrupts those relations. The ultimate spawning place of the parasite in Serres's mythology, as in Burroughs' fiction, is language itself, language which appropriates life and gives nothing in return but "hot air." This hot air generates a system inside which we live as parasites: "Our host? I don't know. But I do know that we are within. And that it is dark in there" (10). Serres asks, finally, if it would be possible to rewrite the system without parasites, to return to the fleeting moment of symbiosis before the fall into parasitism. The question is, of course, rhetorical; the reader cannot offer any answer but the negative one embedded in the question itself. One is never without the parasite for the parasite is the embodiment of difference and therefore the source of all identity, of all change, of life itself.

Parasitic Need

Serres's theory, which owes much to recent developments in post-structuralist and deconstructionist thought, has been both praised and denounced by reviewers as quintessentially contemporary: A theory of the 1980s. Yet, if we look back to Burroughs' work in the late 1950s and early 1960s, we find him already evolving an almost identical model of all human relations as parasitic structures.[1]

In *Naked Lunch*, Burroughs denounces as parasitic all systems of social control which operate through complex networks of institutional bureaucracy:

"A bureau takes root anywhere in the state, turns malignant like the Narcotics Bureau, and grows and grows, always reproducing more of its own kind, until it chokes the host if not controlled or excised. Bureaus cannot live without a host, being true parasitic organisms. . . . Bureaucracy is wrong as a cancer, a turning away from the human evolutionary direction of infinite potentials and differentiation and independent spontaneous action, to the complete parasitism of a virus." (*NL* 134)

Burroughs explains that bureaucracy survives, not unlike the advertising industry, by "inventing needs to justify its existence." Human will and individuality are manipulated by these artificial needs in a hierarchical structure of domination and control. In his fiction Burroughs demonstrates how the need for drugs, sex, or religion is fabricated by a vast parasitic machinery operated by demonic scientists like the ubiquitous Dr. Benway, "manipulator and coordinator of symbol systems, an expert on all phases of interrogation, brainwashing and control." Benway's strategy is the "deliberate attack of an antihuman enemy on [the subject's] personal identity" (*NL* 21). Drawn into the economics of exchange which Burroughs detects behind all human relations, the individual's identity is devoured by a hungry parasitic need.

In the economics of the drug industry, for example, suppliers and addicts alike are dehumanized, turned into sinister vampiric beasts or primitive amoeba-like projections: "Like a vampire bat [the Buyer] gives off a narcotic effluvium, a dank green mist that anesthetizes his victims and renders them helpless in his enveloping presence. . . . the Buyer has lost his human citizenship and was, in consequence a creature without species" (*NL* 18). The drug world forms its own particular bureaucracy in the form of a pyramid of cannibalism, a "pyramid of junk, one level eating the level below. . . . there are many junk pyramids feeding on peoples of the world and all built on basic principles of monopoly" (*NL* xxxviii). This bureaucracy, however, does not remain an external threat to individual life but is internalized in the form of an alien parasite, the "Man Within" or "Mark Inside" who colonizes the will of the addict.

Sexuality in Burroughs' work is directed by the same politics of parasitic power. Monotonous as the drug addict's need, the sexual orgies Burroughs describes are repetitious, mechanical, and impersonal—curiously most obscene when conducted without physical contact. A young hustler describes with distaste the demands of his clients: "they wanta merge with my protoplasm, they want a replica cutting, they wanta suck my orgones, they wanta take over my past experience and leave old memories that disgust me" (*NL* 125). As in the drug pyramid, the goal of sexual contact is the parasitic absorption of one life form by another.

While the need for drugs or sex operates explicitly through the body, religion is seen as an instrument of spiritual or intellectual parasitism. The Benway manipulator reappears here in several theatrical disguises: Christ the carny man, Buddha the pusher, or Mohammed as invented by "an Egyptian ad man on the skids." Religious wisdom is unleashed as the tidal wave of the Wise Man's "Word Hoard" which absorbs, devours, and digests human life: " 'I tell you when I leave the Wise Man I don't even feel like a human. He converting my live orgones into dead bullshit' " (*NL* 116).

The Word Parasite

As Burroughs' cut-up novels make explicit, the parasitic control system operating through drugs, sex and religion is grounded in language, in distorted methods of exchange and communication. In a kind of anthropological fantasy, Burroughs traces this linguistic menace to a virus mutation at the very origins of human life:

Dr. Kurt Unruh von Steinplatz has put forward an interesting theory as to the origins and history of this word virus. He postulates that the word was a virus of what he calls "biologic mutation" affecting a change in its host which was then genetically conveyed. [. . .] He postulates that alterations in inner throat structure were occasioned by a virus illness. And vot an occasion! [. . .] Since the virus in both male and female precipitates sexual frenzy through irritation of sex centers in the brain, the male impregnated the females in their death spasms and the altered throat structure was genetically conveyed. *Ach, Junge*, what a scene is here . . . the apes are molting fur, steaming off, the females whimpering and

slobbering over the dying males like cows with aftosa, and so a stink—
musky, sweet, rotten-metal stink of the forbidden fruit in the Garden of
Eden. [. . .] the forbidden fruit, which was of course knowledge of the
whole stinking thing and might be termed the first Watergate scandal, all
slots neatly into Doc von Steinplatz's theory. (*Job* 13).

Drawing from popular scientific theories about the nature and development of
virus forms as well as from his own satiric inventions, Burroughs postulates a
historical moment at which the word enjoyed a stable and "ancient covenant
of symbiosis" with the human host. He stresses, however, that a virus which
could attain such a state of "wholly benign equilibrium" with its host would
have the strategic advantage of being virtually undetectable. For him the word
is just such an invisible and insidious presence which could threaten human
survival; "It was a killer virus once. It could become a killer virus again" (14).

In the context of this parasitic vision communication is no longer a dialogue
but the manipulative power play of "one-way Sending" which must be exposed. The Factualist Party of *Naked Lunch* issues this urgent telegram:
" 'Emphatically [. . .] we oppose, as we oppose atomic war, the use of
[telepathic] knowledge to control, coerce, debase, exploit or annihilate the
individuality of another living creature. Telepathy is not, by its nature, a one-
way process. [. . .] sending *is* evil [. . .] ' " (*NL* 167–68). As the narrator
concludes, "The Sender is not a human individual. . . . It is The Human
Virus." In its diseased and unnatural form, language infects everything it
sends, "all hate, all pain, all fear, all lust is contained in the word." The de-
humanization of the individual by drugs, sex or religion is traced back here to
the parasitism of language.

For Burroughs the presence of this life-threatening virus is most clearly
manifested in the activity of writing, which he describes as a combination of
biological mutation and demonic possession. The claim of the narrator of
Naked Lunch that he is "never in possession" but rather possessed echoes Burroughs' descriptions in his letters of the experience of writing his routines:
"It's almost like automatic writing produced by a hostile independent entity
who is saying in effect 'I will write what I please' " (*Letters* 20–21). Serres
also describes the composition of his study as the exorcism of a parasite: "It
finally is separate from me. Thus the horrible insect slowly left my room,
through the creaking door, one May morning, in Venice" (253). The problem
for Burroughs is similarly how to exorcize the parasite, the alien which dic-
tates his words and his will; how to gain control of body and writing at once;
how—in his terms—to write his own ticket.

The Mythology of Parasitism

This association of language and parasitism in Burroughs' writing finds a striking parallel in the work of many contemporary theorists. Ideas about language control and social manipulation developed quite independently by Burroughs and Barthes during the late 1950s and early 1960s reflect the negative attitude toward language which pervades much postmodern literature and literary criticism. Burroughs and Barthes have represented with a frightening clarity the abuses of language as a weapon for control and destruction. They have accomplished this task of exposure, moreover, by elaborating an almost identical image system of parasitic forms to represent the linguistic menace within Western civilization.

In *Mythologies*, Barthes examines the invisible system of communication which perpetuates the myths of modern culture, those artificial structures of modern civilization we have come to accept as natural. In one example, Barthes describes a magazine illustration of a black soldier in uniform saluting the French flag. On a primary and perhaps innocent level the man has an individual history which the photograph captures as a specific set of circumstances which converge in his saluting the flag. On the secondary level of myth, however, all individuality and history are absorbed by the generalized concept of French imperialism which the juxtaposition of black soldier and French flag asserts. Barthes diagrams this magazine illustration and other examples of mythical constructs in a simple format:

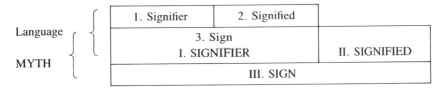

Barthes's diagram of the hierarchy of modern mythology is an inverted version of Burroughs' "pyramid of junk, one level eating the level below." Within this structure, any real meaning conveyed on the level of language becomes merely an empty form serving the production of a secondary mythical meaning. For Barthes the graduation from the primary to the secondary level of signification is not simply a mechanical shift from lower to upper case but a biological metamorphosis of Kafkaesque proportions. Just as Burroughs sees the bureaucratic institutionalizing of needs as a parasitic force which transforms an individual into the "Human Virus," Barthes traces the evolution of potentially self-sufficient meaning into an empty parasitical form in which "the meaning loses its value, but keeps its life, from which the form of the myth will draw its nourishment" (*Mythologies* 118).

In *S/Z*, Barthes studies the convergence of such cultural codes and myths in a single text, Balzac's "Sarrasine." While a system of codes and myths is shown to define and limit Balzac's text, the elements of this system inevitably outlive the text and "emigrate to other texts; there is no lack of hosts" (*S/Z* 205). Like a determined biologist, Barthes tags and pursues these parasitic myths, revealing the terrifying metamorphosis of meaning and life into "empty parasitical form." Like Burroughs' word virus, Barthes's myths do not remain external but enter the host where they try to remain invisible in a "constant game of hide and seek" (*Mythologies* 118). Ultimately the individual is replaced by a "motionless prototype which lives in his place, stifles him in the manner of a huge internal parasite" (*Mythologies* 155).

The Critic-Parasite

Contemporary theory in general shows a marked predilection for similar formulations of linguistic or textual parasitism. The challenge posed by deconstruction against the traditional image of the text is often perceived as an attack by the critic-parasite on the textual host. The conclusion of one hostile review of Serres's book, for example, makes a melodramatic denunciation of the parasitism of contemporary theory itself: "The metaphysical, epistemological and ethical anomalies in Serres's theory indicate where the true parasitism lies: it is in the theory itself" (Cataldo 44).

Accusations of parasitism have become a familiar coin of exchange in the critical marketplace these days. J. Hillis Miller begins his article "The Critic as Host" with what he admits is a parasitic citation of a citation: "At one point in 'Rationality and Imagination in Cultural History' M. H. Abrams cites Wayne Booth's assertion that the 'deconstructionist' reading of a given work 'is plainly and simply parasitical' on 'the obvious or univocal reading'" (217). In what has become a characteristic strategy of deconstruction in such debates, the terms which are accepted "plainly and simply" by traditionalists are (to use Miller's language) "interrogated." In this process the terms "host" and "parasite" are restored to their etymological ambiguity, their meanings are reversed, rendered problematic and equivocal: "What happens when a critical essay extracts a 'passage' and 'cites' it? Is this different from a citation, echo or allusion within a poem? Is a citation an alien parasite within the body of the main text, or is the interpretative text the parasite which surrounds and strangles the citation which is its host?" (217). Miller does not deny the accusation leveled by Booth and Abrams that the deconstructive reading is parasitic on an univocal reading of a text, but he goes on to insist that the idea of an unequivocal meaning is itself a "parasitic virus which has for millennia been passed from generation to generation in Western culture in its languages and in the privileged texts of those languages" (222). Theorists like Derrida or Philippe

Sollers press the point even farther, arguing that all discourse is parasitic on language, all texts already citations of the linguistic system itself.

Miller's etymological interrogation of the term "parasite" reveals an evolutionary pattern very similar to Burroughs' speculative history of "the Word." He uncovers an earlier meaning of parasite as a positive term for the fellow guest who shares the food, who sits in friendship with the host "beside the grain." This meaning is then shown to have given way to a negative designation of the parasite as a "professional dinner guest," one who takes nourishment but offers nothing in return. Miller's analysis traces, in other words, the fall which Burroughs also describes from benign symbiosis to destructive parasitism.

For Miller, as for Burroughs and Barthes, the stage of innocence and mutuality is never more than a remote fiction. The ideal of benign equilibrium is displaced in Miller's argument by a version of literary history as a chain of parasitic appropriations in which each text—as simultaneously parasite *and* host—becomes a "cannibal consumer" of all other texts: "The previous text is both the ground of the new one and something the new poem must annihilate by incorporating it, turning it into ghostly insubstantiality. . . . The new poem . . . is both parasitical on [older texts], feeding ungraciously on their substance, and at the same time it is the sinister host which unmans them by inviting them into its home, as the Green Knight invites Gawain" (225). When Miller asks, "can host and parasite live happily together, in the domicile of the same text, feeding each other or sharing the food?" (217), one may hear the same tone as in Burroughs' ironic question: "Would you offer violence to a well intentioned virus on its slow road to symbiosis?" (*Job* 12). Burroughs sees all relations as a "symbiosis con" masking the parasite's intention to survive at the expense of the host.

Miller describes the parasite as the alien, the uncanny other insinuating itself into the "closed economy of the home" (218). This is, finally, the monolithic power of logocentrism—its "ability to have got itself taken for granted as 'obvious' and single-voiced" (218). Like Burroughs and Barthes, Miller draws our attention to the danger posed by a parasitical form which becomes invisible, "that uncanny alien which is so close that it cannot be seen as strange" (218). In Burroughs' mythology this is how language gains power over human life, by establishing itself within the individual's very nervous system, by becoming confused with the familiar sounds and functions of his own body.

The common goal of Burroughs and many contemporary theorists, then, is to expose the invisible alien in our midst, to expel the language parasite from the body. Their ultimate strategy is to liberate language and the body so the individual may in turn be liberated from the limits imposed by word and flesh. Gérard-Georges Lemaire has described this paradoxical goal as the effort to "possess one's own language within the sphere of language that possesses us so that we can finally be dispossessed of it" (11). What Lemaire says here about language is also true of Burroughs' attitude toward the possession and dispossession of the body, its weaknesses and needs. As we saw in the carny man episode from *Naked Lunch* and in the cut-up narratives in general, the fates of body and word are always inextricably bound in Burroughs' vision.

9 | The Body

The commitment to make visible and tangible the disembodied parasitic machinery of power which rules Western civilization often produces in Burroughs' fiction and in radical critical theory what seems to be an unnatural preoccupation with the body and bodily functions. The sexual and scatalogical content of Burroughs' fiction has often been an obstacle to serious critical interpretation. I think it is crucial, therefore, to recognize that for him as for many contemporary theorists the body is often primarily a site of philosophical and aesthetic debate.

In Burroughs' mythology, word and body come into being simultaneously in a state of "lethal symbiosis" (*TTTE* 23). The word, having no substance, no color, no body of its own, must maintain itself by invading and controlling the body of the host, by predetermining the individual's entire life script: "Look through the human body the house passes out at the door—What do you see?—It is composed of thin transparent sheets on which is written the action from birth to death—Written on 'the soft typewriter' *before* birth—a cold deck built in" (*TTTE* 159). " 'These colorless sheets are what flesh is made from—Becomes flesh when it has color and writing—That is Word And Image write the message that is you on colorless sheets determine all flesh'" (*NX* 30). Intimately spliced in with the very functions and sounds of the body, the word parasite is camouflaged within the host. Life without a body and life without words become equally unthinkable: "Sub-vocal speech is the word organism the 'Other Half' spliced in with your body sounds. You are convinced by association that your body sounds will stop if sub-vocal speech stops and so it happens. Death is the final separation of the sound and image tracks" (*TTTE* 160). Once we are programmed to believe in the absolute *need* for body and word, we have entered the oppressive structure of the "Algebra of Need" and consequently lost all individual will. Burroughs proposes that "once you have broken the chains of association linking sub-vocal speech with body sounds" (*TTTE* 160) you can replace needs with options. He asks us to imagine not only the option of silence or nonverbal methods of communication, but also the option of non-body experience.

The entire machinery of Western culture, however, is organized to repress these options, to keep us in our bodies which provide the perfect site for repressive control. In *Discipline and Punish*, Foucault has described the anonymous power of this machinery and its manipulation of the body: "The human body was entering a machinery of power that explores it, breaks it down and rearranges it" (138). Foucault identifies as "disciplines" the methods "which made possible the meticulous control of the operations of the body, which assured the constant subjection of its forces and imposed upon them a relation of docility-utility" (137). Although for Burroughs it is the machinery of power (language) which enters the body instead of the body which is fed into the power structure, his ultimate goals are identical with those of Foucault: to expose the anonymous and invisible forces which manipulate individual life.

Disembodied Voices

Burroughs explores the same invisible "disciplines" tracked by Foucault, but he perceives them as voices rather than archives, as a ubiquitous system of ventriloquy: "By this time you will have gained some insight into the Control Machine and how it operates. You will hear the disembodied voice which speaks through any newspaper on lines of association and juxtaposition. The mechanism has no voice of its own and can talk indirectly only through the words of others . . . speaking through comic strips . . . news items . . . advertisements . . . talking, above all, through names and numbers" (*TM* 178). In the cut-up novels, this abstract control machine is personified and embodied in the "Death Dwarfs," parasitic creatures specializing in a kind of demonic mimicry:

> Biologic Agent K9 called for his check and picked up supersonic imitation blasts of The Death Dwarfs—"L'addition—laddition—laddition—Garcon—Garcon—Garcon"—American tourist accent to the Nth power—He ordered another coffee and monitored the café—A whole table of them imitating word forms and spitting back at supersonic speed—Several patrons rolled on the floor in switch fits—These noxious dwarfs can spit out a whole newspaper in ten seconds imitating your words after you and sliding in suggestion insults—That is the entry gimmick of The Death Dwarfs: supersonic imitation and playback so you think it is your own voice—(do you own a voice?) (*NX* 76)

Like the anonymous disembodied voice of the drug pusher floating down empty streets these imitative voices insinuate into the body of the victim artificial needs, desires, and fears that control human life. The logocentric system, based on the belief in an epistemological and moral supremacy of voice, presence, identity, and truth, is challenged here by Burroughs' insistence that there is always someone else there when you speak, that you can never *own* a voice. With Mallarmé, with Heidegger, with many contemporary theorists, Burroughs asserts that it is always the voice of language which speaks.[1]

The Body of the Voice

What is perhaps unique in Burroughs' thinking is the notion that this disembodied voice speaks and wields its power from within the stronghold it establishes in the *body* of the human host. As Burroughs sees it, this situation calls for a resistance strategy which begins with reversal: if the word traps us in body, writes us into the body's needs and fears, we must learn to "leave the body behind." If the power of the word depends on its invisibility we must make it visible, force it to take on the body we have cast off. The ultimate aim is to be able to "see the enemy direct" so that it can be expelled.

Burroughs perceives the disembodied voice of language as a strategy of *absent* control rather than *present* self-expression. To expose this strategy he proposes to force the word to reveal its concrete form: "The first step is to record the sounds of your body and start splicing them in yourself. Splice in your body sounds with the body sounds of your best friend and see how familiar he gets. Splice your body sounds in with air hammers. Blast jolt vibrate the 'Other Half' right out into the street. Splice your body sounds in with anybody or anything. Start a tapeworm club and exchange body sound tapes. Feel right out into your nabor's intestines and help him digest his food. *Communication must become total and conscious before we can stop it*" (*TTTE* 50–51). Burroughs' immersion in the physical, as in this experiment, has often been misinterpreted as evidence of an emotional and moral bankruptcy, evidence that he has sold out all spiritual value for bodily sensation. This extreme physicality, on the contrary, is part of Burroughs' project to dissolve the body and exhaust the language parasite, to push linguistic strategy and physical sensation to their limits.

This exposure and exhaustion of the power of the word is, above all, the responsibility of the writer, the victim most insidiously bound to and deluded by the supposed abstract nature of the word:

> The writer does not yet know what words are. He deals only with abstractions from the source points of words. The painter's ability to touch and handle his medium led to montage techniques sixty years ago. It is to be hoped that the extension of cut-up techniques will lead to more precise verbal experiments closing this gap and giving a whole new dimension to writing. These techniques can show the writer what words are and put him in tactile communication with his medium. This in turn could lead to a precise science of words and show how certain word combinations produce certain effects on the human nervous system. (*Job* 27–28)

Burroughs approaches language and the relationship of the author to language with a vigilant and scientific detachment. Taking control of the word by performing a kind of surgical dissection of its functions, he attempts to reveal and transcend the control mechanisms built into our linguistic system.

Exploration of body and word is for Burroughs essentially a strategy of self-defense, and this defensive posture leads him to a deep suspicion and even rejection of both body and word. His intermittent utopian glimpses of liberation are based on the remote possibility of escape from both:

> A trap door opened in the floor of the cubicle—and the subjects lowered themselves into the sense withdrawal tank and floated a few feet apart in darkness with no sound but feedback from the two halves of ten bodies permutated to heartbeat body music vibrating through the tank—Body outlines extend and break here—The stretching membrane of skin dissolves—Sudden taste of blood in his throat as gristle vaporizes and the words wash away and the halves of his body separated like a mold [. . .] Skeletons floated and crab parasites of the nervous system and the grey cerebral dwarf made their last attempt to hold prisoners in spine and brain coordinates—screaming "You can't—You can't"—You can't—Screaming without a throat without speech centers as the brain split down the middle and the feed-back sound shut off in a blast of silence. (*TTTE* 82–83)

As Burroughs describes his own experimental method, "I edit delete and rearrange flesh" (*TTTE* 182). We have seen in *Naked Lunch* and in the cut-up novels that Burroughs dreams at times of generating a new and liberated body by manipulating the traditional forms of word, text, and flesh. But the predominant impulse of his writing is toward "sense withdrawal" and silence, toward the destruction of word and body.[2]

In contemporary theory one notes a similar insistence on the materiality of language, on an exploration of the physical universe of the body. For many of these critics, however, such explorations stem from a much more positive attitude toward word and flesh and serve very different goals. It is not surprising, for example, that as the promoter of an erotics of reading and writing Barthes would examine the relationship of body and language, seeking out language in its materiality. Like Burroughs he stresses the materiality of the word in order to expose the alibis of logocentrism which would disguise words as transparent expressions of self and soul. Unlike Burroughs, however, Barthes's goal is not to destroy language but to immerse himself in its most intimate sensuality.

In an extension of Julia Kristeva's distinction between a "pheno-text" and "geno-text" (*Révolution* 83–85), Barthes designates two orders of the singing voice:

> The *pheno-song* . . . covers all the phenomena . . . everything in the performance which is in the service of communication, representation,

expression, everything which . . . forms the tissue of cultural values . . . which takes its bearing directly on the ideological alibis of a period ('subjectivity,' 'expressivity,' 'dramaticism,' 'personality' of the artist). The *geno-song* is the volume of the singing and speaking voice, the space where significations germinate 'from within language and in its very materiality'; it forms a signifying play having nothing to do with communication, representation (of feelings), expression; it is that apex (or that depth) of production where the melody really works at the language— not at what it says, but the voluptuousness of its sounds-signifiers, of its letters—where the melody explores how the language works and identifies with that work. (*Image* 182)

While the pheno-song "never exceeds culture," the geno-song reaches into the unknown realm outside of culture, into the "materiality of the body speaking its mother tongue" (182). For Barthes the concrete word is not the enemy to be expelled from the body but a kind of promised land of a language outside or before culture and law, a language which can be rediscovered in and through the privileged and idealized sphere of the body. Barthes chooses to explore a level of communication beyond meaning, expression, representation, and sentimentality, communication at its most physical and sensual. He seeks a language "lined with flesh, a text where we can hear the grain of the throat, the patina of consonants, the voluptuousness of vowels, a whole carnal stereophony: the articulation of the body, of the tongue, not that of meaning, of language" (*Pleasure* 66–67).

Both Burroughs and Barthes, then, attempt to achieve communication on a bodily level; but for the novelist communication is made "total and conscious [so that] we can stop it," while for the critic that total communication is an end in itself, absorbing, erotic, blissful. Barthes finds models for this body-to-body communication in listening to a cantor's song:

something which is directly the cantor's body, brought to your ears in one and the same movement from deep down in the cavities, the muscles, the membranes, the cartilages, and from deep down in the Slavonic language, as though a single skin lined the inner flesh of the performer and the music he sings. (*Image* 181–82)

or, in viewing a cinematic close-up:

In fact, it suffices that the cinema capture the sound of speech *close up* (this is, in fact, the generalized definition of the "grain" of writing) and make us hear in their materiality, their sensuality, the breath, the gutturals, the fleshiness of the lips, a whole presence of the human muzzle . . . to succeed in shifting the signified a great distance and in throwing, so to speak, the anonymous body of the actor into my ear: it granulates, it crackles, it caresses, it grates, it cuts, it comes: that is bliss. (*Pleasure* 67)

This close-up of the body and the word which thrusts Barthes into a state of bliss yields for Burroughs only disgust and the desire to escape.

Dismantling the Logocentric Body

Despite these differences, Burroughs and radical theorists like Barthes often adopt almost identical strategies in dealing with the conventional structures of body and word. While Barthes seeks to escape the circumscribed "body of the anatomists and physiologists" in order to enter the limitless "body of bliss" and Burroughs would destroy the body entirely in order to achieve non-body experience, the first stage for either project is the dismantling of the repressive logocentric body and the symbolic system it upholds.

To describe a body or a level of bodily communication which has nothing to do with expression, representation, emotion, or identity is to imagine a body which reverses every premise of logocentric thought. Burroughs and theorists like Barthes and Derrida have developed methods to deconstruct the logocentric body in order to free that other limitless body.

The logocentric body is primarily defined by borders which establish its autonomous, organic unity. Wholeness, clarity, the separate integrity of a self which can be named and represented—these notions form the grounding of traditional systems of meaning and being. The symbolic code which governs the production of meaning gravitates toward this image of a whole body from which it assimilates for itself, parasitically, the "weightiness" of reality and the authority of organic unity: "The symbolic field is occupied by a single object from which it derives its unity (and from which we have derived a certain right to name it, some pleasure in describing it, and what may pass for a privilege granted the symbolic system, the symbolic adventure of the hero, sculptor or narrator). This object is the human body" (*S/Z* 214–15). Serving the linguistic functions of naming and representation and the symbolic notion of organic unity, the logocentric body is clearly an artificial construct of some complexity. But this artifice has disguised itself as nature: "what we assumed—with the complicity of our teachers—was nature is in fact culture, that what was given is no more than a way of taking" (*S/Z* ix). The natural organic body is adopted as the very emblem of logocentrism, which thus conceals its arbitrariness under the glaze of eternal nature. To argue the logocentric position is "plainly and simply" to speak *for* or *as* nature.

As the emblem of eternal and irreversible values the logocentric body necessarily atrophies; ideology produces a body which is, as Barthes describes it, embalmed, benumbed, frozen in an attempt to "stop its transformation" (*Mythologies* 155), to stop the flow of history, change and evolution:

> Bourgeois ideology continuously transforms the products of history into essential types. Just as the cuttlefish squirts its ink in order to protect

itself, it cannot rest until it has obscured the ceaseless making of the world, fixated this world into an object which can be for ever possessed, catalogued its riches, embalmed it, and injected into reality some purifying essence which will stop its transformation, its flight towards other forms of existence. . . . For the very end of myths is to immobilize the world; they must suggest and mimic a universal order which has fixated once and for all the hierarchy of possessions. (*Mythologies* 155)

As monolithic as this body of Western civilization may seem, its structure has fault lines which the deconstructionist and the experimental writer will discover. The very rigidity of the logocentric system necessitates that the borders of the body be carefully policed, that any transgression or movement which threatens that system be immobilized. In order to insure its boundaries, then, the logocentric body is defined by exclusion as well as by inclusion. Everything which has been driven from the body's realm in order to guarantee its purity and integrity becomes a lurking threat of invasion and contamination, the dangerous realm of the abject described by Kristeva:

Taking a closer look at defilement, as Mary Douglas has done, one ascertains [that] filth is not a quality in itself, but it applies only to what relates to a *boundary* and, more particularly, represents the object jettisoned out of that boundary, its other side, a margin.

Matter issuing from them [the orifices of the body] is marginal stuff of the most obvious kind. Spittle, blood, milk, urine, faeces or tears by simply issuing forth have traversed the boundary of the body. [. . .]

It follows from this that pollution is a type of danger which is not likely to occur except where the lines of structure, cosmic or social, are clearly defined. [Douglas 121, 113]

[. . .] Why does *corporeal waste*, menstrual blood and excrement, or everything that is assimilated to them, from nail-parings to decay, represent—like a metaphor that would have become incarnate—the objective frailty of symbolic order? (*Powers* 69–70)

In their efforts to deconstruct the logocentric body, to liberate a new plural body without limits, it is not surprising that Burroughs and other radical thinkers would focus on that which threatens the seamless unity and autonomy of the symbolic body.

The points where self and other, self and world intersect, where the passage from inside to outside overflows the boundaries—these constitute the sites of entry for the radical theorist and for William Burroughs. The bodily functions most intensely implicated in this transgressive movement are digestion and procreation, functions which involve the overflow of "marginal" matter from the body's orifices. The logocentric system attempts to minimize the threat posed by these functions by conceiving of them as linear, irreversible, and hierarchical. Digestion and procreation are contained and controlled as processes of assimilation and filiation which repeat and reinforce the logocentric image of the unified body. But that unified body remains in constant danger of contamination, dismemberment, penetration, and hemorrhage.

Burroughs might be describing a general strategy of deconstruction when he advises, "Reverse all your gimmicks—your heavy blue metal fix out in blue sky—[. . .] your bank of word and image scattered to the winds of morning—" (*TTTE* 134). To reverse and to scatter—this is the "double science" by which deconstruction explodes the logocentric system and its body image. The strategy of Burroughs' fiction and of radical contemporary theory is to reverse the digestive system by an emetic emptying out of the body and to scatter the procreative seed in a non-productive dissemination.

10 | Digestion

In the lively exchange of letters on Burroughs' work that appeared in the *Times Literary Supplement* in 1964, one reader argues that great art is never based on the sex organs and the alimentary tract (Bingham 27). In these next two chapters I will place Burroughs in a literary tradition including such writers as Rabelais, Cervantes, and Sterne in an attempt to demonstrate that indeed there is great art which does not shrink from the body but writes *through* the body and its functions to its own powerful vision.

Burroughs perceives the development of Western civilization as a gradual repression of the life-sustaining functions of digestion and procreation. The centrality of images of digestion in his mythology is already evident in the title of his major novel, *Naked Lunch*. In that novel's introduction he explains the significance of the title:

> Certain passages in the book that have been called pornographic were written as a tract against Capital Punishment in the manner of Jonathan Swift's *Modest Proposal*. These sections are intended to reveal capital punishment as the obscene, barbaric and disgusting anachronism that it is. As always the lunch is naked. If civilized countries want to return to Druid Hanging Rites in the Sacred Grove or to drink blood with the Aztecs and feed their Gods with blood of human sacrifice, let them see what they actually eat and drink. Let them see what is on the end of that long newspaper spoon. (*NL* xliv)

Burroughs reveals how the myths and methods of any given culture hide their artificiality beneath what Barthes has called a "culinary glazing" which disguises culture as nature. The rather nasty project of *Naked Lunch* is to make us see what we are actually being fed; the novel's disturbing images are merely that naked truth without its customary cultural "dressing." The function of Burroughs' imagery is ultimately to disgust the reader, to provoke an emetic purging of his cultural inheritance.

While official institutions and ideologies appear to serve and nurture us, Burroughs argues, they are in fact feeding parasitically off of the human resources of energy and youth: "Into the Interior: a vast subdivision, antennae of television to the meaningless sky. In lifeproof houses they hover over the young, sop up a little of what they shut out. Only the young bring anything in, and they are not young very long" (*NL* 11). In this view abstract ideologies are inimical to life because they must "sop up" and devour life to survive. Culture destroys nature; the inside sustains itself by living off of the outside, by turning youth's "live orgones into dead bullshit."

Perhaps more insidious than its devouring of human life, however, is the way in which civilization as we know it turns man himself into a carnivore, a devourer of other life. Burroughs announces bluntly in *Ticket*, "Message of life written 'We have come to eat'" (100). This is the message of "life written," the message of the life of writing, of life *as defined by* the written word. Burroughs takes the deconstructionist position that writing was always there, even before speech: "I suggest that the spoken word as we know it came after the written word. In the beginning was the Word, and the Word was God—and the word was flesh . . . human flesh . . . in the beginning of *writing*. [. . .] The written word is inferential in *human* speech" (*Job* 11–12). From the first stirrings of human evolution, then, man is always already possessed by language and by the demands of digestion:

> In the pass the muttering sickness leaped into our throats, coughing and spitting in the silver morning. [. . .] dumb animal eyes on "me" brought the sickness from white time caves frozen in my throat to hatch in the warm steamlands spitting song of scarlet bursts in egg flesh [. . .] sound bubbling in throats torn with the talk sickness. faces and bodies covered with pus foam. animal hair thru the purple sex-flesh. sick sound twisted thru body [. . .] We waded into the warm mud-water. hair and ape flesh off in screaming strips. stood naked human bodies covered with phosphorescent green jelly. [. . .] till the sun went and a blue wind of silence touched human faces and hair. When we came out of the mud we had names. (*SM* 177–78)

The mutation caused by the "talk sickness" is the emergence of subjective identity, of a "me" isolated and contained by its binary opposition to all that is "not-me." The survivors of the "talk sickness," those who take on language, subjective identity and name, are driven by an unnameable something inside, a need which makes them dominate and devour other life: "And some did not eat flesh and died because they could not live with the thing inside. [. . .] Came to the great dry plain and only those lived who learned to let the thing surface and eat animal excrement in the brown water holes [. . .] I knew the thing inside me would always find animals to feed my mouth meat" (*SM* 179–80). In the history Burroughs narrates, man climbs up out of these primitive swamps as he evolves, but his need drives him back down into the modern sewers of the city. This monotonous history of digestion and parasitic absorption unravels itself "on a long string of rectal mucus," interminably through "the years. the long. the many" (*SM* 180).

Burroughs perceives the imposing of culture on human consciousness as a kind of forced feeding which ties us to language, to the notion of individual identity, to the hierarchical structures of domination which rule Western thought. In the context of such basic cultural repression, digestion is never nourishing or regenerative but rather doomed to constipation, to exhaustion, and to self-destruction.

A similar history of digestion emerges in the work of some radical theorists, most notably Mikhail Bakhtin, Jacques Derrida, and Jacques Ehrmann. To fully understand the significance of the digestive imagery which pervades Burroughs' work, it will be helpful to examine these critical parallels and to place Burroughs in relation to a literary *tradition* of works which focus on digestion as physical reality and as figurative emblem.

The Economy of Digestion

One early example in this tradition is Rabelais's *Gargantua and Pantagruel*, a work which Mikhail Bakhtin identifies as a model of positive digestion. By locating Rabelais in the spirit of the medieval carnival feast, Bakhtin illuminates his celebration of body and earth, of fertility and hope. The carnival tradition creates what he calls the "grotesque body," a body that is in a perpetual state of becoming: "it is continually built, created, and builds and creates another body" (317). Celebrating fertility, growth, and renewal, the grotesque body digests the world instead of excluding it. "the body swallows the world and is itself swallowed by the world" (317). This swallowing is never appropriative or territorial but rather recreates the mutual economy of borrowing and lending that characterizes the microcosm of the carnival body.

Everywhere in Rabelais's work one finds evidence of this communal body of the people which transcends hierarchical division and domination, functioning by the harmonious interchange of a balanced ecology. In his strange wit and wisdom, Panurge describes the body as an utopian economy where everything flows, interdependent and yet liberated:

> Life consists of blood. Blood is the seat of the soul. Therefore there is only one task entrusted to this microcosm, that is continuously to forge blood. [. . .] To find, prepare, and cook this nourishment, the hands work; the feet move and transport the whole mechanism; the eyes act as guides. [. . .] The tongue makes a test of it; the teeth chew it; the stomach receives it, digests it, and chylifies it. [. . .] leaving the excrements, which are voided by an expulsive mechanism along special conduits, and conduct it to the liver; which transmutes it once more and turns it into blood.
> [. . .] All the members—the feet, the hands, the eyes, and all the rest—absorb it. Thus they become debtors who previously were lenders.

[. . .] In the end it is so refined in the *miraculous network*, that it later becomes the material of the animal spirits, which endow us with imagination, reason, judgement, resolution, deliberation, ratiocination, and memory. (300–301)

The process of digestion here transmutes, as in an alchemical "miraculous network," the physical into the spiritual. No parasitic hierarchies are imposed because each element is nourished by and nourishes the others. Instead of the fixed and divided hierarchy of binary oppositions we find a divine and perpetual circulation.

Within the economy of the body as we find it in Rabelais's fiction, everything is fertile and productive: urine produces the finest wheat crops, excrement cures the dropsy, and Pantagruel's "farts" and "poops" engender entire races. The contemporary world described in Burroughs' fiction, however, is far removed from this utopian model, its economy of digestion produces none of the "miraculous" transformations of Panurge's body system. What we are shown instead is a cycle of diminishing returns, a degenerate capitalist economy headed for bankruptcy:[1]

When a certain stage of responsibility and awareness has been reached by a young banker he is taken to a room lined with family portraits in the middle of which is an ornate gilded toilet. Here he comes every day to defecate surrounded by the family portraits until he realizes that *money is shit*. And what does the money machine eat to shit it out? It eats youth, spontaneity, life, beauty and above all it eats creativity. It eats quality and shits out quantity. There was a time when the machine ate in moderation from a plentiful larder and what it ate was replaced. Now the machine is eating faster. [. . .] People want money to buy what the machine eats to shit money out. The more the machine eats, the less remains. So your money buys always less. [. . .] If the West does not start a nuclear war first their monetary system will fall apart through the inexorable consumption by the machine of life art flavor beauty to make more and more shit which buys less and less life art flavor beauty because there is less and less to buy. [. . .] The time must come when money will buy nothing because there will be nothing left for money to buy. Money will eliminate itself. (*Job* 73–74)

Burroughs is not the first writer to tell us that money is excrement, or—as he asserts elsewhere—that the word is excrement.[2] He has, however, carried this idea to its literal extreme, refusing to evade its implications by treating it as a mere metaphor. Western culture, he insists, propels human life toward a deadly stasis: "metabolism approaching Absolute ZERO. TERMINAL addicts often go two months without a bowel move and the intestines make with sit down adhesions—Wouldn't you?—requiring the intervention of an apple corer or its surgical equivalent" (*NL* xlvi). Constipation, in Burroughs' view, is the characteristic disease of our time.[3] Burroughs would cure such physical and ideological constipation by loosening bowels and throat, by provoking an emetic purging of all established systems and codes. Money, like the body and the word, will eventually "eliminate itself" unless it can be restored somehow to a free and non-repressive circulation.

Burroughs might well recognize in Rabelais a predecessor and collaborator in this venture toward liberation. The narrator of *Gargantua and Pantagruel* repeatedly advises the reader against the danger of obstructing digestion, of withholding or hoarding excrement or farts; and he counsels the contrasting practice of keeping all orifices open to the world, to knowledge, nourishment, and experience. In Rabelais's reformed system of education, the proper digestion of knowledge is often preceded by an emetic purging through which the subject is freed from all predetermined ideas and ideologies. In place of the old obstructive knowledge the narrator offers the reader an inexhaustible flow of wisdom and goodwill in the form of the communal drinking vessel, his text:

> Every honest boozer, every decent gouty gentleman, everyone who is dry may come to this barrel of mine, but need drink only if he wishes. If they wish, and if the wine is to the taste of their worshipful worships, let them drink frankly, freely, and boldly without stint or payment. [. . .] and have no fear that the wine will give out, as it did at the marriage at Cana in Galilee. As much as you draw out at the tap, I will pour in at the bung. In this way the cask will remain inexhaustible, endowed with a living spring and a perpetual flow. (286)

Free of the economics of possession and exchange ("without stint or payment"), the narrator and his audience collaborate freely in generating this freeflowing text.

Rabelais's procedure—first the emetic, then the inexhaustible flow—parallels in many ways Burroughs' writing project. After taking the emetic cure of *Naked Lunch* which immunizes us by exposure, we are offered the more radical treatment of the cut-up text: the dismemberment of bodies and texts in a proliferation of holes and flows, a kind of pan-digestion. Describing his method in *Ticket*, Burroughs stresses the same merging of audience and performer (reader and narrator), the same reversals and permutations of established order and discourse which Bakhtin associates with the carnival spirit of Rabelais. Above all, we find in the utopian moments of Burroughs' cut-ups the Rabelaisian image of a digestive system which is miraculously reversible and communal:

> —(The spectators clicked through a maze of turnstiles)—Great sheets of magnetized print held color and disintegrated in cold mineral silence as word dust falls from demagnetized patterns—[. . .] All music and talk

and sound recorded by a battery of tape recorders recording and playing back moving on conveyor belts and tracks and cable cars spilling the talk and metal music fountains of speech as the recorders moved from one exhibit to another—[. . .] Characters walk in and out of the screen flickering different films on and off—Conversations recorded in movies taken during the exhibit appear on the screen until all the spectators are involved situations permutating and moving—(Since the recorders and movies of the exhibition are in constant operation it will be readily seen that any spectator appears on the screen sooner or later if not today then yesterday or tomorrow as the case may be in some connection—and repeat visitors of course—) [. . .]

A writing machine that shifts one half one text and half the other through a page frame on conveyor belts— [. . .] Shakespeare, Rimbaud, etc. permutating through page frames in constantly changing juxtaposition the machine spits out books and plays and poems—The spectators are invited to feed into the machine any pages of their own text in fifty-fifty juxtaposition with any author of their choice and provided with the result in a few minutes. (*TTTE* 62–65)

Anything spills out, flows out, is spit out of the writing machine in perpetual "fountains of speech"; and anything may be fed into it by the reader. Burroughs, however, sees this positive digestive system as an elusive promised land for the body and the text. What stands stubbornly between the reader or writer and this goal is the elaborate edifice of Western logocentric thought, its image of the body and of digestion. Just as Burroughs isolates the major side effect of language acquisition as the designation of the carnivorous "me," so Bakhtin locates the crisis point in the history of carnival as the emergence of the notion of the individual subjective self.

Digestion Endangered

The eighteenth century, Bakhtin explains, undermines the carnival spirit by shifting the center of gravity from the fertile and communal body of the earth to the individual body, from the physical and sensual to the ideal and abstract. He sees Laurence Sterne's *Tristram Shandy* as the "first important example" of the "subjective, individualistic world outlook" which undermines the regenerative carnival spirit (36). For the isolated and individual body (the "private egotistic form, severed from the other spheres of life") digestion and copulation become sterile and destructive, or merely vulgar. What Bakhtin does not make sufficiently clear is that Sterne himself rejects this historical narrowing and diminishing of the body, attempting, like Burroughs, to challenge its restrictive boundaries. Critical objections to the vulgar or obscene content of both Sterne's and Burroughs' work indicate an analytical blindness to the strategies behind these writers' preoccupation with the body and particularly with the digestive tract.

Following the tradition of carnival humor which "degrades and materializes," Tristram compares his father's idiosyncratic philosophical and linguistic systems to a simple process of digestion: "He pick'd up an opinion, Sir, as a man in a state of nature picks up an apple." This natural procedure, however, is immediately obstructed by conflict and self-interest which transform the life-giving digestion of the apple into a mortal combat: "It becomes his own,—and if he is a man of spirit, he would lose his life rather than give it up" (165). The tortuous and meaningless debate over the individual authority and ownership of ideas and words is inflated to the level of farce by the following hypothetical debate on the subject:

> I am aware that *Didius*, the great civilian, will contest this point; and cry out against me, Whence comes this man's right to this apple? *ex confesso*, he will say,—things were in a state of nature.—The apple, as much *Frank's* apple, as *John's*. Pray, Mr. *Shandy*, what patent has he to shew for it? and how did it begin to be his? was it, when he set his heart upon it? or when he gather'd it? or when he chew'd it? or when he roasted it? or when he peel'd? or when he brought it home? or when he digested?—or when he___?—. For 'tis plain Sir, if the first picking up of the apple, made it not his,—that no subsequent act could.
> Brother *Didius*, *Tribonius* will answer [. . .] the sweat of a man's brows, and the exsudations of a man's brains, are as much a man's own property, as the breeches upon his backside;—which said exsudations, &c. being dropp'd upon the said apple by the labour of finding it, and picking it up; and being moreover indissolubly wasted, and as indissolubly annex'd by the picker up, to the thing pick'd up, carried home, roasted, peel'd, eaten, digested, and so on; 'tis evident that the gatherer of the apple, in so doing, has mix'd up something which was his own, with the apple which was not his own, by which means he has acquired a property;—or, in other words, the apple is *John's* apple. (165–66)

Digestion, then, is offered as a model for the assimilation of preceding texts; to digest is not simply to be nourished by the tradition but to seize the opinions of others, to appropriate them as one's own private property. Once Sterne introduces the notion of ownership digestion becomes an act of territorial aggression, the annexation and fortification of new territory: "Accordingly he held fast by 'em, both by teeth and claws [. . .]—and in a word, would intrench and fortify them round with as many circumvallations and breastworks, as my uncle *Toby* would a citadel" (166).

Sterne's contempt for this brand of self-fortification, for authorial ownership or copyright, is evident in his extension of the digestive analogy: the property acquired and assimilated is no more than the unmentionable "and so on" which marks the end of the alimentary process. The image of Tristram's father building fortifications around his jealously guarded excremental property is a perfect emblem of the constipation which characterizes the eternally fixed and enclosed logocentric body and the conventions it represents. Excrement is fortified and cherished, the nourishing digestive flow obstructed. Thus the total body, the unified body, reconstitutes its borders and closes off access. In the world of *Tristram Shandy* the extent to which the motion and flow of life's fluids is obstructed reflects the burden of the tradition it carries.

Sterne attempts to disrupt this tradition by continually fragmenting his text at every level: displacing the conventional organization of preface, dedication, and chapter breaks; scrambling linear continuity with the digressive-regressive turns of his narrative machinery; fracturing even the continuity of a single sentence or the syllables of a single word. More relevant, perhaps, is his technique of relentlessly returning to the body, to the materiality of the book, the page, the word, to the literalness of the language we devour. One can easily recognize in Sterne's strategies and in his goals the breakthrough achieved by William Burroughs' experimental writing: the multiplication and circulation of body and word.

Digestion Regained

Burroughs' attempt to return to an open and reversible digestion of bodies and texts not only has its precedent in writers like Rabelais and Sterne, but finds even closer parallels in recent critical theory. Discouraged by the persistence of structures of binary opposition and oppression even in writers as daring as Jonathan Swift, Jacques Ehrmann calls for a more thorough liberation from binary opposition, a return to the "fluidity" and "non-pertinence" of a more open knowledge or nonsense.[4] In his essay "The Death of Literature," Ehrmann imagines the subversive goal of a discourse which refuses to fix or "found meaning," a discourse which would not only confront the body and death, but which might—through the liberating freedom of play—escape their limits. He describes this new discourse in terms of the same digestive imagery we have been exploring:

> Since its only viable status is as subversion, [the activity of the reading and writing of signs] can only be a terrorizing one: it consists of setting fire to the powder, of activating the flames—of burning, consuming meaning. [. . .] I could just as well have said that the reading-writing process consists of stirring up shit. It all comes down to the same thing: fire and shit; a childish, childhood game. [. . .]
>
> This game is neither completely free nor completely gratuitous, because we are *implicated* in it: we are that very matter and the subjects who stir it up. Our shit is our history—it is, as we say, our business; it is also we who make it. Conversely, our history is our undoing; literally, it decomposes us. Like death. It *is* our death. We are, therefore, the history of our matter at the same time as the matter of our history. We make and unmake ourselves at one and the same time. [. . .]
>
> Our history is in all its acceptations organic. It digests us and we di-

gest it: it consists in absorbing the signs, which, in turn, absorb us; it is the nourishing and fecal matter of the signs that we consume and secrete. [. . .] The chemistry of our history corresponds to the economy of our discourse. A paradoxical circuit through which we both communicate with and escape from ourselves. (251–52)

Ehrmann's conclusion posits the same paradoxical hope we found expressed by Burroughs in *Naked Lunch*, "The way OUT is the way IN" (*NL* 229), and in *The Wild Boys*, " 'The way out is the way through' " (82). As Cary Nelson has described Burroughs' method, "Scatology becomes eschatology." The acknowledgment that speech is defecation, Nelson explains, "signals an end to talk" and we "purge ourselves of [the] common product [of language and shit], history" (221).

In the work of theorists like Ehrmann, Barthes, and Derrida—as in Burroughs' fiction—there is a return to the body which has as its ultimate goal an escape from the body. The digestive system is often the conduit for that escape. In "Economimesis," for example, Derrida explores the digestive imagery in Kant's *Critique of Judgement*, exposing the philosopher's determination to displace the body and sensual tasting with an intellectual and ethical notion of "ideal" taste. Derrida, for his part, will return insistently in his commentary on Kant and in subsequent texts to the actual body, to the physical functions of digestion and excretion.

Derrida reveals in the philosophical sphere the same moment of crisis Bakhtin describes in the literary development of grotesque realism. While in Rabelais's economy of the body the spiritual and physical nourished each other in harmonious interdependence, Derrida reveals how Kant's body system establishes a strict hierarchical relationship between the actual tasting of food and drink and the idealized tasting of ideas of beauty and morality. Unlike the liberated and limitless digestion at the carnival feast, the digestion favored by Kant is a closed and carefully regulated system. Derrida paraphrases Kant's position:

Because the outside appears purposeless, we seek purpose within. There is something like a movement of interiorizing suppliance, a sort of slurping by which, cut off from what we seek outside, from a purpose suspended outside, we seek and give within, in an autonomous fashion, not by licking our chops, or smacking our lips or whetting our palate, but rather (what is not entirely something else) by giving ourselves orders, categorical imperatives, by chatting with ourselves through universal schemas once they no longer come from the outside. (14)

This autonomous process of "idealizing interiorization," Derrida explains, is the basis of our system of morality.

In Kant's system the body is hierarchically structured around the mouth, the organ of expression and of communication by analogy. In this context the mouth is situated within a tightly closed circuit of mouth-to-ear, in fact displaced entirely from its relation to the alimentary system and to the external world. In the grotesque body of the carnival, the mouth is also central and dominant, but it is a gaping mouth, receptive and open to all external stimuli. Derrida points out that the idealized digestion described by Kant is dependent on its denunciation of actual tasting; thus a superior disgust with bodily pleasure emerges as the supporting element in Kant's system of aesthetic judgment. As Derrida puts it, "What is already announced here is a certain allergy in the mouth, between pure taste and actual tasting" (16).

As we learned from the carnival man's story, the victory of an idealizing philosophy over the actual body is a temporary delusion, a "phantasm" in Derrida's terms. Hovering outside the borders of the text, the joke, or the philosophic question, there always remains the abject realm of the *truly* indigestible, that which "one cannot resign oneself to mourn," to overcome by digesting. That which "does not allow itself to be digested, or represented, or stated" (21) is given a word (by Kant): the disgusting or vomit. "The word vomit," Derrida explains, "puts the thing in the mouth; it substitutes . . . oral for anal" (25). To speak of vomit—of the excluded, the disgusting, the other, of death—is to construct what Derrida calls a "paregoric parergon," a painkilling remedy which "softens with speech."

By linking speech with an opium derivative, Derrida (like Burroughs) suggests the addictive nature of language. Because the linguistic representation of the disgusting or vomit establishes the excluding borders of Kant's system, philosophy is shown to be addicted to and dependent on the very elements it seeks to suppress. As Derrida argues with characteristic deconstructive perversity, "[vomit] is then for philosophy, still, an elixir, even in the very quintessence of its bad taste" (25).

This paradoxical status of vomit as an elixir, its ambivalent alternation of pleasure and pain, of attraction and repulsion, also appears in Burroughs' conception of the addictive power of Western thought and culture. All variations of the junk equation—the addiction to body image, to subjective identity and self-expression, to the power of the word—produce the same impression of a digestive system gone haywire, turned against itself. Burroughs describes Western man as the carnivore, the addicted "Meat Eater" who embodies the vicious cycle of indigestion produced by distorted notions of desire and need: "Several Meat Eaters lay in vomit, too weak to move. (The Black Meat is like a tainted cheese, overpoweringly delicious and nauseating so that the eaters eat and vomit and eat again until they fall exhausted.)" (*NL* 55). Like Derrida's provocative assertion that vomit is the elixir of philosophy, Burroughs' naked lunch of the addictions of Western culture is a deconstructive strategy. It is in this philosophic context that we must understand such

elements in Burroughs' fiction as the scenes of coprophagy which have pro-
voked outrage not only in the literary arena but in the courtroom.

In *Glas*, a text often as scatalogical as anything one might find in Bur-
roughs' novels, Derrida makes an aggressive move against the tyranny of
Kant's system of idealized tasting and isolated subjectivity. In his discussion of
Genet he returns to actual digestion, to the very slurping, the licking of chops,
smacking of lips, and whetting of the palate excluded from Kant's philosophy.
Digestion no longer functions as a metaphor (under the rule of the mouth), but
is returned to its literal materiality. Derrida describes the new textuality in
Glas as an antibody to body images of power and presence (xxv). Against the
fortified and regulated body, the logocentric body, Derrida will generate something resembling the body experienced by Barthes in the "grain" of the text, in
the "pulsions" which mark an energy beyond meaning, beyond self-expression, beyond subjectivity. The power of the logocentric body resides in its hierarchical organization, the subordination of lower to upper body functions,
of digestion to thought, of anus to mouth. *Glas* parodies and explodes these
divisions by juxtaposing and intermingling body and mind, Genet and Hegel
in the two facing columns of his text.

In the Genet columns of *Glas* there is, as in Barthes' descriptions of the
"grain," a preoccupation with the lips and mouth, the sensual and material
reality of language. The word "glas" in its many lexical meanings, in its several etymologies (real or imagined), is dissolved by the sound of "gl": "It is
not a word—gl hoists up the tongue but does not set store by it and always lets
it fall back, does not belong to it—even less a name, hardly a propername"
(263b).[5]

If "glas" in its lexical meaning is the death knell of the physical body, the
heralding of the soul's transcendence of the body, then Derrida's insistence on
the materiality of "gl" reconstitutes that physical body: "gl: the stricture of
the orifice—gullet of strangling—informs a block of casein, for example, a
belch, a fart, a remains to make in all cases it falls" (286b). In *Glas* everything falls—name, family, meaning, ideology—everything runs the gamut of
the gullet. As Gayatri Spivak points out, the legend of the text's production
is repeatedly told as the production of remains: a constipation or constriction
triumphantly released and dispersed. Because he has no intention of ending
up like Walter Shandy fortifying excrement, Derrida defines his ungraspable
text as a gas, the temporarily suspended fart or belch, the disappearing trace
of decomposition or digestion.

Derrida also describes his critical method as the careless movement of a
great dredging machine from which much inevitably escapes, undigested, to
reconstitute itself elsewhere. So to fall (as excrement falls from the body) is to
be freed, freely disseminated, to escape the fixed confines of the body, individual self, name, book. In this context excrement once again might become

productive, regenerative, and liberating as it was in the medieval carnival world.

The iconoclastic operations of Burroughs' experimental writing, what he has called the "cement mixer" of his writing machine, resemble in many ways the "dredging machine" of Derrida's deconstruction. As in *Glas*, everything falls in Burroughs' fiction: in the mosaic collages of *Naked Lunch* where "pearl and opal chips fall in a slow silent rain through air clear as glycerine," where a body "leaps out into space. Masturbating end-over-end, three thousand feet down [. . .] to shatter in liquid relief in a ruined square paved with limestone" (*NL* 94, 98); or in the recurrent refrains of descent and release which punctuate the cut-up triology, announcing "Word falling— Time falling—'Love' falling—Flesh falling—Photo falling—Image falling" (*TTTE* 105).

The reader will not find in Burroughs the kind of Rabelaisian joy in the body and in language that surfaces in Ehrmann or Bakhtin, for ultimately Burroughs intends to leave behind body and language. Determined to break free of the body and its digestive function, to break free of the addiction to that "paregoric parergon" of language, Burroughs pursues for himself and offers to his readers the austere and often repellent emetic cure by apomorphine. "Apomorphine," he explains, "is no word and no image" (*NX* 47). Apomorphine is directed not only at the death of language, but at the dispersal of the self-enclosed interiorizing, idealizing ego—the self as carnivore. Apomorphine sets the individual consciousness free of the body, allows the subject to observe his own body from a decentered and detached outpost: "He reached for his stash of apomorphine and slipped a handful of tablets under his tongue—His body twisted forward and emptied and he jetted free and drifted to the ceiling—Looked down on quivering bodies—crab and centipede forms flashed here and there—" (*NX* 86). Beyond the rigidity of single identity and name, revolutionary agents who have used the drug are able to "[exchange] identities as articles of clothing, circulate in strata of hustlers" (*NX* 87). Above all, apomorphine releases the subject from the claustrophobic body system addicted to the digestion and reproduction of its own image. Burroughs describes this condition through the figure of the "Death Dwarf," a creature manipulated by remote control: "Images—millions of images—That's what I eat—Cyclotron shit—Ever try kicking *that* habit with apomorphine?—Now I got all the images of sex acts and torture ever took place anywhere and I can just blast it out and control you gooks right down to the molecule—I got orgasms—I got screams—I got all the images any hick poet ever shit out— [. . .] And I got millions and millions and millions of images of Me, Me, Me, meee" (*NX* 45).

Reduced to a diminutive puppet obsessed by his fear of death, man is trapped within a vicious cycle which turns everything into images of "Me,

Me, Me, meee." The digestion of the world, which in the Rabelaisian body transmuted not only into generative sperm but into ideas and feelings, produces nothing here. It leads only to repetition, to the infinite replication of the "me" which marked man's first stirrings from the swamps. As Bakhtin laments, to be estranged from the collective body of the people, to become an isolated subjectivity, is to be reduced to the biological body which "merely repeats itself." The fate of reproduction (of procreation, repetition, representation) is linked here to the fate of digestion, and both together trace the evolution of identity and language into the postmodern world.

11 | Procreation

In the history of Western civilization, as Burroughs perceives it, procreation moves toward a sterile repetition which increasingly resists evolution and change. In this chapter I will consider Burroughs' treatment of reproduction first in relation to the work of several other fiction writers who have focused on the liberation or repression of procreative energy, and then in relation to several branches of contemporary theory which directly challenge the sterility and stasis of Western culture.

Burroughs attributes the polarization of reproductive energy to structures of binary opposition which set two incompatible sexes in perpetual conflict, channeling the flow of creative energy into a parasitic economy based on power and property. He proposes, with characteristic dramatic provocation, nothing less than the destruction of all established formulas of nation, family, and reproduction (*Job* 50). To dismantle conventional modes of reproduction, both sexual and textual, is to open the way for new and monstrous births, for unthinkable transformations. This tendency toward unnatural and inhuman novelty constitutes a strong affinity between the work of William Burroughs and that of contemporary theorists like Roland Barthes, Jacques Derrida, and the philosophical collaborators Gilles Deleuze and Félix Guattari. The latter two in particular coincide with Burroughs in their perception of the gradual degeneration of the procreative principle in the restricted arenas of sexual dualism, family, and society. They also share with the novelist futuristic visions of possible avenues of escape and liberation.

These flights are often violent and unspeakable, iconoclastic gestures which mark what Derrida has called (in describing deconstruction) the birth of something "as yet unnameable . . . under the species of the non-species, in the formless, mute, infant and terrifying form of monstrosity ("Structure" 265). The monstrous textual births which have been generated by contemporary radical theory and by the extravagant fictions of William Burroughs are products of an alternative mode of reproduction: reproduction as dissemination, as a liberated and infinite spawning of bodies and words.

From Fertility to Sterility:
The Development of the Novel

Before examining these alternative modes of reproduction, it will be helpful to trace the historical changes in the notion of procreation as reflected in several major works of fiction. These works reveal a history of the gradual repression of procreative energy which has lead to our current impasse and the need for radically new formulations of creativity. Mikhail Bakhtin has charted this progression in his study of the flowering and decline of the medieval carnival spirit of challenge and renewal. In the development of narrative fiction from Rabelais to Sterne and beyond, he examines the struggles of several novelists against growing threats to textual and sexual fertility.

As we saw in the history of digestion, Bakhtin finds an early model for the ideal conditions of reproduction in the carnival tradition of grotesque realism in the age of Rabelais. He describes, for example, the ambivalent carnival image of the earth as both grave and womb: "[The opposition of life and death] is completely contrary to the system of grotesque imagery, in which death is not a negation of life seen as the great body of all the people but part of life as a whole—its indispensable component, the condition of its constant renewal and rejuvenation. Death is here always related to birth; the grave is related to the earth's life-giving womb" (50). Where the individual is absorbed into the communal body of the people, Bakhtin explains, death and rebirth are merely part of an eternal cycle, the death of the old body making way for the birth of a new and renewed body. The testicles do not contain (as in Burroughs' death dwarf figure) "millions of images of Me, me, meeee," but rather the seeds of the entire human stock. As Panurge argues, "When a man loses his head only the individual perishes; but if the balls were lost, the whole human race would die out" (309). He proposes further that any criminal about to lose his head should be " 'allowed to poke like a pelican, until his spermatic vessels are so drained that there isn't enough in them to write the letter Y. [Thus he might] die without regret, leaving a man for a man' " (362). Here procreation reconciles one to death by reaffirming the continuity of a communal and natural cycle of life.

The carnival tradition harmonizes death and rebirth in the context of the material bodily principle of the earth, but its effects extend to the context of language and writing as well. The aging Gargantua, for example, writes a letter to his son in which he asserts his faith in an immortality made possible for man by the divinely granted "method of seminal propagation" (193). Gargantua describes this immortality as the ability to be present (in his son) even when he is absent, and specifically as the ability to continue through Pantagruel "visiting and conversing with men of honor and my friends." To be

able to converse even in one's absence is not only the gift of "seminal propagation," but also of what Gargantua praises as the "divine inspiration" of printing (194). Rabelais justifies his own work in very similar terms in a letter to
his patron: "my sole aim and purpose in writing [these chronicles] down was
to give such little relief as I could to the sick and unhappy, in my absence"
(435). The divine gifts of procreation and writing, then, arise as compensa-
tion for—and as a reminder of—man's mortality. Writing and death coincide
here, but they are assimilated and neutralized in the miraculous network of the
carnival's fertile cosmos.

This miraculous network, however, is endangered by the progress of Western civilization. The gradual decline of carnival fertility despite intermittent
literary efforts to reverse this entropic tendency can be traced through the evolution of the novel. In Cervantes' *Don Quixote* one still finds positive carnival
images of death merging joyously into rebirth, and the mating of the realm of
the spirit with that of the body still bears fruit:

> "Every day, Sancho," said Don Quixote, "you grow less simple and
> wiser."
> "Yes," replied Sancho, "for some of your worship's wisdom must stick
> to me. Since lands of themselves barren and dry, with mucking and till-
> ing come to yield good fruit. I mean that your worship's conversation has
> been the muck, which has been cast upon the sterile ground of my dry
> wit, and the time of my service and communion with you has been the
> tillage. And so I expect to bear fruit of my own, which may be a bless-
> ing, and won't disgrace me, I hope, or slither off the paths of good breed-
> ing you have beaten in this parched understanding of mine." (539)

As early as in Cervantes' novel, however, Bakhtin sees the beginning of the
reduction of "the material bodily principle." The body has begun to narrow its
boundaries, becoming individual and isolated rather than communal.

One can easily find evidence in Cervantes' text to support Bakhtin's gener-
alization. For example, the threat of sterility referred to jokingly by Sancho
(" 'the sterile ground of my dry wit' ") echoes the narrator's opening remarks
about the limitations of his own "sterile and ill-cultivated genius." In part, the
narrator blames the frailty of his literary progeny on precisely his own estrangement from the earth's fertile energies:

> And so, what could my sterile and ill-cultivated genius beget but the
> story of a lean, shrivelled, whimsical child . . . much like one engen-
> dered in prison, where every discomfort has its seat and every dismal
> sound its habitation? Calm, a quiet place, the pleasantness of the fields,
> the serenity of the skies, the murmuring of streams and the tranquility of
> the spirit play a great part in making the most barren muses bear fruit and
> offer to the world a progeny to fill it with wonder and delight. (25)

With the development of the art of printing in Cervantes' time, reproduction of the word (and of ideas and flesh) begins to appear problematic, becoming a source of anxiety and fear as well as wonder. Between the publication of the first and second parts of Don Quixote's adventures, Cervantes suffers the dubious honor of being crudely imitated in print. The penning of the false "Part Two" of Quixote's exploits by Alonso Fernandez de Avellaneda raises the issue of the authentic and inauthentic fathering of texts, making procreation and identity increasingly uncertain. The "divine inspiration" of printing in which Gargantua had such naive faith poses genuine dangers for Don Quixote and Sancho. The two heroes find themselves haunted in Cervantes' own "Part Two" not only by their literary likenesses from the now circulating "Part One," but also by the unsettling spectres from Avellaneda's counterfeit sequel. The Sancho who so firmly proclaimed his identity earlier in the novel ("Sancho I was born, and Sancho I expect to die") is now unsettled by doubts:

> "Tell me brother squire, about this master of yours. Is he not one about whom a history has been printed called *The Ingenious Gentleman Don Quixote de la Mancha. . . ?*"
> "That's the man, my lady," answered Sancho, "and his squire Sancho Panza by name, who is, or should be in that history is myself, unless I was changed in my cradle—I mean changed in the press." (663)

Accustomed to swear "by the mother who bore [him]," Sancho finds he can no longer pronounce that oath without self-conscious equivocation. The extent of his involvement with Quixote and with the written word measures the extent of his estrangement from the material bodily principle of the fertile earth and the mother's body.

By the eighteenth century it is clear that something has gone wrong not only with digestion, but with procreation as well; the regenerative fertility of the carnival spirit has been dangerously repressed and constricted. Sterne's *Tristram Shandy* dramatizes the uncertain identity and immobilizing self-consciousness that usher in the modern era. In Sterne's novel, the process of procreation is removed from the regenerative earthly principle and subjected to continual dangers and accidents. The carnival bodily principle which still survives in Sancho Panza is displaced here by language—not the fertile cornucopia of words, lists, and stories which accumulate and flow joyously in Rabelais, but the linguistic machinery of legal, medical, and scholarly rhetoric, the engine of auxiliary verbs, the oblique cuts and slashes of Sterne's wit. Tristram's description of himself as one more attached to his remarks than Sancho Panza was to "his ass's FURNITURE" reflects this shift clearly. As Sterne demonstrates, Tristram's obsession with words keeps him from life, and he wastes his time in pursuit of his endangered witticisms while all the rest of the world is "a-May-poling."

The abundant fertility of Rabelais's *Gargantua and Pantagruel*, in short, is replaced in *Tristam Shandy* by images of castration and impotence. Conception is harried, birth difficult, future progeny threatened. Tristam's world is claustrophobically domestic, the family circle immobilizing. In an attempt to reinfuse his world with some of the liberality and spirit of Rabelais and Cervantes, Tristam promotes (though he does not always practice) "pure Shandyism" which "opens the heart and lungs, and like all those affections which partake of its nature, it forces the blood and other vital fluids of the body to run freely thro' its channels, and makes the wheel of life run long and chearfully round" (255).

Social and philosophical constraints, however, already restrict the free flow of Sterne's "pure Shandyism." The vital fluids of life are fed through the vast machinery of Western civilization; the binary mechanism which separates life/death, inside/outside, solemnity/wit constructs a vertical hierarchy of values and an irreversible linear model of history or narrative. Sterne chafes against this machine and its rules, but he is ultimately caught within its gears.

Reproduction as Production

With the development and rise of the realistic novel in the nineteenth century, reproduction functions more abundantly, but only within a carefully controlled system. The fortifying of the body's boundaries which we saw in Walter Shandy's constipated protection of his theories and systems is extended here to the context of literary reproduction. Under the law of representation, logocentric thought solidifies into patriarchal structures of hierarchy and domination, repressive patterns which reflect or are reflected in the dominant structures of familial, economic, and political life.

Barthes is a particularly helpful guide through this stage of our history because he explores, particularly in his study of Balzac, how the laws of realism and representation dictate particular forms of textual and sexual reproduction. Barthes attributes the increasingly constricted process of reproduction in the nineteenth century to the dominance of the metaphor of the author as father of the text: "the impulse, the origin, the authority, the Father, whence his work would proceed, by a channel of *expression*" (*S/Z* 211). The author reigns as the father-producer of the literary work which is his product and his effigy. This model of reproduction, unlike the medieval carnival image of earthly fertility, is a controlled flow of desire, life, and semen. Realistic narrative, for Barthes, typifies the "readerly" work; it is a "calculation" producing only a limited plenitude, a "simple—temporary—suspension of affinitive, already magnetized elements, before they are summoned together to take their place, economically, in the same *package*" (*S/Z* 182). The realistic work reproduces within a capitalist economy oriented toward the marketing of a consumable product.

At every level of such a work, the flow of meaning is coerced and directed: "the *author* is always supposed to go from signified to signifier, from content to form, from idea to text, from passion to expression; and, in contrast, the *critic* goes in the other direction, works back from signifiers to signified" (*S/Z* 174). The flow of life is trapped, predetermined in the binary structure of language itself: "the discharge, the emanation, the spiritual effluvium overflowing from the signified toward the signifier."

The alibi of organic reproduction which supports the "readerly" work culminates in the image of the text as a pregnant female body waiting to be "delivered": "[Any] classic (readerly) text is implicitly an art of Replete Literature: literature that is replete: like a cupboard where meanings are shelved, stacked, safeguarded (in this text nothing is ever lost: meaning recuperates everything); like a pregnant female, replete with signifieds which criticism will not fail to deliver" (*S/Z* 200–201). The promised delivery of meaning and truth, the solution of the text's enigma, is a birth which closes and kills the plurality of the text. While the convergence of death and birth in the carnival tradition is positive and productive, the effect here is negative and irreversible.

In Burroughs' fiction and theory we often find this same evolutionary tale of the fall from a liberated fertility to the controlled manipulation of reproductive energy. As he sees it the evolution of Western thought moves toward a sterile and dehumanized economy of word and flesh. Burroughs has a nightmare vision of the repressive channelling of creative seminal fluids by an anonymous and impersonal machine: "Through transparent walls he could see hundreds of other prisoners in cubicles of a vast hive milked for semen by the white-coated guards—The sperm collected was passed to a central bank— [. . .] At the center of this pulsing translucent hive was a gallows where the prisoners were hanged after being milked for three weeks—" (*TTTE* 23). The insidious machinery of Western culture demands that all life and youth be sacrificed in the procreation of new life as commodity. At his most pessimistic Burroughs seems to imply that the individual cannot evolve beyond his role as the doomed host to this parasitic economy. The regenerative juxtaposition of birth and death which Bakhtin finds in the fertile world of the carnival grotesque has come here to an historical dead end.

The Way Out

In the remote hope of finding a way out of the repressive structures of Western culture, however, Burroughs persists in his dissection of its forms. His first step is to isolate sexual dualism as the origin and model for all other forms of hierarchical domination. He perceives the economy of re-production as built on the forced interaction of two incompatible life forms—male and female. The only possible relationship between two sexes defined in binary opposition to each other is one of conflict. A civil war is continuously enacted on the battleground where all procreation takes place:

> The war between the sexes split the planet into armed camps right down the middle line divides one thing from the other—
> [. . .] On the line is the Baby and Semen Market where thc sexes meet to exchange the basic commodity which is known as the "prop-erty"—Unborn properties are shown with a time projector. [. . .] Bio-logical parents in most cases are not owners of the property. They act under orders of absentee proprietors to install the indicated stops that punctuate the written life script—With each Property goes a life script—(*SM* 157–58)

This fantasy represents procreation as a mechanical and indifferent mode of production in which human life is alienated and processed. There is no winner in this war between the sexes; manipulated by "absentee proprietors" of the reproductive machine, both men and women are robbed of individual will and desire.

Burroughs implies that the Wall of Antithesis, the Either/Or of sexual du-alism, not only divides but destroys. In the deliberately repellent persona of Herr Doktor Kurt Unruh von Steinplatz, Burroughs offers the following re-sponse to the "woman question" as posed by a female reporter: " 'Vy not cut off the head? Chickens can live so without the head nourished from tubors it is of course the same with womans. So brought to her true purpose of bearing strong male children she finds her simple contentment is it not? I appeal to you as a woman of good will to facilitate my experiments'" (*Job* 100–101). The good doctor's modest proposal, like Swift's, is meant to expose and undermine the attitudes and abuses already in place in Western culture. He merely states the naked facts with a nasty and unabashed bluntness: to have a "monopoly [on the] baby thing" is, in effect, to have your head cut off, to be reduced to a single body function. Like the young men in the semen factory who are milked and then hung, women too are metonymically reduced to a single function, to their reproductive organs.

When Burroughs remarks obliquely in *Naked Lunch* "male and female cas-trated he them," he implies that the definition of sexual difference as binary opposition is in itself a kind of castration, a dismemberment or decapitation which disenfranchises both sexes. One way out of the current impasse of pro-creation is to challenge, wherever possible, the restrictive structures of sexual difference and division.

Castration: Threat and Escape

In a kind of oriental strategy of assimilation rather than direct opposition Burroughs resists the castrating threat of sexual dualism by performing his own gestures of cutting, amputating, and dismembering bodies and texts. In Burroughs' experimental writing methods and in some of the more innovative forms of contemporary literary theory, there seems to be an assertion that one way out of the repressive channelling of conventional modes of reproduction is to break open the seamless enclosure of the work's logocentric body, to liberate it by castration or dismemberment.

Using a method similar to Burroughs' cut-up writing technique, for example, Barthes generates in *S/Z* something resembling the ideal text which defies all rules and boundaries, all marketability. Barthes's analysis not only dismembers Balzac's text in a castration which releases and multiplies the text's plurality, but also focuses explicitly on the thematic implications of castration in the narrative.

As for Burroughs, the problems of reproduction begin for Barthes with the idea of sexual difference as a castration. Sarrasine's virility is defined for him in opposition to La Zambinella's apparent femininity. His phallic certainty is itself derived from the castrating gesture of the binary opposition of the sexes: male/female. Imposed as the measure of sexual difference, the phallus is always already a castration. In the story's action, La Zambinella's ambiguous sexual identity (a castrato disguised as a woman) is treated by his/her entourage as a joke being played on the enamoured hero. As Barthes explains, this playing with sexual ambiguity castrates again by removing the "slash of separation" which established sexual difference. What Barthes accomplishes in his theoretical carvings and digressions in *S/Z* is the removal of the phallus-as-castration. There are, as Barbara Johnson has pointed out, two modes of castration for Barthes: the negative mode which reduces plurality to structures of binary opposition and univocal readings, cutting the multiple braid of the text's meanings; and a positive mode which functions as a cutting free, a cutting loose from all restrictive structures.[1]

Barthes describes, for example, the pleasure of reading an author like the Marquis de Sade:

> Sade: the pleasure of reading him clearly proceeds from certain breaks (or certain collisions): antipathetic codes (the noble and the trivial, for example) come into contact; [. . .] the language is redistributed. Now *such redistribution is always achieved by cutting.* Two edges are created: an obedient, conformist, plagiarizing edge (the language is to be copied [. . .]) and *another edge*, mobile, blank (ready to assume any contours), which is never anything but the site of its effect: the place where the death of language is glimpsed. [. . .] Neither culture nor its de-

struction is erotic; it is the seam between them, the fault, the flaw, which becomes so. (*Pleasure* 6–7)

Although his work does not celebrate the same erotics of textual pleasure that we find in Barthes, Burroughs' more detached and scientific cut-up method produces the same discontinuity and transgression, the same scandal of palpating the "Divide Line" and breaking open the packaged text. The solidity of the conventional mimetic text which generates "Identical Replicas" of the world or of the self is shaken by Burroughs' writings experiments which perforate and permutate all the "edges" of the discourse. Like de Sade, he makes breaks, collisions, and cuts through which the death of logocentric language and its methods of reproduction "can be glimpsed."

Derrida, too, plays with and against castration as part of his strategy to replace the rule of sexual dualism with an indeterminate anatomy and new modes of reproduction: "Dissemination 'is' this *angle* of the play of castration which does not signify, which permits itself to be constituted neither as a signified, nor a signifier, no more presents than represents itself, no more shows than hides itself. Therefore in and of itself it is neither truth (adequation or unveiling) or veil. It is what I have called the graphic of the hymen, which can no longer be measured by the opposition veil/nonveil" (*Positions* 86–87). In dissemination the phallus becomes a hymen; not in its negative sense as absent phallus, but as escape from duality, as the incalculable angle of the play *between*. The hymen is simultaneously that which separates desire from its fulfillment and the marriage consummation which removes the obstruction.[2] Instead of setting out in the mode of conventional analysis to fill every hole with the universal phallus (as Hartman puts it), Derrida proceeds by what he calls "invagination." This transsexual surgery moves beyond the mere reversal of sexual identity to the transcendence of sexual difference; invagination folds the outside in, creates a confusion of outside/inside, center/margin, male/female, dispersing all binary oppositions which follow in their wake. In his experimental writing Burroughs utilizes similar methods of cutting up (dismembering, castrating) and folding in (invagination) of multiple texts in order to disrupt conventional structures of binary opposition and power. The hymen and invagination are not so much markers of the ascendance of a female principle as they are emblems of something beyond the binary opposition of the sexes, beyond the conflict and domination to which sexual dualism leads.

In *Glas* Derrida confronts even more explicitly the repressive structures of family and reproduction and counters them with innovative forms of juxtaposition, interruption, cutting, and splicing. The two columns of the text, in which Derrida reproduces the words and ideas of Hegel and Genet, are forced into a kind of erotic intimacy, a peculiar mating device by which the philosopher and the novelist are alternated, reversed, and intermingled to produce a composite monstrosity equal to the most grotesque inventions of Rabelais or Burroughs.

In this hybrid text Derrida enacts the confrontation of two reproductive systems: one associated through Hegel with the father, family, genealogy, and property; the other associated through Genet with the mother, sexual perversion, the fetish, and theft. *Glas* reveals that what threatens procreation in the realm of Hegel is the dominance of the name of the father, the ossification of an ideology of absolute knowledge. Hegel's description of the erecting of India's phallic statues becomes emblematic of the paradox of a phallic hardening which procreates and perpetuates itself by means of its stoney sterility. As Derrida explains in the Genet column, however, the force which erects also entombs; the philosophic institutions which assimilate, interiorize, and idealize maintain themselves by embalming, entombing, inscribing the name of the father on the crypt. Derrida's relentless punning reminds us that the tomb (*tombe*) will eventually fall (*tombe*). While phallic columns are raised up in the Hegel column, the reproduction of tradition-name-self is fractured and scattered in the fragment which opens the Genet column: "what remains of a Rembrandt torn in neat little pieces, and screwed to the shithouse" (7b, my translation). If remains (the remains of Hegel and patriarchal history) are immortalized in one column, monumental tradition (Rembrandt) is reduced to ruins in the other. The phallic god is buried in excrement.

Burroughs assembles these same elements in a characteristic mosaic at the end of *Naked Lunch*: "So where is the statuary and the percentage? Who can say? I don't have The Word. . . . Home in my douche bag . . . The King is loose with a flame thrower and the king killer, tortured in effigy of a thousand bums, slides down skid row to shit in the limestone ball court" (*NL* 227). As in Derrida's *Glas*, the patriarchal figures of authority, truth, and power—the statuary, The Word, the King and his adversary—end up "screwed to the shithouse." Burroughs' narratives return repeatedly to images of young boys hardened into marble flesh or limestone mollusks, images of the dangerous sterility and numbness produced by the addictions of Western culture. In the mosaics of *Naked Lunch* and the cut-ups of the subsequent novels the statuary is exploded, the shell breaks open, the limestone hut crumbles in ruins to release and disseminate the imprisoned energy of the text.[3]

For Derrida and for Burroughs liberation from the monuments of Western culture, release from the laws which govern and restrict dissemination, can only be achieved by violent means. These conventional laws—Gayatri Spivak enumerates them as the laws of "genealogy and hence of textuality, of Law and hence of language, of sexual difference and hence of the phallus (plus or minus) as the signifier" ("*Glas*-Piece" 41)—operate by the threat of castration. As Barthes reveals in his reading of Balzac's "Sarrasine," the hero is castrated because his actions have been motivated by the *fear* of castration.

Derrida reasons similarly that the tactic to be used against what he calls "phallogocentrism" and its threat of castration is castration itself.

In removing the phallus from its powerful position as "transcendental signifier," Derrida makes the castrating gesture. As in Barthes's *S/Z*, Derrida's gesture of castration becomes a positive process leading to regenerative dissemination rather than impotence: "'"Dissemination *affirms* (I do not say produces or controls) endless substitution, it neither arrests nor controls play ('Castration—in play always . . .'). And in doing so, runs all the risks, but without the metaphysical or romantic pathos of negativity" (*Positions* 86). *Glas* can never be packaged for it adopts the economy of the plural text—the text as a continuous movement between two irreconcilable points, between Hegel and Genet[4]: "If I write two texts at once, you cannot castrate me. However much I delinearize, I erect. At the same time, I divide my act and my desire. I—show off the division and always escape you, I sham without intermission and come nowhere. I castrate myself—I hold myself thus—and I 'play at coming'" (77b). To escape castration, Derrida will castrate himself, and even as he accepts the double bind in which this action traps him, it is without anxiety, "in play": "For if my text is (were) impregnable, it will (would) not be taken nor held. Who would be punished in this economy of the undecidable? But if I lineate, if I set going a line and believe—nonsense—I am writing only one text at a time, it amounts to the same thing and it is still necessary to reckon with the cost of the margin. I gain and lose in each case my forked tongue" (77b). Derrida accepts the adventure of what he calls the "*genetic* indetermination [and] seminal adventure of the trace" ("Structure" 264). Derrida's place in the scattered family structure of *Glas* (in which Spivak recognizes Hegel as father, Genet as mother, and Derrida as child), is like Burroughs' place in his collective and anonymous cut-up narratives. Their place is a displacement, for both Derrida and Burroughs break the textual and genealogical chain to enter the "irreducible and *generative* multiplicity" of dissemination (*Positions* 45).

In *Anti-Oedipus*, Deleuze and Guattari similarly envision "active and positive lines of flight" beyond the structures of family drama, beyond Oedipal conflict and castration fear, flight into a "deterritorialized" and polymorphous realm of desire.[5] Reproduction in this realm takes place on the level of molecular conjunctions and disjunctions of fragments without fixed identity or gender. In this flow, castration and dismemberment lead miraculously and almost mockingly—as in the fertile world of Rabelais's imagination—to limitless production: "each partial object produces and cuts again, reproduces and cuts at the same time" (*Anti-Oedipus* 69). This sort of ubiquitous and inexhaustible metamorphosis which flows through and dissolves sexual dualism is at work in the seemingly effortless gender changes and asexual reproduction often depicted in Burroughs' work.

Deleuze argues in *Dialogues* that Anglo-American literature in particular aspires to *la fuite*—flight, escape, extension beyond organizational structures and fixed identity, flights of "becoming" (34). Such flights produce liberating metamorphoses which displace or decenter established patterns of power. Even for such alleged "phallocrats" as D. H. Lawrence or Henry Miller, Deleuze concludes, the writing process produces an alchemical transformation, a woman-becoming, a *devenir-femme* (55). In this process, the writer is aligned with the outside, with the margin, with minority, with the female. "Woman," Deleuze explains, is not the writer but the minority-becoming, the *devenir-minaurité*, of his or her writing. This radical feminist or minority impulse forms the vanguard of contemporary theory and, I would suggest, resembles in many ways the revolutionary energy behind the fiction of William Burroughs.

The Woman Question

To claim an alliance between Burroughs and feminist theory seems unlikely, if not perverse. For if one of his methods of resisting sexual dualism is to dismember or castrate the castrating power of sexual dualism, another method—simpler and more direct—is to eliminate women altogether from the arena of reproduction. Despite the apparent solidarity of the sexes (united as fellow victims of conventional modes of reproduction), Burroughs seems to blame women for the emergence of sexual dualism:

Q: How do you feel about women?
A: In the words of one of the great misogynist's plain Mr Jones, in Conrad's *Victory*: "Women are a perfect curse." I think they were a basic mistake, and the whole dualistic universe evolved from this error. (*Job* 116)

While Eric Mottram evades Burroughs' misogyny by stressing his relation to traditions of bisexuality, androgyny, and hermaphroditism,[6] there are those who speak of Burroughs' "tactical misogyny," implying that if he doesn't like women it is because he hopes for the appearance of the "new woman." Arguing rather bluntly against this position, Philippe Mikriammos insists that at worst Burroughs hates women and at best he envisions with a cold smile their disappearance (*William Burroughs* 101–2).

Burroughs has, in recent years, modified the sort of provocatively misogynistic statement that characterized his early attacks on sexual dualism. He insists in response to a reviewer of *The Place of Dead Roads*, "I have often said that it is not women *per se*, but the dualism of the male-female equation that I consider a mistake" (*New York Review* 45). It is nevertheless undeniable that women play little if any role in Burroughs' utopian fictions. His invention in *The Wild Boys* of an ideal race of male adolescents who have "never seen a

woman's face nor heard a woman's voice" and who reproduce by some mysterious method of parthenogenesis is just one example of Burroughs' readiness
to imagine a world without women.[7]

Although there is evidence that Burroughs *has* somewhat revised his attitude toward women since the 1970s, what is significant for an analysis of procreation in Burroughs' work is not his personal feelings about women, but
more specifically his response to the role assigned to women in the conventional modes of reproduction and family structure. For it is the figure of the
mother in particular who arouses his most vitriolic resentment, and it is through
his treatment of the mother that Burroughs' alleged misogyny takes some surprising and ironic turns.

Burroughs sees the matriarchal figure as the primary obstruction to innovative modes of reproduction. Her domination of reproduction and child rear-
ing is not only the central support of a repressive family structure but functions ultimately as the model for the national state. At each level—from
sexual reproduction, to family relations, to national boundaries—power is established by the dominance of a single group which represses all others. Burroughs recognizes this power structure in the ideology of the American South
and the dominant position of women within that culture: "This whole worship
of women that flourished in the Old South, and in frontier days, when there
weren't many, is still basic in American life; and the whole Southern worship
of women and white supremacy is still the policy of America. They lost the
Civil War, but their policies still dominate America. It's a matriarchal, white
supremacist country" (*Job* 122). The myth of the American South not only
represents an almost parodic exaggeration of sexual stereotypes, but it also
evokes the image of division and conflict within, of a struggle for survival
which pitted North against South, black against white, an old world of for-
malized traditions against a new and changing world. Burroughs aims some of
his most vicious early satires against this reactionary mentality, a mentality
locked into patterns of binary opposition and hierarchy. The goal of such reactionary thinking, which Burroughs associates with the American South, is
stasis: the perpetuation of established institutions and the repression of the
evolutionary energy which springs from desire.

Burroughs perceives that the mother, as defined by conventional notions of
sexual difference and family structure, is a necessary instrument in a larger
system of patriarchal power which seeks to dominate the individual from his
earliest moments of life. Using again a kind of oriental strategy of taking over
the weapons of the enemy, Burroughs seems to escape the tyranny of the
mother by appropriating her maternal and reproductive power for himself.[8]
More in the interest of explanation than justification, I would stress that much
of the violence against women in Burroughs' fiction can be best understood as
part of this strategy of assimilation: to take the place of the mother Burroughs

must first displace her. To take on the maternal role is to confuse both sexual dualism and family structure, to confound the power structures which limit and rule conventional reproduction.

We have seen something of this strategy in Barthes's privileging of the "grain of the voice" ("the materiality of the body speaking its mother tongue") over the laws of logocentrism (the symbolic realm of the father). Barthes associates the pre-Oedipal mother of the bodily realm with certain "pulsional incidents," a throbbing erotics of textual pleasure that may well seem as excessive, as forbidden and abject as anything in Burroughs' sexual Garden of Delights. Defying all taboo and propriety, Barthes asserts rather obscenely that the writer is playing always with the mother tongue, playing with his mother's body. Barthes's pursuit of bliss acknowledges no forbidden territory and charts an intimate course through the body of language itself.

Burroughs' relation to the mother's body is violent and destructive rather than erotic, but like Barthes he sees an intimate link between the maternal body and language. His simultaneous assimilation and rejection of the maternal produces some ambivalent and fascinating permutations in his fiction. In the following be-bop revision of *Hamlet* from *Naked Lunch*, for example, Burroughs dismantles and reshuffles conventional family structure and reproduction and at the same time scrambles the established form of the father's literary masterpiece:

> He turns into a Rock and Roll hoodlum: "I screw the old gash—like a crossword puzzle what relation to me is the outcome if it outcome? My father already or not yet? I can't screw you, Jack, you is about to become my father, and better 'twere to cut your throat and screw my mother playing it straight than fuck my father or *vice versa mutatis mutandis* as the case may be, and cut my mother's throat, that sainted gash, though it be the best way I know to stem her word horde and freeze her asset. [. . .] Male and female castrated he them. Who can't distinguish between the sexes. I'll cut your throat you white mother fucker. Come out in the open like my grandchild and meet thy unborn mother in dubious battle. Confusion hath fuck his masterpiece." (*NL* 40)

The threatening matriarchal "word horde" which is terminated by the decapitation of the mother ("I'll cut your throat") finds itself cut loose from the mother's body to become a liberating flood. Anatomically, the "sainted gash" which indicates the mother's vagina is displaced to her slashed throat, where the flood of language may be most economically released. The tyranny of one orifice (the mother's vagina) is dispersed by the creation of other holes which will restore free circulation.[9]

This convoluted logic is repeated in *The Soft Machine* where Burroughs "rewrites" Melville's *Billy Budd*. He invents a scene in which Billy's mother mysteriously takes over his body at the moment of his execution:

"Gentlemen," say Captain Verre "I can not find words to castigate this foul and unnatural act whereby a boy's mother take over his body and infiltrate her horrible old substance right onto a decent boat and with bare tits hanging out, unfurls the nastiest colors of the spectroscope."

A hard faced matron bandages the cunt of Radiant Jade—

"You see, dearie, the shock when your neck breaks has like an awful effect [. . .] It's a *medical fact*—All your female insides is subject to spurt out your cunt the way it turned the last doctor to stone [. . .].

"I have come to ascertain death not perform a hysterectomy," snapped the old auntie croaker munching a soggy crumpet with his grey teeth—A hanged man plummets through the ceiling of Lord Rivington's smart mews flat—Rivington rings the Home Secretary:

"I'd like to report a leak—"

"Everything is leaking—Can't stem it—*Sauve qui peut*" snaps the Home Secretary and flees the country disguised as an eccentric Lesbian abolitionist— (*SM* 170–71)

The irrepressible tide which flows from the mother's body or from the hanged body of Radiant Jade carries the narrative into the next routine. In the wake of the flood, the agent of repression—in the figure of the Colonialist "Home Secretary"—is driven from the occupied territory in a liberating skirmish of deterritorialization. The "word horde" which was originally associated with the dominating "bad" mother, is now a liberated and liberating tide which overflows all boundaries and releases from domination.

In the "Atrophied Preface" which concludes *Naked Lunch* Burroughs claims for himself the "word horde" he has associated with the ambivalently revered and despised maternal figure: "Now I, William Seward, will unlock my word horde" (230). He claims his identity as a writer by leaving behind his patronym, moving into and through the mother's body and assimilating its power. In *Junkie* Burroughs first identifies himself publicly as a writer by taking on his mother's family name, signing his first novel with the pseudonym "William Lee."[10] In the later cut-up novels he continues to identify himself primarily with the persona of Willy Lee, appearing as Inspector Lee of the Nova Police. Through his writing Burroughs becomes, in a sense, his own mother.

In his essay "The New Mutants," Leslie Fiedler notes a certain tendency toward what he calls feminization among American novelists of the sixties. He describes these writers as promoting a "post-male, post-heroic world" and anticipating a "post-Humanist sexuality." Burroughs emerges in his view as the "chief prophet" of a group of young men trying to "assimilate into themselves (or even to assimilate themselves into) that otherness, the sum total of rejected psychic elements which the middle-class heirs of the Renaissance have identified with 'woman'" (516). To be new men, he remarks, "these children of the future seem to feel they must not only become more Black than White but more female than male" (516). Fiedler seems to recoil from this tendency as from a dangerous flirtation with passivity, and he scolds "hetero-sexual writers [who] have permitted homosexuals to speak for them . . . even to invent the forms in which the future will have to speak" (521). Revealing his patriarchal perspective on sexual difference and reproduction, Fiedler elaborates on the analogy between this feminization and the worlds of homo-sexuality and drug addiction: "What could be more womanly . . . than per-mitting the penetration of the body by a foreign object which not only stirs delight but even (possibly) creates new life?" (522).

As a result of the developments in post-structuralism, deconstruction, and feminist theory in the last fifteen or twenty years, our understanding of the impulse to feminize discourse has advanced significantly beyond Fiedler's view of that phenomenon. In light of these more recent theoretical writings, Burroughs' relationship to the female and to the maternal appears much more suggestive and complex.[11]

In the context of a traditional patriarchal system like that invoked by Fiedler, the maternal body is present as the empty hole which must be filled by a universal and transcendental signifier (the phallus) or as the pregnant body of the text to be delivered of its meaning by the critic-physician. In con-trast to these carefully defined functions, the maternal body returns in radical contemporary theory—and surprisingly in the work of William Burroughs—in the fullness of its carnivalesque ambivalence: it is both the bottomless cask from which all life's abundance flows and the gaping maw of the grave. As we saw in the two parodies from *Naked Lunch*, the maternal body manifests itself simultaneously as language in the procreative fullness of play and as a threat-ening and destructive flood. The intrusion of the ambivalent image of the ma-ternal body into the patriarchal structures of Western thought is a disruption of the code, a scattering and disseminating of all that has been channelled and controlled.

Burroughs adopts an anti-patriarchal perspective from which he isolates sexual dualism as the basic problem in Western civilization and thought. There are some surprising affinities between this position and radical feminist the-ory. Julia Kristeva, for example, identifies a power which she calls "woman" as "something that cannot be represented, something that is not said, some-thing above and beyond nomenclatures and ideologies." Since it does not refer to anatomical difference, this revolutionary phenomenon can be discovered, she insists, even in the writing of certain men, particularly in those "modern texts" which test "the limits of language and sociality—the law and its trans-gression, mastery and (sexual) pleasure—without reserving one for males and the other for females" ("Woman" 137–38). The aversion to binary opposi-tion, to definitions and naming, to all repressive boundaries and laws which characterizes Burroughs' theoretical position has been ironically reinscribed by Kristeva under the sign of "woman."

In *La révolution du langage poétique*, Kristeva associates liberated discourse with the pre-oedipal phase of development, and consequently with the deterritorialized space of the mother's body, a realm outside of or anterior to patriarchal authority and regulation. She compares the artist's radical impulse toward "becoming-a-mother" to the risky indeterminacy of Heraclitus's flux or Epicurus's atoms: "Cells fuse, split and proliferate; volumes grow, tissues stretch, and body fluids change rhythm, speeding up or slowing down" ("Motherhood" 237). In this process which returns to us from a "prelinguistic, nonrepresentable memory" (239) we encounter a language which is at once ephemeral and nonsignifying. The collective, sexually indeterminate, constantly shifting permutations of Burroughs' experimental prose can be recognized in this redefinition of a maternal space in which sexual difference, identity, and language dissolve.

In the feminist poetics of Hélène Cixous we find something very much like those alternative modes of reproduction toward which Burroughs and other radical theorists aspire. Cixous replaces sexual dualism with infinite intersections, "a crowning display to new differences," "radical mutations" and the merging of many voices with the voice of the writer ("Sorties" 97). The mother still exists in this world, but she stands "outside her role functions: the mother as nonname and source of goods" ("Medusa" 251). Without a single name or under many names, the power of the creative mother stems from "the presence in the inventing subject of an abundance of the other, of the diverse . . . a springing forth of self that we did not know about—our women, our monsters, our jackals, our Arabs, our fellow-creatures, our fears" (97). The otherness Cixous identifies here with women and monsters is described elsewhere in her work as a mysterious "third one" who runs along the borderline, refusing inclusion in any binary structure (*Illa* 7). When the established structures have been thus thrown off balance, she argues, the poet "slips something by, for a brief span, of woman" ("Medusa" 249).

The similarities between Cixous and Burroughs are striking: their call for continuous evolutionary change and for open biological mutation; their desire for a collective, collaborative writing process; their habitation of the space between. The terms in which Cixous celebrates and identifies with the work of Jean Genet might easily be applied to Burroughs' experimental work as well: "a text which divides itself, breaks itself into bits, regroups itself, [possesses] an abundant, maternal, pederastic femininity" ("Sorties" 98).

Beyond Man, Woman, and Humanism

While this intersection of Burroughs with feminist theory is highly suggestive, there are basic obstacles to such an unlikely union. The feminization of discourse one may detect in Burroughs' fiction is never an end in itself, and such gestures as his assimilation of the maternal function are merely skirmishes in a larger battle, single lines of attack among many others. While he may promote a kind of sexual indeterminacy by playing with castration and with the mother's body, by inventing images of androgyny and hermaphroditism, Burroughs envisions ultimately the explosion of *all* bodies and texts in the constantly shifting gears of his inhuman writing machine. To achieve the most thorough dismantling of conventional modes of reproduction, the most radical dissemination of procreative energy, we must look beyond man, woman, and humanism.

Derrida draws his emblem for dissemination, for example, not from the human sphere, but from the operations of botanic reproduction, evolving a theory of procreation by "antherection." Outside of the human context of sexual difference and family structure, Derrida is free to elaborate this most radical rewriting of reproduction. Like grafting and pollarding, terms Derrida uses to describe intertextuality, antherection suggests the paradox of cutting off to add on, encouraging growth by amputation. Spivak explains how Derrida uses this notion to designate the filling up of the anther or seed pod with seeds, but also to suggest *anti*-erection, the necessary breaking or cutting open of the anther to release and scatter the seed. By a tortuous route of linguistic play, Derrida arrives at the assertion that in the logic of dissemination, castration is a prosthesis. Here is Derrida's text as presented within and alongside Spivak's valuable commentary and translation:

[Antherection] describes the cracked doubling (or reversal-displacement) structure. First, as the time of dissemination, for the fall of the anther must precede fertilization: "All this for nothing, for no effective insemination. The anther is the garment that encloses the pollen before fertilization . . . . What we shall from now on call *antherection*: time of the erection countered [contra-band], cut down by its contrary—in the place of the flower. Enanthiose [pun on *enantiosis*: saying one thing and meaning the opposite]. The repeated cutting crosses over indefinitely upon itself. Whence this effect of capitalization [columning as well as hoarding] but also of unlimited effusion" [146–49b]. [. . .]

Antherection is, then, a nickname for the detumescence that lets the seeds fly, where castration enables a sort of life to proliferate and continue as it is indefinitely diffused [. . .]. [As Derrida explains,] "One must not simplify the logic of antherection. It does not erect itself *against* or *in spite of* castration, *in despite of* the wound or the infirmity, castrating castration. It binds, castration [*ça bande, la castration*; the placing of the comma makes subject and predicate interchangeable here]. The infirmity itself is bandaged or bound [*se panse*: pun on *se pense* = "is thought"] to bind itself. That it is which, as one still says in the old language, *produces* erection: a prosthesis" [156–57b]. ("*Glas*-piece" 28–29)

Derrida's account of the expansive carelessness of the chance scattering of seed, "for nothing, for no effective insemination," describes a method of procreation which defies restrictive channelling and the market economy. Barthes has similarly described the scandalous text of bliss as "the trace of a cut, of an assertion (and *not of a flowering*)" (*Pleasure* 20). Barthes and Derrida imagine an insemination which need not culminate in or be justified by a final product, but which may lead to infinite disseminations, to the free circulation of texts, identities, and ideas.

Beyond Nature: The Machine

Finally, the botanical metaphor is insufficient for the kind of radical and monstrous births envisioned by Burroughs and by contemporary theorists at their most extreme. Their introduction of botanic or organic imagery to describe futuristic visions of new ways of writing and thinking is, more often than not, ironic.

The conventional notion of the organic blossoming of the text is perhaps most self-consciously parodied in Deleuze and Guattari's *Rhizome*. In this short text, the authors develop a comprehensive typology of literary texts based on three different methods of botanical growth: the conventional tap root text, the more daring modernist rootlet, and the radical rhizome text. The first two belong to structures of "arborescences," tree-like constructs which return every branch, arrange every outgrowth hierarchically around a center, origin, root. The rhizome formation, on the contrary, comprises an ideal decentered system, characterized by its continual circulation of states (*Rhizome* 62). The botanical analogy is driven underground here to reveal the structure *behind* or *beneath* the blossom. In their concept of the rhizome, Deleuze and Guattari move toward the notion of the text as a non-hierarchial network or system, as a complicated machine which expands beyond the confining myths of Western culture. The rhizome establishes a rapport with sexuality, with animal, vegetable, with natural and artificial things, with many becomings (63).

Burroughs shares with Deleuze and Guattari this vision of a network of conjunctions and disjunctions of desire extending well beyond human heterosexual reproduction or organic growth. As he explains in *The Job*, "It is simply a perception that sex is a very widespread phenomenon in the interconnection of living matter and non-living matter as well" (113). Burroughs' vision of pansexuality at times takes the form of a Yeatsian panorama of some omnipresent life force: "Pictures of men and women, boys and girls, animals, fish, birds, the copulating rhythm of the universe flows through the room, a great blue tide of life" (*NL* 81). In the cut-up novels, however, this flow becomes a more indeterminate series of ephemeral transformations produced by a vast machine: "The two beings twisted free of human coordinates rectums merging in a rusty swamp smell—spurts of semen fell through the blue twilight of the room like opal chips—the air was full of flicker ghosts who move with the speed of light through orgasms of the world—tentative beings taking form for a few seconds in copulations of light" (*TTTE* 7).

This free circulation of bodies is, of course, a corporeal model of what Burroughs is doing with texts and with language in the cut-up novels, where the copulating rhythm of the universe is displaced by the pulsating energy of his cut-up writing machine. One glimpses here the possibility of a regenerative convergence of destruction and creation not unlike that found in Rabelais and the carnival grotesque. One of the most striking differences between that earlier iconoclastic tradition and its modern counterpart is the shift from organic to mechanical models of reproduction.

Burroughs and radical theorists who construct similar alternative methods of reproduction acknowledge that in some basic way the organic model of fertility which formed the basis of the carnival grotesque is no longer viable. Organic reproduction and the fertile energies of the earth and the body have gradually become, since Rabelais, mere metaphors developed by Western culture to disguise its repressive mechanisms under what Barthes calls the "alibi of Nature." The life-giving flows of earthy fertility have been channelled and have atrophied in the service of artificial and arbitrary institutions of power. Barthes's image of the machinery of the writerly text as a telephone network gone haywire, Derrida's venture into futuristic technologies of communication in the "Envois" of *La Carte Postale*, and Burroughs' cut-up writing machine—all of these technological fantasies displace the organic model of reproduction with a vast mechanism of dissemination. Unlike the machinery of Western culture which channels creative life and desire into predetermined patterns, these radical machines of indeterminacy and chance never repeat themselves.

The most elaborate development of this machinery of desire and dissemination, the vision which perhaps comes closest to a contemporary version of the carnival grotesque, is Deleuze and Guattari's *Anti-Oedipus*. The parallels with Burroughs' experimental vision and methods are so striking here that Serge Grunberg has suggested that the French philosophers have failed to acknowledge a major debt to the American novelist for their conceptual framework.[12]

In their collaborative work Deleuze and Guattari attempt to deconstruct Western culture, to liberate desire by means of a new critical perspective which they call "schizoanalysis." Working against the restrictive channelling of desire into the enclosed theater of the family, into the rigid configurations of oedipal conflict and castration fear, they evolve a model for a machinery of desire which would produce continuous pulsations, flows, and breaks in every realm of human and non-human activity.

Anti-Oedipus calls for a purgative surgical procedure which would first remove all conventional constraints: "Destroy, destroy. The task of schizo-analysis goes by way of destruction—a whole scouring of the unconscious, a complete curettage" (311). As Rabelais's digestive purge preceded the imbibing of new knowledge, Deleuze and Guattari perform an abortion of the still-born corpus of Western culture. All repressive structures governing dualistic thought, mimetic representation, the structure of the family and genealogy, are dismantled. All value—stylistic, social, political, ontological—resides in the explosive energy of desire which continually produces and destroys itself.

In the high-tech utopia of desire envisioned in *Anti-Oedipus* there are no monuments, no fixed identities or totalities which might impose a hierarchy or a center. Everything circulates, connections are broken and reformed in perpetual metamorphoses. The subject is never fixed in body, name, or relation but is absorbed in an evolutionary flux: "It is a strange subject, however, with no fixed identity, wandering about over the body without organs, but always remaining peripheral to the desiring machines . . . being born of the states that it consumes and being reborn with each new state" (16). This free and uncertain subject escapes the claustrophobic enclosure of the family to pursue nomadic wanderings in an uncertain wilderness.

Such a peripheral and uncertain territory is not without dangers and shocks—it corresponds both to the monstrous freedom of the carnival and to the mad and marginal world of the abject. One recognizes in this nightmare world the shifting geography, the permutating architecture, and the dissolving identities of Burroughs' experimental fiction.

The conjunctions and disjunctions of Burroughs' fiction with the writings of radical contemporary theorists provide fertile, if uncertain, ground for a better understanding of both. As critical theory continues to move fearlessly into and through the uncharted and uninhabited realms explored by theorists like those considered in the preceding chapters, we may hope to rediscover and reevaluate more writers like William Burroughs, prophetic writers who have slipped through the gaps left by conventional, humanistic methods of literary judgment and analysis.

Afterword

William Burroughs' experimental writing elicits extreme responses from critics and readers. Some dismiss this phase of his career as a temporary aberration which he was to renounce (as he *did* renounce Scientology) once he had discovered its limits; others remain staunchly loyal to the cut-up techniques and the texts it produced, insisting that even the work which follows *Nova Express* is still rooted in this experimental method. The writer himself has a much more flexible attitude. Maintaining a healthy skepticism about his experimental writing, he insists even in early statements about the use of cut-ups that it may work for some writers and not for others, that it is to be understood as *experiment*, not as didactic argument or aesthetic platform. Burroughs never perceived the cut-up techniques as a system to live by but as a tool to be used and then discarded, like apomorphine. The overtly experimental writing style of the early novels never became, for him, an addiction. As he has remarked in another context, "I think anybody incapable of changing his mind is crazy" (Bockris 42).

Many critics see the change of direction in Burroughs' style after the cut-up novels as evidence that his experiments had led him to a "brilliantly lit dead end" (Solotoroff 253). The more moderate style of *The Wild Boys* and *Exterminator!* is welcomed as a mellowed and more temperate accommodation to convention. *Naked Lunch* and the cut-up trilogy appear to some, in retrospect, as Burroughs' repeated failure to produce the organically unified narrative which they perceive in *Cities of the Red Night*. From this perspective *Cities* is hailed as the apotheosis of Burroughs' career, and the renegade is welcomed back into the narrative fold. Ironically, a careful reading of *Cities* reveals that Burroughs is still using both montage and cut-up effects in that novel, and one wonders if the alleged dramatic shift in Burroughs' style is not actually a gradual evolution in what traditional critics will recognize and tolerate as successful narrative.

Burroughs himself presents the situation in much less dramatic terms. A harsh critic of his own writing, he declares *Nova Express* not wholly successful and finds *The Ticket That Exploded* contains too much undifferentiated cut-up material. He remarks dispassionately in an interview in 1965, "Occasionally I have the sensation that I'm repeating myself in my work, and I would like to do something different—almost a deliberate change of style" (Knickerbocker 164). In considering Burroughs' comments about his return to conventional storytelling, one sees clearly that he is a very pragmatic man. He insists repeatedly in interviews that the writer must consider his audience: "So, so far as writing goes, you can't get away from a narrative style altogether because they won't read it. . . . I just don't think there's any substitute for it. I mean—people want some sort of story in there. Otherwise they don't read it. What are they going to read? That's the point" (Skcrl "Interview" 11). With a very clear sense of the "rules to observe," Burroughs outlines the way to write a best seller: "You're aiming for the general public, and there are all sorts of things the general public doesn't want to see or hear. A good rule is never ask the general public to experience anything they cannot easily experience. You don't want to scare them to death, knock them out of their seats, and above all, you don't want to puzzle them" (Bockris 27). As an example of his own effort to find a subject matter that would have a broader appeal than the all-male adolescent utopia of *The Wild Boys*, Burroughs sketches out the plot of a novel which "concerns an incestuous family of father, mother, two brothers and two sisters—completely interchangeable sexual combinations. . . . Yes, I thought it might have more popular appeal" (Palmer 52). While such remarks could be taken at face value, I sense here a certain sly and mocking tone which should discourage reading them as the sober pronouncements of a reformed experimentalist.

It is certainly true that Burroughs never wanted to be the leader of an obscure avant-garde elite, that he would like to have more popular success. James Grauerholz—Burroughs' secretary, collaborator, and friend—stresses that his own most important contribution to the recent novels has been his insistence that Burroughs "should really make [them] have boundaries. . . . [*Cities*] has boundaries, it has a beginning . . . there are outside limits" (Zurbrugg, "Interview" 26). So Burroughs writes a novel with "a beginning, a middle and an end"; he quiets the audience with familiar continuities "to spare The Reader stress of sudden space shifts and keep him Gentle" (*NL* 218). We might see here another compromise not without its ironic or parodic intent, and certainly a compromise which still allows Burroughs to pursue his subversive vision.

Burroughs' dissection and scrambling of straightforward narrative in his experimental novels exposes, with clinical detachment, the nature and function of beginning, middle, and end. In *The Soft Machine*, he explores the obsessive repetition of fresh beginnings, new starts which are always haunted by the stale sense of familiarity; in *Ticket* he manipulates the passage of time, experimenting with alternatives to linear sequence; and in *Nova Express* he rehearses endlessly the features of "endingness" until they are turned inside out like the hide of a skinned rabbit. Having exposed and examined the beginning, middle, and end of narrative sequence, Burroughs may now feel free to return to traditional forms as an artistic *choice*, free of illusions and without any sense of coercion.

The goal of Burroughs' experimental writing in *Naked Lunch*, *The Soft Machine*, *The Ticket That Exploded*, and *Nova Express* is to bring to the writer (and to the reader as well) a total understanding of his medium, the word. The advanced training of the revolutionary cadets in *Ticket* enables them to slip their bodies on and off like interchangeable overcoats. It is possible that Burroughs the writer has come out of *his* experimental training with a control of language and literary convention which enables him to return "quite deliberately" to what he describes as "carefully elaborated" and "precise" narrative structure.

Burroughs has often suggested that conventional, even classical narrative form could be used to "escape the imprisonment of words and to achieve things that you think could not be achieved in words" (*Job* 55). The boundaries and limits of Burroughs' recent novels, then, may be no more than a mirage. It is perhaps too early, as Jennie Skerl has suggested, to decipher the subversive intentions at work in the current phase of Burroughs' writing. Careful and detailed analyses of his recent novels will have to be made before we can hope to penetrate beneath their polished surface. And who can anticipate in what new reincarnations William Burroughs may appear before the end of his literary career.

Notes

Chapter 1

1. Michael Goodman's *Contemporary Literary Censorship: The Case History of Burroughs' Naked Lunch* narrates the fascinating encounters between Burroughs' novel and the American legal system. Goodman fills in the often farcical scenarios of suppression and seizure of *Naked Lunch* from its earliest excerpts published in *Chicago Review*, to the litigation with the post office over the issue of *Big Table* containing sections of the novel, to the intervention of the customs office, and finally to the Boston censorship trial. Goodman also includes information and insightful chapters on the composition and critical reception of *Naked Lunch*.

2. Charles Russell similarly reprimands Burroughs for operating within such a self-enclosed semiotic context that his revolutionary aims are of "questionable efficacy" (37).

3. John Calder argues that Burroughs is a "scientist in literature who must have freedom to experiment," yet he continues to defend the author primarily as a moralist (*TLS* 947).

4. Mary McCarthy shares Lodge's view that Burroughs is a satirist whose aims are prescriptive, but she attributes the failure of *Naked Lunch* as moral instruction to the poetic power of Burroughs' style: "The book is alive, like a basketful of crabs, and common sense cannot get hold of it to extract a moral" (*Writing* 51). George P. Elliot makes an interesting distinction between Swift's satire, in which the ugliness is in the object being satirized, and Burroughs' work, in which the ugliness is in the style itself. The object under attack in Burroughs' fiction, as Elliot sees it, is the reader. While he seems to find Burroughs' desire to alter the reader's consciousness inferior to Swift's aim to incite his reader to reformative action, Elliot's distinction between the two authors underlines the extent to which Burroughs' writing focuses on language and communication, on the processes of reading and interpretation.

5. Mikriammos writes of *Naked Lunch*, "Vu, pensé, rêvé, imaginé, halluciné: pas de différences et de limites—tout est à prendre littéralement. Littéral contre littéraire . ." (*William Burroughs* 44).

6. Critics are divided on the significance of the shock effect of Burroughs' work. Lionel Abel argues that "nowadays" the only way for some people to feel in touch with reality is by means of shocking images like those in *Naked Lunch* (109–12); and Ronald DeFeo, writing nine years later, dismisses the novel as trash because social and legal changes have removed its "shock value" (150–53). On the other side of the issue,

Clive Bush argues that through Burroughs' work we learn that "our incapacity to face [Conrad's 'The horror! the horror!'] may exist in proportion to its power over us" (128). In other words, Burroughs' aim is not to shock us but to defuse the shock effect, the horror effect, of certain images.

7. Several critics adopt perhaps the most productive position that drug addiction in Burroughs' work is simultaneously figurative and literal: see Jerry Bryant in *The Open Decision* (199–228), R. G. Peterson in "A Picture is a Fact" (37), and Jennie Skerl in *William S. Burroughs* (36).

8. Jennie Skerl explains Burroughs' position as a recognition that we cannot get rid of body and word but we can regulate them (72). Burroughs describes in the *Rolling Stone* interview the "optional" position he eventually takes in regard to flesh as well as language: "The more precise your manipulation or use of words is, the more you know what you're actually dealing with, what the word actually is. And by knowing what it actually is, you can supersede it" (Palmer 53).

9. For a discussion of absence in Burroughs' style see Serge Grunberg (168).

10. Frank McConnell points out that "the images of Interzone tend toward an allegorization of the drug life (which for Burroughs, the poet, would be, of course, re-addiction), and are continually reduced to the anti-allegorical, minimal visions which are perhaps the single greatest imaginative triumph of *Naked Lunch*" (677).

Chapter 2

1. John Vernon's reading of the carny man story in *The Garden and the Map* is another good case in point. The overriding principal of "either- or polarities" (88) which he identifies as characteristic of Burroughs' style, is of course the binary grid through which his own psychoanalytic reading is channeled. While he is moving in the right direction when he focuses without flinching on the importance of the body in *Naked Lunch*, Vernon reads the text's body images as Burroughs' *reinforcement* of the polarities of hierarchical, binary thought: the body is divided into external/internal, into upper ("consciousness and a mental structure")/ lower ("sexual energies and anal violence"), and these divisions are cited as evidence of Burroughs' schizophrenic vision (94). When he comes to the talking anus story, Vernon reads the tale as an example of the triumph of one pole in this dualistic vision, as the body turning on and devouring itself (105).

2. Tony Tanner's *City of Words* contains one of the best discussions of Burroughs' work. For his analysis of the notion of language as power see particularly pages 117–18. See also Cary Nelson's excellent essay on Burroughs in *The Incarnate Word* (108–29) and John Tytell's *Naked Angels* (111–39).

3. Grunberg's analysis might be more fitting for a text like Diderot's *Bijoux Indiscrets*, in which a sultan acquires a magic ring which has the power to endow a woman's vagina with speech. By means of this device, Diderot exposes not only society's muzzling of desire (all the women of the court buy jeweled muzzles to silence their sexual orifices), but suggests that the voice of the body will always speak the uncensored truth. Burroughs' skepticism about the ability of *any* language to communicate truth would seem to make Grunberg's approach here inappropriate.

4. Derrida demonstrates in "Economimesis" how an idealist philosophy would transform both the lower body function and the outside world into internalized elements of the subjective self. The mouth rules, he explains, by a system of analogy which makes every other orifice of the body a mere semblance, an inferior imitation of the oral cavity (14–16).

5. As Mikriammos points out, there is no dialogue in *Naked Lunch*, just your need meeting with my need in speech (*William Burroughs* 54).

6. The final legal farce in Le Petomane's history involves a case of libel brought by his successor at the Moulin Rouge, a female petomane. This woman had been described in the press as a tasteless fraud for performing by means of a bellows hidden beneath her skirts. She lost her case, and thus saved Le Petomane the expense of pursuing his own legal action against this false usurper of his reputation and uniqueness.

7. On Burroughs' use of ventriloquy effects see Françoise Collin (63) and Mary McCarthy (*Writing* 46). Collin stresses the indeterminacy of the origin of the voice in Burroughs' narratives; McCarthy focuses more on the hostile or threatening quality of "ventriloquial voices produced, as it were, against the will of the ventriloquist, who has become their dummy." This general description of Burroughs' prose style is dramatized explicitly in the carny man story.

8. As Peter Michelson puts it, in the carny man story "function displaces humanity" (151).

9. Mikriammos describes two silences in Burroughs' work: one which carries the risk of sterility and the other which is a positive and generative force (*William Burroughs* 66).

10. Vernon describes the amputation of body and language in *Naked Lunch* as a "schizophrenic atomism," a living-in-fragments. While Vernon assesses this quality in a psychoanalytic context, I will trace it through language and rhetoric. The metonymic tendency Vernon describes here operates as a challenge to the metaphorical structures of totality, unity, and organicism which rule Western thought.

11. The most important critical texts would include Paul de Man's *Allegories of Reading*, Gérard Genette's *Figures III*, and David Lodge's *The Modes of Modern Writing*. All studies of metaphor and metonymy rely heavily on Roman Jakobson's essay "Two Aspects of Language and Two Types of Aphasic Disturbances." The only specific reference to metonymy in Burroughs' work is from the French camp. Serge Grunberg refers to an oscillation in Burroughs' novels between metaphoric and metonymic meanings (of the addict's needle, for example), but he seems to be using the rhetorical terms in a specialized psychoanalytic sense in which the oscillation is connected to narcissism (40, 59).

12. See, for example, Paul Ricoeur's "The Metaphoric Process as Cognition, Imagination and Feeling."

13. Lodge himself sees many of the problems posed by Jakobson's theory, particularly its neglect of the element of choice, and he offers a valuable redefinition of metonymy which would stress its poetic potential. As metaphor is associated with substitution, he argues, metonymy could be associated with deletion or with what he calls the "*condensations* of contexture" (*Modes* 76). What preserves the figurality of metonymy for Lodge is that the deletion is illogical or arbitrary. So the illogicality of metonymy would correspond in complexity and suggestiveness to the ambiguity of

metaphor. I think this is a crucial amendment to Jakobson, but oddly Lodge does not apply this insight in his analysis of *Naked Lunch*. For an excellent overview of what has been happening to metaphor and metonymy in critical theory see Hans Kellner's "The Inflatable Trope."

14. Mary McCarthy traces the scientific definition of the term "mosaic" which appears so often in *Naked Lunch*: "a plant-mottling caused by a virus." She goes on to describe Burroughs' planetary perspective in which "history shrivels into a mere wrinkling or furrowing of the surface, as in . . . one of those pieced-together aerial photographs known in the trade as (again) mosaics" (*Writing* 45). The mosaic style of *Naked Lunch*, for McCarthy, is directly linked to Burroughs' scientific and science-fiction vision, the vision which will dominate the cut-up novels.

15. Cohen's ingenious translation of Cervantes' puns in this section works out quite well for my analysis, but he has taken some liberties with the original. In the Spanish, Sancho misunderstands "equinoctial line" as *leña* (which means literally "firewood" but figuratively "rough play" or "a beating"). His confusion about Quixote's reference to the "computations of Ptolemy" produces the vulgar response: "que vuesa merced me trae [por testigo] de lo que dice a una gentil persona, puto y gafo, con la anadidura de meon, o meo, o no sé como" (210–11). Although Cohen's use of "amputation" as the play on "computation" does not appear here, Sancho's scrambling of Quixote's phrase is full of negative terms such as bugger, leper, and puling baby.

16. My allusion here is to Kafka's "On Parables," which plays with the notion of a special truth that is to be found only "in parable." For an extended and rather dazzling analysis of Kafka's text and a fruitful psychoanalytic development of the metaphor/metonymy opposition see Charles Bernheimer's *Flaubert and Kafka: Studies in Psychoanalytic Structure*.

17. In a very interesting study of literary metamorphosis, *The Gaping Pig*, Irving Massey contrasts the violence behind physical metamorphosis with the cooperative and synthesizing function of metaphor. Much of what he says about metamorphosis, defining it as a grotesquely literalized metaphor, is true of metonymy as it is used by Burroughs. Massey sees metamorphosis as hostile to binary opposition and as a "testimony to the sinister powers of language" (185–86). While metaphor bridges the gap between man and beast, he argues, metamorphosis imposes an inescapable physical continuity. In his reading of Ovid, Massey stresses the author's replacement of the fixed structure of "stable moral principles" with a metamorphic energy, an "irresistible and largely meaningless violent change, usually impelled by erotic forces" (23). One can see the parallels between this opposition of morality and erotic energy and the opposition of metaphoric closure and metonymic drive within a narrative like Burroughs' *Naked Lunch*.

18. While metaphorical naming is seen in conventional rhetoric as leading to the expansion and elevation of the self, the reductive pinch of metonymic naming most often takes the form of attack or insult. Consider the difference between the metaphorical predication of "she's brainy" or "he's ballsy" and the metonymic insult of being dubbed "a brain" or "a prick." The metaphorical "man is an ass" by means of which Cervantes elevates and enriches our world and our image of ourselves becomes in Burroughs' fiction the unpleasant metonymic assertion that "man is an asshole."

19. See, for example, Paul Ricouer's "Metaphor and the Main Problem of Hermeneutics."

20. Georges Poulet gives a very similar description of reading as enforced ventriloquy: "[Here] I am thinking a thought which manifestly belongs to another mental world, which is being thought in me just as though I did not exist. [. . .] this *thought* which is alien to me and yet in me, must also have in me a *subject* which is alien to me. [. . .] Whenever I read, I mentally pronounce an *I*, and yet the *I* which I pronounce is not myself" (56). For Burroughs, the alien 'I' of the text is not the voice of the author but of language.

21. This idea of Burroughs' text as a subtraction machine appears in Ihab Hassan's "The Subtracting Machine" (16) and in Mikriammos's *William Burroughs* (8). Both critics are playing here on the fact that Burroughs' paternal grandfather made an important advancement in the design of the modern adding machine.

22. For an analysis of the significance of the interstice in Burroughs' style see Marshall McLuhan's "Notes on Burroughs" (518).

Chapter 3

1. Serge Grunberg elaborates on Burroughs' use of the "metaphor" of the magnetic band (138). Although his "dream analysis" method leads him repeatedly into this sort of figurative transcription of Burroughs' efforts to make the word concrete and literal, Grunberg's speculations are always provocative and insightful.

2. See Nicholas Zurbrugg's "Burroughs, Barthes, and the Limits of Intertextuality." Zurbrugg pursues a detailed comparison of intertextuality in deconstruction and in Burroughs' work, with some particularly interesting observations about the latter set in the context of performance art and "intermedia."

3. Tytell argues that although the cut-up narratives share the same vision, Burroughs is always *extending* that vision (135).

4. Mikriammos argues that Burroughs' work does not consist, as some critics have claimed, of lazy and mechanical repetition, but that he perfects the use of "*déjà lu*" ("already read") for maximum effct (52).

5. Burroughs draws this notion from Wilhelm Reich's theories about human orgasm. See Reich's *The Function of the Orgasm* (New York: Noonday Press, 1971).

6. Gaétan Brulotte describes Burroughs' scrapbook device: "Le scrapbook c'est en effet, comme son nom l'indique, le 'livre' du *scrap*, c'est-à-dire un recueil de morceaux, de fragments, de bribes, de rebuts, et en même temps, le *scrap* du livre, sa démolition même, la déchéance de sa fonction (qui est la communication d'un sens diégétiquement structuré) . . . . Le scrapbook est donc un lieu d'accumulation, l'exhibition d'une épaisseur, d'une massification . . . . Et la technique du cut-up lui parut comme le moyen rêvé d'augmenter la production des textes" (34–35).

7. In David Lodge's *The Novelist at the Crossroads* (210) and Alvin Seltzer's *Chaos in the Novel* (330–35) we find two typical examples of literary critics' distress at Burroughs' use of chance in his compositons.

8. In *The Job* Burroughs acknowledges that "John Cage and Earl Brown have carried the cut-up method much farther in music" (33). Tanner (128), Hassan ("Silence" 78), and Kostelanetz ("Nightmare" 129) discuss Burroughs' affinity with Cage and other artists using chance techniques for composition.

9. I have borrowed and revised Michael Riffaterre's description of the "automatism effect" practiced by Dada and Surrealist writers to suggest that Burroughs' achieve-

ment is similarly to have created the *effect* or *illusion* of indeterminacy for the reader: "automatism effect [is] what makes the appearance of automatism (regardless of whether this appearance is obtained naturally or by artifice)" (224). Lemaire argues, similarly, that Burroughs' cut-ups "reach a point *indicative of* unreadability" (20).

Chapter 4

1. Jennie Skerl attributes the limitations of the cut-up technique in *The Soft Machine* to the fact that it "analyzes existing structures and breaks them apart but does not produce a new order" (57). Hassan says of the novel, "The theory no doubt, is attractive. Its results, however, often appear banal or inchoate; and in long stretches of the book gibberish prevails over revelation" ("Subtracting" 15).

2. After completing my own work on the cut-up novels, I read Michael Skau's excellent essay, "The Central Verbal System: The Prose of William Burroughs." Skau focuses on many of the same devices which I discuss here, and gives helpful examples of Burroughs' distortions of the shape of the page, of conventional spelling and syntax, and his use of refrains. See also Oxenhandler on the counterpoint between refrains and the "deeper rhythm" in the surrounding text (183).

3. This strategy of speed up to explosion appears throughout Burroughs' work in increasingly technological form. An orgy in *Soft Machine*, for example, is broken up by a rebel who seizes control of the projector; half the spectators are eventually caused to explode "from altered pressure chunks of limestone whistling through the air" (83). In *Nova Express*, Burroughs describes many similar tape and film experiments which apply this same rhythmic weapon against the word, the body, and time, "in explosive bioadvance out of space to neon" (130). The use of alternating rhythm patterns is the basic stylistic device of *The Ticket That Exploded*, and will be discussed in detail in chapter 5.

Chapter 5

1. Jennie Skerl discusses the accentuation of technology in *Ticket*, contrasting the gangster and vampire images of *The Soft Machine* with the virus and film metaphors of *Ticket*.

2. Cary Nelson and Michael Skau both approach Burroughs' cut-up narratives as a challenge to conventional methods of reading. See also Tony Tanner (130), and Lemaire (14).

3. Several critics discuss Burroughs' use of alternation or pulsating rhythms. Oxenhandler links this quality to a tradition of writers of "ambivalence and indeterminacy" (like Kafka and Beckett) for whom there is no contradiction, only flux (199). Vernon discusses Burroughs' alternating expansion and contraction of space, rather than rhythm (91).

4. For a more detailed summary of the nova mythology see Skerl 50–52 and 58–63.

5. See Michael Skau's analysis of the popular song lyric cut-up (406).

6. See Craig Werner's *Paradoxical Resolutions* for a discussion of this same section of *Ticket* (114–19). Werner argues against Ihab Hassan's assertion that Burroughs is aiming for bodiless silence, and he cites the events in the basement and loft as ex-

amples of the "bodied silence" he feels is Burroughs' goal. Werner's theory that in *Ticket* Burroughs "urges physical sexual consummation as an antidote to ghost eroticism" (117) is convincing, and he elaborates clearly and insightfully on the entire system of negative or absent power which manipulates human life in the novel. I think, however, that he stops short of the final stage of Burroughs' program, which is ultimately the escape from the body through the exhaustive exposure of its pleasure and pain. This escape *almost* succeeds in the "silence to say goodbye" chapter of *Ticket* which I will discuss below.

7. See E. E. Cummings, *Complete Poems: 1913–62* (276). For a stylistic comparison of Burroughs and Cummings see James Tanner's "Experimental Styles Compared."

8. This image of the black hole persists even in Burroughs' recent work, *Cities of the Red Night*. This narrative is initiated by "a black hole, a hole in the fabric of reality" (26) and terminates in a spinning and spiraling anus which becomes another "BLACK HOLE" (329), a hole "blown . . . in time with a firecracker" (332). For a fine analysis of this novel and the significance of its holes and gaps, see Steven Shaviro's "Burroughs' Theatre of Illusions: *Cities of the Red Night*."

9. This combination of dashes and ellipses is also characteristic of Céline's most experimental writing, a resemblance noted by Skerl (70). Julia Kristeva's study of Céline, *Powers of Horror*, discusses many of the same stylistic effects I have found in Burroughs' prose.

Chapter 6

1. Alan Ansen describes Burroughs' "distinguishing feature [as] the mania for contacts. One sometimes feels that for him drugs and sex exist only to provide opportunities for making appointments. It is a revealing clue to his tremendous isolation" ("Frying pan" 66). Mottram associates the "melancholy within the borderlands" of Burroughs' fiction with the sensibility one finds in Kafka's diaries and fiction. He quotes Kafka's confession, "I have but very rarely crossed out of this borderland between loneliness and community; I have taken root in it more than in loneliness itself" (29).

2. With a good deal less anxiety, it would seem, Derrida too asks us in *La Carte Postale* to imagine a postal system in which no communication would ever arrive at its destination, a system which would consist only of relays and deferrals. The aim of this "mise en abîme" is to destroy the postal system as we know it: a system based on the specific identities of senders and recipients (72). Derrida, like Burroughs, would usher in a new age of technological and collective modes of discourse.

3. Even (or especially) such direct statements as these fail to escape Burroughs' self-conscious ambivalence about writing as a means of self-expression and making contact. In the first example it is not Burroughs who describes his "purpose" in writing *Naked Lunch*, *The Soft Machine*, and *Nova Express*, but Inspector Lee, a fictional character based on Burroughs' first pseudonym, Willy Lee. So while Burroughs seems at first to be reporting unequivocally his authorial intentions, when we look for him in the text he isn't exactly there. In the second instance, it is more than likely that Burroughs' "creeping opponents" have given up reading his works long before he provides them with this helpful, if somewhat hostile, clarification of his intentions.

4. See Anthony Hilfer's "Mariner and Wedding Guest in William Burroughs' *Naked*

Lunch" for an interesting reading of Burroughs' aggressive capturing and manipulation of his audience. See also Michael Leddy's "Departed have left no address." Leddy traces Burroughs' anxiety about self-revelation and his relationship to the reader through the different meanings of the word "deposition." Etymologically the word suggests both concealing *and* revealing of the self, and with some license, Leddy suggests, might be said to indicate a "put-down" (de-position) of the reader.

5. On the role of collaboration in Burroughs' work see Mikriammos (*William Burroughs* 28–29), Skerl (71–72), and Mottram (19–20). It is clear from these critics' summaries of the pattern of Burroughs' writing career that collaboration served repeatedly to "cure" the author of writing blocks and of his disappointment in what he had already written.

6. Burroughs worked once as a copywriter, a profession which demonstrates perhaps the inherent deceptions practiced by all "copy-writing," all mimetic representation which produces an artificial imitation of the world. Things are never quite what they are represented to be in the context of advertising, as Burroughs shows us in the "Trak Trak Trak" parody in *The Soft Machine* (35–36). The relation of copywriting to copyrighting is also suggestive of the mistaken way language is treated as commodity to be bought and sold. Burroughs' use and abuse of found texts is very similar to the interrogation of textual authority by contemporary literary theory. Barthes's distinction between the conventional literary "work" and the radical literary "text" is based on the association of the former with fathering, ownership, and copyright (*Image* 160). The most relentless and witty play on the notion of copyrighting is probably Derrida's skirmish with Searle in "Limited Inc."

7. Mottram discusses Burroughs' discovery of Dutch Schultz's last words as an example of a found text (15). The affinity between the cut-up style and the patterns of the dying man's delirium suggests that Burroughs' method is in some way a confrontation with death, and a way of passing beyond it.

8. In her article "At the Margin of Discourse: Footnotes in the Fictional Text," Shari Benstock sees the use of footnotes by Fielding, Sterne, and Joyce as a way of raising questions about textual authority. She argues that the technique itself reveals an intense ambivalence on the author's part toward text, speaker, and audience. Benstock's article not only corroborates my general remarks about the structural significance of footnotes, but her specific readings of *Tristram Shandy* and *Finnegans Wake* uncover a pattern of the ultimate convergence of multiple lines of discourse which will also be evident in *Nova Express*.

9. See Allan Johnston's "The Burroughs Biopathy: William S. Burroughs' *Junky* and *Naked Lunch* and Reichian Theory" (107–20).

10. For a similar play on the authority of signatures see Derrida's "Signature Event Context" (194).

11. Mottram quotes the phrase "my writing arm is paralyzed" as evidence of Burroughs' exhaustion at the end of the trilogy which has "drained off too much energy"(109), rather than as a rejection of the writing addiction.

Chapter 7

1. For a discussion of Barthes's understanding of "third meanings" in Eisenstein's film stills see Zurbrugg's "Burroughs, Barthes" (91–92).

Chapter 8

1. Michel Serres had, in fact, been working on these ideas since the mid-sixties. See, for example, *Hermes Vol. I: La Communication* (Paris: Minuit, 1968) which contains essays Serres wrote at least as early as 1966.

Chapter 9

1. For a discussion of the role of "voice" in Burroughs' written style and in his distinctive manner of reading his work in performance, see Mikriammos's "Vox Williami, vox monstruorum." Mikriammos identifies the voice as the invisible body which carries language from inside the body, from inside the cacaphony of the body's many sounds. It is the voice which establishes and links the biological body and the body of language (100). Burroughs' work stresses that connection. In Burroughs' recordings of his narratives Mikriammos hears the labored intake of breath with which Burroughs begins each phrase, as though indicating his intense ambivalence toward the necessity of speech. Or perhaps, he speculates, the writer breaths loudly as one does before spitting or whistling—in order to seize the audience's attention. Voice and breath are made concrete and audible by Burroughs to draw our attention to their function as the ceaseless coming and going between the world and the self (102). Finding in Burroughs' style of speech a minimal use of the lips and an intensification of the impression that the voice comes directly from the throat, Mikriammos connects the American writer with Roland Barthes' notion of the "grain" of the voice (103).

2. Burroughs' critics may be divided into those who perceive him as committed to—even obsessed with—the body (McLuhan, Fiedler, Werner) and those who perceive him as anti-body (Nelson, Hassan). Grunberg describes Burroughs' radical writing as a means of access to another body, a new body (of the page and of the flesh) which will be liberated, plural, born through silence but generating its own language (81, 127).

Chapter 10

1. Grunberg makes some very interesting comparisons between Marx and Burroughs (32–34). The notion of Burroughs' relation to an economy of writing, digesting, and reproducing is also explored by Bush (128) and McConnell (675–78).

2. See Nelson (221) and Brulotte (34–41) for a discussion of this connection in Burroughs' work, and Octavio Paz's *Conjunctions and Disjunctions* for a more general discussion of the association of language and excrement (19–23).

3. Grunberg discusses constipation as a side effect of heroin addiction, proposing some ingenious psychoanalytic readings of such indigestion (48, 54, 82).

4. I refer here to Ehrmann's essay "Le dedans et le dehors," a brilliant analysis of patterns of binary opposition in *Gulliver's Travels*. Ehrmann explores Swift's iconoclastic attacks on social, philosophical, medical, and political abuses perpetrated by dualistic thinking, but he concludes his essay with the sad discovery that Swift himself is ultimately drawn into the same patterns of thought. He finds that contemporary theory, too, is often imprisoned within binary opposition (40).

5. I acknowledge a large debt here to Guyatri Spivak's analysis of *Glas* in *"Glas*

piece" and I am particularly indebted to her for the translations of Derrida's text which I quote in this and the following chapter. Page references cited after these translated passages refer to the original French text. In addition to Spivak's work on Derrida, I have found helpful readings of *Glas* in Geoffrey Hartman's *Saving the Text* and Maria Ruegg's "The End(s) of French Style."

Chapter 11

1. See Barbara Johnson's "The Critical Difference" (2–9).

2. See Derrida's discussion of the "hymen" in *Dissemination* (220).

3. In a letter to Allen Ginsberg, Burroughs contrasts the beauty of Venice, "a dream congealed in stone. And it is someone else's dream. The final effect is to me nightmarish—" with the constantly "changing combinations" which make up the beauty of Tangier. "No stasis horrors here," he concludes (*Letters* 154).

4. For this section of *Glas* I have borrowed Vincent Leitch's translation. See his *Deconstructive Criticism* (205–10).

5. Leslie Fiedler has suggested a parallel somewhat closer to home for Burroughs in Norman O. Brown's projected sexuality of the future in *Love's Body*. I am more convinced by Mottram's argument that Burroughs' work is ultimately anti-sexual (129). He quotes the novelist's assertion that "speaking for myself, the one thing I find sexy is creation, to create on paper a sexy person—sexy to me that is. And if it is a real creation, it will be interesting to other readers as well" (201).

6. Eric Mottram has pursued more fully Burroughs' relation to the religious and literary traditions associated with bisexuality, androgyny, and hermaphroditism (163–73). He sees beyond Burroughs' overt misogyny the desire for an "alchemical hermaphroditic power" which has its roots in many ancient civilizations and which re-emerges in the American tradition of self-reliance and self-sufficiency. This tradition, he claims, "comes to fruition" in Burroughs' work.

7. Burroughs has remarked in relation to the idea of all-male communities that lesbians should be free to form similar homogeneous groups. Catherine Stimpson has pointed out that Burroughs alone, among the "beat" writers with whom he is often linked, is able to consider the idea of lesbianism without horror, and even with a certain relief ("The Beat Generation" 392). Stimpson suggests that Burroughs' indifference is in the end less manipulative and repressive of women than the ambivalent and ultimately dehumanizing veneration of women by bisexual or heterosexual men.

8. Kristeva makes a similar argument about Lautréamont's efforts to usurp the maternal function (*La révolution du langage poétique* 319–34, 464–69).

9. The most direct intersection of Burroughs with feminist theory is Françoise Collin's "Coupes/coupures." She discusses the general horror of birth as the desire to be one's own origin, and finds in Burroughs in particular the desire to be his own mother. She describes his efforts to "remplacer le trou originel par un autre trou" (71). Writing is for Burroughs, Collin asserts, a substitute for birth: "Le corpus de l'oeuvre burroughsienne comme corps an-historique, morcelé, acentrique, est un corps-femme. Il ne se symbolise pas dans un organe. Il ne prend pas origine dans un moment. C'est un corps sans organes? Un corps sans l'Organe" (72). She sees Burroughs' fiction staged in a night of limitless space-time, a uterine space (67). Neil Oxenhandler sees the war

between the sexes as an externalization of the inner struggle in the child between oral (submission to the mother) and anal (submission to the father). He sees Burroughs as freeing himself from his pre-oedipal mother by becoming his own mother, feeding himself with words, transmuting the passive reception of pain to active enjoyment of it (192, 198). Serge Grunberg's Lacanian reading of Burroughs' misogyny leads him to perceive his rejection of the mother as a rejection of the spoken word (96), as a denial of the giver of milk, of the mirror, of language, a denial of the civilizing mother (68, 112).

10. For an interesting discussion of Burroughs' maternal inheritance, see Skerl (2–3). Skerl describes the Lee technique practiced by Burroughs' maternal grandfather (a liberal Methodist Episcopal pastor) and his maternal uncle (an early public-relations man and apologist for capitalism): "Ivy Lee was a conciliator who taught his clients to acknowledge public opinion and accommodate social change in order to preserve their power. Lee . . . believed that the way to persuade the masses was through 'symbols and phrases' not reason and facts. Lee was often attacked by radicals and reformers who denounced him as a sinister manipulator." Skerl's impression of the trilogy of Burroughs' experimental novels is that in these works he "seems to acknowledge, and at the same time, ironically reject the Lee heritage in his use of the family name as a pseudonym." She describes his political stance, given his particular family history, as "the rebellion of a disaffected insider." Perhaps this same ambivalence is at work in Burroughs' simultaneous identification with and rejection of the maternal power within himself.

11. Since this book went to press I have read Alice A. Jardine's fascinating study, *Gynesis: Configurations of Woman and Modernity.* I have clearly taken some liberty, and avoided the complexities of the issue, in describing Kristeva and Cixous as radical feminist theorists. The phenomenon I identify here in Burroughs' work and in contemporary theory would more accurately be designated as what Jardine calls "gynesis": a settling on "the concept of 'woman' or 'the feminine' as both a metaphor of reading and topography of writing for confronting the breakdown of the paternal metaphor—a tool for declaring war in the Image" (34). Ironically, Jardine discusses Burroughs briefly on the final pages of her book, but because she is contrasting American and French patterns of thought, I think she is led to underestimate his affinity with the continental theories she associates with gynesis.

12. The closest American parallel to the radical theory of Deleuze and Guattari is the "hipsterism" movement. See Skerl (2–11) for a discussion of the elements of indeterminacy, flux, energy, and transgression associated with this period and its artistic output.

Works Cited

Abel, Lionel. "Beyond the Fringe." *Partisan Review* 30 (Spring 1963): 109–12.

Adams, Robert. Review of *The Soft Machine*. *Hudson Review* 15.3 (Autumn 1962): 420–30.

Ansen, Alan. "Anyone who can pick up a frying pan owns death." In *White Subway*. William Burroughs. London: Aloes seolA, 1965: 64 71. Originally published in *Big Table* 2 (Summer 1959): 32–41.

Bakhtin, Mikhail. *Rabelais and His World*. 1965. Trans. Helene Iswolsky. Cambridge, Mass.: MIT Press, 1968.

Barthes, Roland. *Image-Music-Text*. 1961–75. Trans. Stephen Heath. New York: Hill and Wang, 1977.

———. *Mythologies*. 1957. Trans. Annette Lavers. New York: Hill and Wang, 1972.

———. *The Pleasure of the Text*. 1973. Trans. Richard Miller. New York: Hill and Wang, 1975.

———. *Roland Barthes*. 1975. Trans. Richard Howard. New York: Hill and Wang, 1977.

———. *S/Z*. 1970. Trans. Richard Miller. New York: Hill and Wang, 1974.

Benstock, Shari. "At the Margin of Discourse: Footnotes in the Fictional Text." *PMLA* 98.2 (March 1983): 204–25.

Bernheimer, Charles. *Flaubert and Kafka: Studies in Psychopoetic Structure.* New Haven: Yale University Press, 1984.

Bingham, Madeline. Letter to *Times Literary Supplement* 3228 (10 Jan. 1964): 27.

Bockris, Victor. *With William Burroughs: A Report from the Bunker*. New York: Seaver, 1981.

Borges, Jorge Luis. *Labyrinths*. New York: New Directions, 1964.

Brulotte, Gaétan. "Le déchet." In *Le Colloque de Tanger*, edited by Gérard-Georges Lemaire, 29–44. Paris: Christian Bourgeois, 1976.

Bryant, Jerry H. *The Open Decision: The Contemporary American Novel and Its Intellectual Background*. New York: The Free Press, 1970.

Burgess, Anthony. Letter to the *Times Literary Supplement* 3227 (3 Jan. 1964): 9.

———. *The Novel Now: A Guide to Contemporary Fiction*. New York: Norton, 1967.

Burroughs, William S. *The Book of Breeething*. Berkeley: Blue Wind, 1975.

———. "Censorship." *Transatlantic Review* 11 (Winter 1962): 5–10.

———. *Cities of the Red Night*. New York: Holt, Rinehart and Winston, 1981.

———. *The Exterminator*. With Brion Gysin. San Francisco: Auerhahn, 1960.

————. *Exterminator!* New York: Viking Press, 1973.

————. *The Job.* With Daniel Odier. New York: Grove Press, 1970.

————. *Junkie: Confessions of an Unredeemed Drug Addict.* [By "William Lee."] New York: Ace Books, 1953.

————. *The Last Words of Dutch Schultz: A Fiction in the Form of a Film Script.* London: Cape Goliard, 1970.

————. Letter to *New York Review of Books* 19 (July 1984): 45.

————. *Letters to Allen Ginsberg, 1953–1957.* New York: Full Court, 1982.

————. *Minutes to Go.* With Sinclair Beiles, Gregory Corso, and Brion Gysin. Paris: Two Cities, 1960.

————. *Naked Lunch.* 1959. New York: Grove Press, 1966.

————. *Nova Express.* New York: Grove Press, 1964.

————. *The Place of Dead Roads.* New York: Holt, Rinehart and Winston, 1983.

————. *The Soft Machine.* 1961. New York: Grove Press, 1967.

————. *The Third Mind.* With Brion Gysin. New York: Viking Press, 1978.

————. *The Ticket That Exploded.* 1962. New York: Grove Press, 1968.

————. *White Subway.* London: Aloes seolA, 1965.

————. *The Wild Boys.* New York: Grove Press, 1971.

————. *The Yage Letters.* San Francisco: City Lights Books, 1963.

Bush, Clive. "Review article: An Anarchy of New Speech: Notes on the American Tradition of William Burroughs." *Journal of Beckett Studies* 6 (Autumn 1980): 120–28.

Cage, John. *Silence.* Middletown, Conn.: Wesleyan University Press, 1973.

Calder, John. Letter to *Times Literary Supplement* 3221 (21 November 1963): 947.

Caradec, F., and Jean Nohain. *Le Petomane.* Trans. Warren Tute. Los Angeles: Sherbourne Press, 1968.

Cataldo, Peter J. "An Underfed Pest." *Chronicles of Culture* (April 1983): 43–44.

Cervantes Saavedra, Miguel de. *El Ingenioso Hidalgo Don Quijote de la Mancha.* Madrid: Espasa-Calpe, 1957.

————. *The Adventures of Don Quixote.* Trans. J. M. Cohen. New York: Penguin, 1950.

Ciardi, John. "Book Burners and Sweet Sixteen." *Saturday Review* 42 (27 June 1959): 22.

Cixous, Hélène. *Illa.* Paris: Des Femmes, 1980.

————. "The Laugh of the Medusa." 1975. Trans. Keith Cohen and Paula Cohen. In *New French Feminisms,* edited by Elaine Marks and Isabelle Courtivron, 245–64. Amherst: University of Massachusetts Press, 1980.

————. "Sorties." 1975. Trans. Ann Liddle. In *New French Feminisms,* edited by Elaine Marks and Isabelle Courtivron, 90–98. Amherst: University of Massachusetts Press, 1980.

Collin, Françoise. "Coupes/coupures." In *Le Colloque de Tanger,* edited by Gérard-Georges Lemaire, 63–72. Paris: Christian Bourgeois, 1976.

Creely, Robert. "A New Testament." *A Quick Graph,* 327. San Francisco: Four Seasons Foundation, 1970.

Culler, Jonathan. *On Deconstruction: Theory and Criticism after Structuralism.* Ithaca: Cornell University Press, 1982.

————. *The Pursuit of Signs: Semiotics, Literature, Deconstruction.* Ithaca: Cornell University Press, 1981.

Cummings, E. E. *Complete Poems: 1913–62.* New York: Harcourt, Brace, Jovanovich, 1972.

Davis, Robert. Review of *Ticket. Hudson Review* 16.3 (Summer 1963): 280–89.

Day, Dorothy. Letter to *Times Literary Supplement* 3228 (10 Jan. 1964): 27.

De Feo, Ronald. *Modern Occasions* (Winter 1972): 150–53.

Deleuze, Gilles. *Sacher-Masoch: An Interpretation.* Trans. Jean McNeil. New York: George Braziller, Inc., 1971.

Deleuze, Gilles, and Félix Guattari. *Anti-Oedipus: Capitalism and Schizophrenia.* 1972. Trans. Robert Hurley, Mark Seem, Helen Lane. New York: Viking Press, 1977.

————. *Rhizome.* Paris: Editions de Minuit, 1976.

Deleuze, Gilles, and Claire Parnet. *Dialogues.* Paris: Flammarion, 1977.

De Man, Paul. *Allegories of Reading: Figural Language in Rousseau, Nietzsche, Rilke, and Proust.* New Haven: Yale University Press, 1979.

Derrida, Jacques. *La Carte Postale: de Socrate à Freud et au-delà.* Paris: Flammarion, 1980.

————. *Dissemination.* 1972. Trans. Barbara Johnson. Chicago: University of Chicago Press, 1981.

————. "Economimesis." 1975. Trans. R. Klein. *Diacritics* 11 (1981): 3–25.

————. *Glas.* Paris: Editions Galilee, 1975.

————. "Limited Inc." Trans. Samuel Weber. *Glyph* 2 (1977): 162–254.

————. "Living On: Border Lines." Trans. James Hulbert. In *Deconstruction and Criticism.* Harold Bloom et al., 75–176. New York: Continuum, 1979.

————. *Of Grammatology.* 1967. Trans. Guyatri Spivak. Baltimore: Johns Hopkins University Press, 1976.

————. *Positions.* 1972. Trans. Alan Bass. Chicago: University of Chicago Press, 1981.

————. "Signature Event Context." Trans. Samuel Weber and Jeffrey Mehlman. *Glyph* 1 (1977): 172–97.

————. "Structure, Sign and Play in the Discourse of the Human Sciences." 1967. Trans. Alan Bass. In *The Languages of Criticism and the Sciences of Man: The Structuralist Controversy,* edited by Richard Macksey and Eugenio Donato. Baltimore: Johns Hopkins University Press, 1972.

Ehrmann, Jacques. "The Death of Literature." In *Surfiction,* edited by Raymond Federman, 229–53. Chicago: Swallow Press, 1975.

————. "Le dedan et le dehors." *Poétique* 9 (1972): 31–40.

Eliot, T. S. *"The Waste Land": A Facsimile and Transcript of the Original Drafts.* Edited by Valerie Eliot. London: Faber and Faber, 1971.

Elliot, George P. "Destroyers, Defilers, and Confusers of Men." *Atlantic Monthly* 222 (Dec. 1968): 74–80.

Fiedler, Leslie. "The New Mutants." *Partisan Review* 32.4 (Fall 1965): 505–25.

————. *Waiting for the End.* New York: Stein and Day, 1964.

Foucault, Michel. *Discipline and Punish: The Birth of the Prison.* 1975. Trans. Alan Sheridan. New York: Pantheon, 1977.

Genette, Gérard. *Figures III*. Paris: Editions du Seuil, 1972.

Ginsberg, Allen. In *The Beat Book*, edited by Arthur and Glee Knight. California, Pa.: the unspeakable visions of the individual series, 1974.

———. "On Burroughs' Work." *Reality Sandwiches, 1953–1960*. San Francisco: City Lights Books, 1963.

———. Responses in "Excerpts from the Boston Trial of *Naked Lunch*," xviii–xxxiv. *Naked Lunch*. New York: Grove Press, 1966.

Goodman, Michael. *Contemporary Literary Censorship: The Case History of Burroughs' Naked Lunch*. New Jersey: The Scarecrow Press, 1981.

———. *William S. Burroughs: An Annotated Bibliography of His Works and Criticism*. New York: Garland, 1975.

Grunberg, Serge. *"A la recherche d'un corps": Langage et silence dans l'oeuvre de William S. Burroughs*. Paris: Editions du Seuil, 1979.

Gysin, Brion. Excerpts from *Here to Go: Planet R-101*. *Research* 4.5 (1982): 44–51.

Hartman, Geoffrey. *Saving the Text: Literature/Derrida/Philosophy*. Baltimore: Johns Hopkins University Press, 1981.

Hassan, Ihab. "The Literature of Silence: From Henry Miller to Beckett and Burroughs." *Encounter* 28 (January 1967): 74–82.

———. "The Novel of Outrage, a Minority Voice in Postwar American Fiction." *American Scholar* 34 (Spring 1965): 239–53.

———. "The Subtracting Machine: The Work of William S. Burroughs." *Critique* 6 (Spring 1963): 4–23.

Hilfer, Anthony. "Mariner and Wedding Guest in William Burroughs' *Naked Lunch*." *Criticism* 22 (1980): 252–65.

Hoffman, Frederick. *The Mortal No: Death and the Modern Imagination*. Princeton University Press, 1964.

Jakobson, Roman. "Linguistics and Poetics." In *Style and Language*, edited by Sebeok. Cambridge, Mass.: MIT Press, 1960.

———. "Two Aspects of Language and Two Types of Aphasic Disturbances." In *Fundamentals of Language*, 69–96. The Hague: Mouton, 1956.

Jardine, Alice A. *Gynesis: Configurations of Woman and Modernity*. Ithaca: Cornell University Press, 1985.

Johnson, Barbara. "The Critical Difference." *Diacritics* 8.2 (June 1978): 2–9.

Johnston, Allan. "The Burroughs Biopathy: William S. Burroughs' *Junky* and *Naked Lunch* and Reichian Theory." *Review of Contemporary Fiction* (Spring 1984): 107–20.

Kellner, Hans. "The Inflatable Trope as Narrative Theory: Structure or Allegory?" *Diacritics* 10 (Dec. 1980): 14–28.

Knickerbocker, Conrad. "William Burroughs." In *Writers at Work: The Paris Review Interviews*, edited by Alfred Kazin, 143–74. New York: Viking, 1967.

Kostelanetz, Richard. "From Nightmare to Serendipity: A Retrospective Look at William Burroughs." *Twentieth Century Literature* 11 (1965–66): 123–30.

Kristeva, Julia. "Motherhood According to Giovanni Bellini." 1975. In *Desire in Language*, 237–70. Trans. Thomas Gora, Alice Jardine, Leon S. Roudiez. New York: Columbia University Press, 1980.

———. *Powers of Horror: An Essay on Abjection*. 1980. Trans. Leon S. Roudiez. New York: Columbia University Press, 1982.

————. *La révolution du langage poétique*. Paris: Editions du Seuil, 1974.

————. "Woman Can Never Be Defined." 1974. Trans. Marilyn A. August. In *New French Feminisms*, edited by Elaine Marks and Isabelle Courtivron, 137–41. Amherst: University of Massachusetts Press, 1980.

La Capra, Dominick. "Who Rules Metaphor." *Diacritics* 10 (Dec. 1980): 15–28.

Leddy, Michael. " 'Departed have left no address': Revelation/ Concealment Presence/ Absence in *Naked Lunch*." *Review of Contemporary Fiction* (Spring 1984): 33–39.

Leitch, Vincent. *Deconstructive Criticism: An Advanced Introduction*. New York: Columbia University Press, 1983.

Lemaire, Gérard-Georges. "23 Stitches Taken." In *The Third Mind*, 9–24. New York: Viking Press, 1978.

Levine, Paul. "The Intemporate Zone: The Climate of Contemporary American Fiction." *Massachusetts Review* (1967): 505–23.

Lodge, David. *The Modes of Modern Writing: Metaphor, Metonymy, and the Typology of Modern Literature*. Ithaca: Cornell University Press, 1977.

————. *The Novelist at the Crossroads*. London: Routledge and Kegan Paul, 1971.

Mailer, Norman. Responses in "Excerpts from the Boston trial of *Naked Lunch*," x–xviii. *Naked Lunch*. New York: Grove Press, 1966.

Massey, Irving. *The Gaping Pig*. Berkeley: University of California Press, 1976.

McCarthy, Mary. "Déjeuner sur l'herbe: *The Naked Lunch*." *New York Review of Books* 1.1 (1963): 4–5.

————. *The Writing on the Wall*. New York: Harcourt, Brace, Jovanovich, 1970.

McConnell, Frank. "William Burroughs and the Literature of Addiction." *Massachusetts Review* (1967): 665–80.

McLuhan, Marshall. "Notes on Burroughs." *Nation* 199 (28 Dec. 1964): 517–19.

Michelson, Peter. "Beardsley, Burroughs, Decadence, and the Poetics of Obscenity." *TriQuarterly* 12 (Spring 1968): 139–55.

Mikriammos, Philippe. "Vox Williami, vox monstruorum." In *Le Colloque de Tanger*, edited by Gérard-Georges Lemaire, 99–106. Paris: Christian Bourgeois, 1976.

————. *William Burroughs*. Paris: Seghers, 1975.

Miller, J. Hillis. "The Critic as Host." In *Deconstruction and Criticism*. Harold Bloom et al., 217–53. New York: Continuum, 1979.

————. *The Disappearance of God: Five Nineteenth-Century Writers*. 1963. Reprint. Cambridge, Mass.: Belknap Press of Harvard University Press, 1975.

————. "Stevens' Rock and Criticism as Cure, II." *Georgia Review* 30 (1976): 330–48.

————. "Theory and Practice: Response to Vincent Leitch." *Critical Inquiry* 6 (1980): 609–14.

Mottram, Eric. *William Burroughs: The Algebra of Need*. London: Marion Boyars, 1977.

Moorcock, Michael. Letter to *Times Literary Supplememt* 3221 (21 Nov. 1963): 947.

Nelson, Cary. *The Incarnate Word*. Urbana: University of Illinois Press, 1973.

Odier, Daniel. *The Job: Interviews with William S. Burroughs*. 1969. New York: Grove Press, 1974.

Ovid. *Metamorphoses*. Trans. Rolfe Humphries. Bloomington: Indiana University Press, 1955.

Oxenhandler, Neil. "Listening to Burroughs' Voice." In *Surfiction*, edited by Raymond Federman, 181–201. Chicago: Swallow Press, 1975.

Palmer, Robert. "William Burroughs." *Rolling Stone* 11 (May 1972): 48–53.

Paz, Octavio. *Conjunctions and Disjunctions*. 1969. Trans. Helen R. Lane. New York: Viking Press, 1974.

Peterson, R. G. "A Picture is a Fact: Wittgenstein and *Naked Lunch*." In *The Beats: Essays in Criticism*, 30–39. London: McFarland, 1981.

Poulet, Georges. "The Phenomenology of Reading." *New Literary History* 1.1 (Fall 1969): 53–73.

Rabelais, François. *The Histories of Gargantua and Pantagruel*. Trans. J. M. Cohen. New York: Penguin, 1955.

Ricoeur, Paul. "Metaphor and the Main Problem of Hermeneutics." *New Literary History* 6.1 (Autumn 1974): 95–110.

———. "The Metaphoric Process as Cognition, Imagination and Feeling." In *On Metaphor*, edited by Sheldon Sacks, 141–57. Chicago: University of Chicago Press, 1978.

———. *The Rule of Metaphor: Multi-Disciplinary Studies of the Creation of Meaning in Language*. 1975. Trans. Robert Czerny. University of Toronto Press, 1977.

Riffaterre, Michael. "Semantic Incompatabilities in Automatic Writing." In *About French Poetry from Dada to "Tel Quel,"* edited by Mary Ann Caws, 223–41. Detroit: Wayne State University Press, 1974.

Ruegg, Maria. "The End(s) of French Style: Structuralism and Post-Structuralism in the American Context." *Criticism* 21 (1978): 189–216.

Russell, Charles. "Individual Voice in Collective Discourse: Postmodern American Fiction." *Sub-stance* 27 (1980): 29–39.

Said, Edward. "Problem of Textuality: Two Exemplary Positions." *Critical Inquiry* (Summer 1978): 673–714.

Seltzer, Alvin J. *Chaos in the Novel: The Novel in Chaos*. New York: Schocken Books, 1974.

Serres, Michel. *The Parasite*. Trans. Lawrence R. Schehr. Baltimore: Johns Hopkins University Press, 1982.

Shaviro, Steven. "Burroughs' Theatre of Illusions: *Cities of the Red Night*." *Review of Contemporary Fiction* (Spring 1984): 64–74.

Shklovsky, Viktor. "Art as Technique." In *Russian Formalist Criticism: Four Essays*, edited by Lee T. Lemon, 3–24. Lincoln: University of Nebraska Press, 1965.

Skau, Michael. "The Central Verbal System: The Prose of William Burroughs." *Style* 15.4 (Fall 1981): 401–14.

Skerl, Jennie. *William S. Burroughs*. Boston: Twayne Publishers, 1985.

———. "An Interview with William S. Burroughs." *Modern Language Studies* 12 (Summer 1982): 3–17.

Solotoroff, Theodore. "William Burroughs: The Algebra of Need." *The Red Hot Vacuum*, 247–53. New York: Atheneum, 1970.

Sontag, Susan. "The Aesthetics of Silence." *Styles of Radical Will*, 3–34. New York: Farrar, Straus and Giroux, 1966.

Spitzer, Leo. "Linguistic Perspectivism in the *Don Quijote*." *Linguistics and Literary History*, 41–86. Princeton University Press, 1948.

Spivak, Gayatri Chakravorty. "*Glas*-piece: A Compte Rendu." *Diacritics* 7 (Fall 1977): 22–43.

————. "Love me, Love my ombre, elle." *Diacritics* (Winter 1984): 19–36.

Sterne, Laurence. *The Life and Opinions of Tristram Shandy, Gentleman*. Boston: Houghton Mifflin, 1965.

Stimpson, Catherine. "The Beat Generation and the Trials of Homosexual Liberation." *Salmagundi* 58–59 (Fall-Winter 1982–83): 373–92.

Stull, William. "Quest and the Question." In *The Beats: Essays in Criticism*, edited by Lee Bartlett, 14–29. Jefferson, N.C.: McFarland, 1981.

Tanner, James E., Jr. "Experimental Styles Compared: E. E. Cummings and William Burroughs." *Style* 10 (1976): 1–27.

Tanner, Tony. *City of Words: American Fiction 1950–1970*. New York: Harper and Row, 1971.

Tytell, John. *Naked Angels: The Lives and Literature of the Beat Generation*. New York: McGraw Hill, 1973.

Vernon, John. *The Garden and the Map: Schizophrenia in Twentieth-Century Literature and Culture*. Urbana: University of Illinois Press, 1973.

Wain, John. Review of *Naked Lunch*. *New Republic* 147 (1 Dec. 1962): 21–23.

Warren, Austin, and Rene Wellek. *Theory of Literature*. 3rd ed. New York: Harcourt, Brace and World, 1956.

Weinstein, Arnold. "Freedom and Control in the Erotic Novel: The Classical *Liaisons dangereuses* versus the Surrealist *Naked Lunch*." *Dada/Surrealism* 10/11 (1982): 29–38.

Werner, Craig. *Paradoxical Resolutions: American Fiction Since James Joyce*. Urbana: University of Illinois Press, 1982.

Wilson, Terry. "Brion Gysin: A Biography/Appreciation." *Research* 4.5 (1982): 39–43.

Zurbrugg, Nicholas. "Beckett, Proust, and Burroughs and the Perils of 'Image Warfare.'" In *Samuel Beckett: Humanistic Perspectives*, edited by Morris Beja, 172–87. Columbus: Ohio State University Press, 1983.

————. "Burroughs, Barthes, and the Limits of Intertextuality." *Review of Contemporary Fiction* (Spring 1984): 86–106.

————. "Burroughs, Grauerholz, and *Cities of the Red Night*: An Interview with James Grauerholz." *Review of Contemporary Fiction* (Spring 1984): 19–32.

Index

A Note on the Author

Robin Lydenberg is an associate professor of English at Boston College. A graduate of Barnard College, she received her Ph.D. in comparative literature from Cornell University. In addition to several articles about aspects of the work of William Burroughs, Professor Lydenberg has published studies of such diverse authors as Lautréamont and Isak Dinesen. Her work has appeared in a number of journals, including *Contemporary Literature, Diacritics, Review of Contemporary Fiction, Esprit Créateur, Comparative Literature Studies*, and *Modern Fiction Studies*.